AF413643

My Gift to You

Learn lessons of New Wave Leadership you can apply to daily living right now.
Becoming your better, your best self is an uncomplicated process
you can work into your day. How you think, learn, practice,
and especially do things matters. With this gift, you can learn
to live well with meaning, thrive, and help others thrive.

Visit the link below to access your free gift and receive periodic resources
and tips for **Becoming a New Wave Leader:**
http://AffinitasPublishing.org/resources/

Praise for *Becoming a New Wave Leader: Principles and Practices to Live and Lead Well*

A deeply compelling argument for values in leadership. In a troubled age the message of Jim Klopovic's *Becoming a New Wave Leader* is less new than eternally relevant and more important than ever. Brilliantly crafted, entertaining and instructive, a must-read for current and future leaders.

– Stanley McChrystal, General, USA, Ret.,
Partner, McChrystal Group

Becoming a New Wave Leader confirmed many of my beliefs about how to lead a successful company but also gave me many other ways to consider leadership. All business leaders need to read this well written and researched book. It may be more relevant in today's world than at any other time in history.

– Ed White, Chairman/CEO, Field2Base, Inc.

In the heart of his excellent new book *Becoming a New Wave Leader*, James Klopovic writes, "Knowing right from wrong takes continuous, serious contemplation and practice." So does exceptional leadership. Few understand this as the author does. Through smart, age-old, practical and most important proven insights, the author shows why success boils down to a handful of deceivingly simple, powerful principles. The book's gift isn't just clarifying why these things matter but how to make them real. Becoming a New Wave Leader is worthy of your time.

– Larry Robertson, award-winning author of
Rebel Leadership: How to Thrive in Uncertain Times

A rare book for its clarity and compelling case for being our best, *Becoming a New Wave Leader* is an engaging work of scholarship for all of us. It presents a realistic, very useful process for developing personal growth into constructive leadership and discusses implications for solving individual and community challenges. As an extensive and layered work on the conceptual origins of what great character looks like, how one can aspire to it, and the importance of it in leadership, this book stands out. Solutions to community problems are realistic and possible with a mindful leader's investment in collaboration based in well-being and civility. Answers focus on what works, such as an integrated flow of top-down and bottom-up creative energies. Fun to read and uniquely informative, this book leaves an indelible impression. I will refer to it often and recommend it even more.

– Deborah Heil, Ph.D., Practicing Clinical Psychologist

Becoming a New Wave Leader provides a proven and practical path to leveling up your leadership skills. It's simultaneously succinct yet comprehensive and offers time-tested, field-proven principles that can immediately be put into practice. The book is full of anecdotes that will bring to life concepts and simple truisms that future leaders must learn and experienced leaders would do well to revisit.

– Michael Young, Ph.D., Director of Performance, Athletic Lab

Practical and effective, *Becoming a New Wave Leader* delivers a proven approach to leadership that anyone can apply who wishes to unlock his or her potential and obtain the apex level of leadership.

– Olin O. Oedekoven, Ph.D., President & CEO,
Peregrine Global Service

Jim Klopovic's life story led him from Ohio farm kid to Air Force officer, from a Doctor of Public Policy degree to public policy expert. His life forms the foundation for this clear, practical, and accessible guide to effective leadership today and especially tomorrow. Compelling storytelling illustrates principles appropriate for both seasoned and aspiring leaders. A must-read for anyone interested in ethical leadership.

– Katherine Pecka, Executive Communications Consultant, Vox Optima

Becoming a
NEW WAVE LEADER

---

*Principles and Practices
to Live and Lead Well*

Other Books by James Klopovic

In Print

Your Moral Compass: A Practical Guide for New Wave Leaders (2020)
Available from: *https://affinitaspublishing.org/your-moral-compass/*
and *https://www.amazon.com*

Volume II of the Capacity Building Series. *Decriminalizing Mental Illness: A Practical Model for Building Sustainable Crisis Intervention Teams* (2019)
Available from: *https://affinitaspublishing.org/dmi/*
and *https://www.amazon.com*

Little Stories: A Legacy of Learning, Laughing and Loving
Available from: *https://affinitaspublishing.org/little-stories-a-legacy-of-learning-laughing-and-loving/* (2019)

The Honest Backpacker: A Practical Guide for the Rookie Adventurer over 50 (2017)
Available from: *https://affinitaspublishing.org/the-honest-backpacker/*

Effective Program Practices for At-Risk Youth: A Continuum of Community-Based Programs (2003)
Available from: *http://www.civicresearchinstitute.com/epy.html*

Capacity Building Series

Volume I. *Building Capacity from the Bottom Up: The Key to Sustaining Local Services* (In the pipeline)

Volume II. *Decriminalizing Mental Illness: A Practical Model for Building Sustainable Crisis Intervention Teams*
(In print. See above.) Available from: *https://affinitaspublishing.org/dmi/*
and *https://www.amazon.com*

Volume III. *Accelerating Juvenile Reentry: A Practical Capacity Building Model for Sustaining Aftercare* (In the pipeline)

Volume IV. *Accelerating Adult Reentry: A Practical Capacity Building Model for Sustaining Post-Release Transitional Services* (In the pipeline)

Becoming a
NEW WAVE
LEADER

*Principles and Practices
to Live and Lead Well*

James Klopovic
with
Nicole Klopovic

Go from inaction and uncertainty to collaboration, respect, and well-being

AFFINITAS PUBLISHING

Becoming a New Wave Leader: Principles and Practices to Live and Lead Well
by James Klopovic with Nicole Klopovic

Copyright © 2021 by James Klopovic and Nicole Klopovic

Published in the United States by Affinitas Publishing

Except as noted, the web addresses referenced in this book were live and correct at the time of the book's publication but may be subject to change.

Cover and interior design: Nick Zelinger, NZ Graphics
Editing: Peggy Henrikson, Heart and Soul Editing
Virtual Assistance: Kelly Johnson, Cornerstone Virtual Assistance, LLC
Indexing: Michelle Guiliano, Line-by-Line Indexing

Publisher's Cataloging-In-Publication Data
(Prepared by The Donohue Group, Inc.)

Names: Klopovic, James, author. | Klopovic, Nicole, author.
Title: Becoming a new wave leader : principles and practices to live and lead well / James Klopovic, with Nicole Klopovic.
Description: First edition. | [Morrisville, North Carolina] : Affinitas Publishing, [2021] | Includes bibliographical references and index.
Identifiers: ISBN 9798985011906 (paperback) | ISBN 9798985011920 (hardcover) | ISBN 9798985011913 (ebook)
Subjects: LCSH: Leadership. | Conduct of life. | Character. | Virtue. | Self-actualization (Psychology) | Neurosciences—Philosophy.
Classification: LCC BF637.L4 K56 2021 (print) | LCC BF637.L4 (ebook) | DDC 158.4—dc23

ISBN: 979-8-9850119-0-6 (paperback)
ISBN: 979-8-9850119-2-0 (hardcover)
ISBN: 979-8-9850119-1-3 (e-book)

Library of Congress Control Number: 2021913835

10 9 8 7 6 5 4 3 2 1

First Edition

Printed in the United States of America

To Don Martin (1945–2020), my one true friend of a lifetime.
As Cicero explains, *“Even when absent, friends are near. . . .”*

Whatever you are, be a good one.
– Abraham Lincoln

Contents

Preface

We need to redefine . . . the way that we interact with other human
beings. . . . We have to reconsider how we choose and carry out
our work, structure our communities, and bring up our children.
We have to imagine another way to live.
– Lynne McTaggart

These extraordinary times offer us more hope for a bright future than ever before. Why is this so? Our focus and perspective make all the difference. Rather than wallow in our challenges, we can choose innovation and determination to answer our most vexing difficulties, resulting in previously unseen individual and collective leaps forward. We are now in the latest and arguably greatest leap forward in technology. For example, breakthroughs in gene editing will, over time, markedly improve humanity if used ethically. Imagine curing more and more of our major diseases and maladies.

Yes, these are the best of times—not to be squandered! Steven Pinker concurs in his brilliant book *Enlightenment Now: The Case for Reason, Science, Humanism and Progress.* He uses historical reference, data, and logic to explain why we are in a new age of enlightenment. This insightful work is a supporting reference for the New Wave Leader.

One of Pinker's students asked the serious question "Why should I live?" His answer provides the perfect backdrop and rationale for *Becoming a New Wave Leader* (The italics in the quotation are his.)

"In the very act of asking that question, you are seeking reasons for your convictions, and so you are committed to reason as the meaning to discover and justify what is important to you. And there are so many reasons to live!

As a sentient being, you have the potential to *flourish.* You can refine your faculty of reason itself by learning and debating. You can seek explanations of the natural world through science, and insight into the human condition through the arts and humanities. You can make the most of your capacity for pleasure and satisfaction, which allowed your ancestors to thrive and thereby allow you to exist. You can appreciate the beauty and richness of the natural and cultural world. As the heir to billions of years of life perpetuating itself, you can perpetuate life in turn. You have been endowed with a sense of *sympathy*—the ability to like, love, respect, help, and show kindness—and you can enjoy the gift of mutual benevolence with friends, family, and colleagues.

And because reason tells you that none of this is particular to you, you have the responsibility to provide to others what you expect for yourself. You can foster the welfare of other sentient beings by enhancing life, health, knowledge, freedom, abundance, safety, beauty and peace. History shows that when we sympathize with others and apply our ingenuity to improving the human condition, we can make progress in doing so, and you can help to continue that progress."[1]

We have devoted ourselves to gaining formal education, skills, professional development, and especially experience. We're capable; we can do the job. What more could we add if we continuously improve our character and well-being, truly thriving in our work and relationships? Most important, how much more positive influence could we have on those around us, thus helping to uplift the conscious-ness and conscientiousness of the world? The time is right for the MAGNUS–OVÉA New Wave Leader, who can do just that.

LIVE with Virtue—*STRIVE* with Character—*THRIVE* for a Lifetime

Introduction to the Theory of New Wave Leadership

New Wave Leadership is a new general theory of human behavior that synthesizes the teachings of Ancient sages, principles modeled by our nation's Founding Fathers, and ideas espoused by today's philosophers, scientists, and leaders.

Becoming a New Wave Leader is simply pursuing being your best. It is the lifelong pursuit of the Cardinal Virtues of Justice, Wisdom, Courage, and Temperance with Character born of humility and self-analysis. The result is learning to thrive.

New Wave Leadership is based on conscientiousness—the foundation for not only surviving but thriving, even during a chaotic day. With that base, we can consider how to unceasingly enhance personal performance, leadership capacity, resiliency, antifragility,[2] and, primarily, continuous well-being. Constantly developing these capacities will lead to improvements in individual performance as well as organizational effectiveness and productivity. MAGNUS–OVÉA New Wave Leaders *LIVE* with Virtue—*STRIVE* with Character—*THRIVE* for a Lifetime.

From Wellness to Well-being to Thriving–Proof, Practicality, Practice

New Wave Leadership is symbolized by the mythological Phoenix, representing renewal and resurrection, continually rising from the flames and ashes to not just survive but thrive. When we thrive, we find we are largely content with ourselves and reasonably happy. Phoenix Factors, which we will explore in Chapter 11, explain and illustrate the possibilities. While the factors are ideals, they are realistic because they are practical. Even if only a few factors are realized, they are well worth pursuing because anyone in pursuit of these ideals is much the better for the effort. Possibilities are remarkable when even an individual, and certainly an agency or organization, commits to one of the factors and shows the way for another New Wave organization, which then paves the way for the next . . . and the next . . . and the next.

This book explains the *journey* of becoming a New Wave Leader—being the best you were meant to be. This journey is a process because as we reach a certain level of competence, we become aware of what's next, what's possible; and thus the journey continues. The intention is to learn to live virtuously and build character. Then learning how to be antifragile becomes possible, which is only one facet of this journey. Virtue is primary as learning the difference between right and wrong and making just decisions is basic to good character. Character is co-primary as it determines how we function as individuals in human systems. How we relate with good character to others involves our values, ethics, and conscientiousness. The resulting character-based mindset will support effective individual and leadership capacity and overall well-being. Our well-being then enables us to thrive even through difficulties.

Explaining this shift from wellness to well-being to thriving with regard to leadership helps clarify this new theory as it is applied, analyzed, tested, adjusted, and validated. We begin with this assertion:

Continuously educating and developing people in virtuous character building to the point of thriving will result in measurable advancements in personal effectiveness, organizational performance, and community well-being, thereby improving general well-being beyond the individual.

The tenets of this theory are inspirational, motivational, and above all, practical. How actions are accomplished matters. The habit of daily—no, minute-to-minute—character-building may not be quite as measurable as science demands. However, even as this nascent theory takes shape, people are reporting results that are ultimate arbiters of its value. These include:

- improved personal effectiveness,
- increased organizational progress, and
- more satisfaction with services and providers.

What the wise and revered Ancients and notable Americans prescribed for personal conduct is often subverted given the demands of a rapidly changing world. Governance, private and public, must evolve with time-honored principles or face diminished, even corrupted results.

Becoming a New Wave Leader is based on a new concept, MAGNUS–OVÉA, a process of continuous improvement. It details how we learn to think and behave to be accomplished, effective, and also happy. *Note:* The happiness this journey builds isn't the temporary kind based on fortuitous circumstance. No. It means contentment with who we are, what we're doing, and the legacy we're creating. The process is:

- rooted in ancient philosophy,
- verified by modern science,
- practical in application, and
- a map for our New Wave of leadership.

Public Services–for Example

We begin with local public agencies as the segue to governance in the private and private nonprofit sectors. Municipalities are also where we can observe how service is evolving. Local towns and counties are where the fruits of government and its governance are realized . . . or not. They are perfect incubators for how (or often how *not*) to provide services. At this level, we can more easily see where difficulties manifest and how they're best solved.

The New Wave program works, and it will work anywhere. It must work. Why? Because some of the greatest minds in history have promoted the efficacy of building character and a moral foundation for all actions and transactions. New Wave Leadership describes a life well lived.

Benjamin Franklin is one such example of a public servant guided by the ancient philosophy of virtuous living and service—and an example in every way of the modern New Wave servant. His influence on and gifts to society were extensive. We can imagine him as a major administrator in post-revolutionary Philadelphia. His remarkable progress and accomplishments were anchored in character-based, virtuous, and healthy living—with continuous improvement even to his very last day. He was never idle, always curious, kind, and looking for ways to use his talents and skills to benefit society. Thus he thrived, improved an entire generation of Americans as well as those who followed, and was even a boon to the whole of mankind. He understood that civic duty, giving back, was and is paramount to a life well lived.

You may be thinking *yes, but he was a genius and most of us aren't*. The point is, he possessed the worldview of New Wave Leaders, which we all can adopt or work toward as we are able. Granted, he was inordinately talented, but thus he saw his responsibilities as equally inordinate. He worked harder than anyone to use his gifts well. "Persistence at purpose matters," he would say. Challenges to him were opportunities to reach higher, do more, and have greater impact on his neighbors and business associates, his city and country, and the world and history itself. Can we learn from Dr. Franklin? Absolutely. Chapter 4 delves further into his amazing life and legacy to give us insights.

Foreshadowing Capacity Building and the New Wave Professional

In studying the work of Ben Franklin, the important question arises: How did he take his ideas from conception to permanence? The answer is, he focused on how he might fulfill an idea or deliver a service by creating a matrix of local resources to support solutions to local problems and needs. That approach became a model for his greatest accomplishments. With this methodology, he foresaw and employed the theory of Capacity Building, the sequential process of planning, operating, and sustaining an idea with matrices of relevant agencies or services. Such an approach is an effective way to develop ideas into permanent working solutions.[3]

Why is that important? It means we can work beyond delivering basic services to promoting well-being and establishing places where people can thrive and be happy and pass these lessons on to their children and theirs and so on. The overall aim of governance, private and public, can and should be to help people *flourish*, not just survive. We can build capacity for positive change through the collaboration of multiple resources to realize long-term goals that solve problems and continuously contribute to the common good. Thus, as Aristotle proclaimed, the whole becomes much greater than the sum of its parts.

These New Wave Leaders concentrate on living virtuously with character, pursuing well-being and balance in life. They provide role models to strengthen families, agencies, organizations, and communities.

The change agents in moving from "silo" services to a cross-agency collaborative matrix are New Wave professionals. They are technically skilled, professionally developed, and morally grounded. The foundation of this shift in focus is the character development and education of the individual leader. These New Wave Leaders concentrate on living virtuously with character, pursuing well-being and balance in life. They provide role models to strengthen families, agencies, organizations, and communities.

Everyone is responsible for becoming a New Wave Leader. Those managing and leading are particularly positioned to model and establish the culture to develop New Wave employees. One way is to adopt a pre-hire to post-retirement process and philosophy. Currently, it's common in every sector to hire for skills and fire for character. The New Wave agency reverses that to hire for character and fire for (deficient) skills (which rarely happens), looking to hire and develop people who have intellect and compassion. Then, each department adopts career-long progressive skill-building and especially character education and development from new hire to agency leadership. It also adopts programs that develop beyond wellness to well-being, considering a long life beyond a career, during which we can live our most productive years . . . if we are prepared.

Let's look more closely at what's involved in becoming a New Wave Leader, as well as the concept of MAGNUS–OVÉA and its beneficial results.

New Wave MAGNUS-OVÉA Leadership: The Essentials

The New Wave professional continuously models character by pursuing virtues and holistic living, which blesses the individual with health, accomplishments, respect, and contentment.

Living virtuously as described by the Ancients is committing to live a good life, giving of our talents and ourselves as best we can to uplift our immediate sphere of influence. The best part of this *becoming* is that it's never finished. We keep growing, energized by our inevitable progress even as we fail, learn, and try again. One must merely begin with conviction. Let's look at how the New Wave MAGNUS–OVÉA theory came about.

MAGNUS

This theory is based on the wisdom of ancient oriental as well as occidental philosophers beginning with Socrates and Aristotle and progressing through subsequent philosophers and thinkers. This ancient term *MAGNUS* also means great. Cicero, the ultimate Roman statesman, lawyer, and scholar, understood that it's natural to be good and that happiness is a product of giving to others and contributing to society. This sharing is how we survived then dominated as a species.

New Wave MAGNUS–OVÉA Leadership is a fresh look at how we function individually and especially in collaboratives motivated by a clear vision. It recognizes the march of civilizations and thus reflects, updates, and carries forward the ancient concept of what and how it is to be our ever-improving best while being aware of how we fit in and affect those around us, beginning with family. It's the necessary modernization of what, how, and who we are in this age of genomics in which we can probe our physical origins, cure diseases, and improve our human species. Gene editing with CRISPR[4] is our greatest and most solemn innovation, in which we can, ". . . boost our bodies and enhance our babies to have better muscles, minds, memory, and moods."[5]

The New Wave Leader, then, influences and inspires others and aspires to humbly accomplish more. Not the least of these accomplishments might be nurturing a moral, balanced child to follow in his or her footsteps.

Yet, living the Good (moral/virtuous) Life alone is not the whole story. We must also commit to strengthening our overall well-being: body, mind, and spirit, as the Ancients proclaimed. Thus, we exercise our bodies and minds and learn moderation in all things. We study and practice the Cardinal Virtues of Justice, Wisdom, Courage, and Temperance as they apply to daily living. Then we can apply such values as love, kindness, forgiveness, gratitude, and peace. This is not a "soft" view of how to live life; in fact, it's tough to stay focused day by day, even minute by minute, but it's well worth the persistence and discipline. Pursuit of the Journey and these kinder goals is based heavily in large bodies of science and evidence, which we explore in this book.

OVÉA =

What sparks and accelerates our progress? Enter OVÉA, which represents the "chemistry" of the New Wave MAGNUS–OVÉA Leader and good citizen. OVÉA is a major theme to which we will return often throughout the book.

- *Others* – Giving. We gain gratification and leave a legacy when we give back to improve the lives around us and beyond us.

- *Values* – Character. Primarily, we gain values and develop character through introspection/self-awareness and humility. When we give respect, we are respected. When we give happiness, we are happy.

- *Ethics* – Morals. It's natural to live the Good Life when we have a moral compass.[6] This compass keeps us heading in a self-sustaining direction that enhances all our relationships.

- *Acceleration* – Inspiration. The daily process of continually learning more, improving more, doing more, and especially becoming more inspires us and those who witness our progress. It's the spark that keeps us committed. Becoming a New Wave MAGNUS–OVÉA Leader is exciting!

While it may seem as if this "becoming" takes Herculean effort, it's actually a process, a habit of moderation, or what the Ancients called *sophrosyne*. It involves searching for the Golden Mean between the extremes of excess and deficiency that are harmful and difficult. Becoming a New Wave MAGNUS–OVÉA Leader is highly practical and realistic—and for anyone. It's not about perfection but rather awareness and modification of how one thinks and acts to continuously improve. Its pursuit is simple, suitable, and sustainable: One finds the path *simple* and easy when its practice becomes habitual. Being an individual endeavor, it's *suitable* to everyone. Likewise, because it's a self-fulfilling pursuit, it's *sustainable*. In fact, the process has volumes of significant and accruing scientific support.

Science, Theory, Practicality, and Application

Science has proven that as we model what it is to be good and do good, we are rewiring our brains through processes called *neuroplasticity* and *synaptic pruning*. Our brain adjusts to this way of character-based personal and professional development to support us in being accomplished and happy. This is a choice that it easily made. In other words, our neuronal pathways are continually being modulated by what we practice; the evolving brain wants to be efficient, effective, and especially organized.[7]

We also have hormonal support when we do something good for ourselves and especially for others. A release of feel-good hormones compels us to do more of the same. As mentioned, the Ancients over 2,400 years ago intuited that to live virtuously and want to be good and do good is *innate* to humanity. Somehow, they understood that we have a positive neurophysiologic reaction to being virtuous, living holistically with character, and being other-focused.

> **Becoming MAGNUS–OVÉA is highly practical and realistic—and for anyone. It's not about perfection. It's about awareness and modification of how one thinks and acts to continuously improve.**

Later in this book, we further discuss the science and philosophy that underpins and validates our journey of becoming.

Initial reports from New Wave professionals in the field are most promising. People are greatly, if not dramatically and permanently, bettering their lives. After practicing what we explain, a student of the Journey exclaimed, "You saved my life!" But no. That individual *committed* to the Journey and did the *work*.

In other words, once you have the information and the guidance, it's up to you to consciously trigger, support, and guide this growth with your study, thoughts, and actions. If you choose to put yourself on a continuous journey to becoming MAGNUS–OVÉA, you can get better and better at life. Likewise, if you tell your body and psyche that you prefer a life of complaint, mediocrity, and laziness, your brain will facilitate those choices. If you want a constantly improving and happy life, the best choice is obvious. And once on the journey, it's *fun*.

How to Use This Book

Resolve to put the suggestions in this book to work. Nothing happens until something moves, as Einstein reminded us. More specifically:

- *Read actively* – Keep a pencil and highlighter handy. Underline, highlight, write your thoughts in the margins or a notebook. Do keep a journal; Leonardo DaVinci did, and thus we have his legendary art and innovations to marvel at and guide us.

- *Think* – Digest the ideas and suggestions. Then think about how they apply to your life and life in general.

- *Understand* – Consider how this book can shape your life for the better and thus help shape the world around you.

- *Plan* – Determine how to *use* the information herein to live virtuously with meaning, character, good health, and the realization of genuine happiness.

- *Act* – Put your plan to work and *practice* till living well becomes habitual. Act you must.

Thank you for any efforts you make toward becoming a New Wave Leader.
You are on your way simply by reading this far.

SECTION I:

EVOLVING INTO THE NEW WAVE

Here's to the crazy ones. . . . The ones who see things differently . . . [who] push the human race forward. . . . Because the people who are crazy enough to think they can change the world are the ones who do.

– Steve Jobs, from Apple's "Think Different" ad, 1997

Section Overview

This section begins the discussion of how leadership has developed and must evolve. World, national, and local events demand a new look at how we conduct our lives as individuals, communities, and leaders. How can we be our best and leave a legacy that contributes to the common good? Imagine what happens when we think and act that way.

Here, we put New Wave Leadership into historical context.

Chapter 1: Lessons from the Evolution of Governance – The New Wave traces four evolutionary waves in governance as our country developed, using community safety and security as an example. It introduces the promise of the fifth wave—the New Wave.

Chapter 2: Introducing the MAGNUS–OVÉA New Wave Leader begins the discussion on how to become the leader of today and tomorrow.

Chapter 3: New Wave Leadership – A Fundamental Shift establishes the language and basic concepts of New Wave Leadership.

Chapter 4: Ben Franklin – Our First New Wave Leader provides an example of how to lead and reveals the implications for leadership now and into the future.

Chapter 1

Lessons from the Evolution of Governance – The New Wave

Those who fail to learn from history are doomed to repeat it.
– Winston Churchill

History teaches us what works and what doesn't, if we are aware and make the effort to learn. At the very least, it can keep us from repeating mistakes if we pay attention.

We have examined and continue to study municipal governance—its roots, laws, principles, and practices. We discovered governance has come in four eras or waves: the establishment era, the political era, the reform era, and the most recent problem-solving era.[8]

We arrive now at what we observe is the fifth wave of public governance evolution—one for community well-being based on the New Wave MAGNUS–OVÉA servant. It's a return to the past, a return to the Ancients, for guidance on how to live the Good Life of contented accomplishment. It's not coincidental that governance is at the edge of the next evolutionary stage of progress—the New Wave.

Thus we study public services for the lessons, perhaps secrets, certainly insights, for how we can be better as individuals and how we can better conduct governance in any sector, public or private. This also has implications for how we progress as a republic.

The bulk of public services are top-down, centrally controlled services in agency "silos," similar to the private sector. The model is largely good but not entirely applicable. Experience and common sense demonstrate that top-down programming can be complemented by bottom-up energies. The next-wave servant will do well to focus on bottom-up construction of service ideas to build community well-being. Why? When problems are defined and solutions designed locally with local leadership, it generates ownership. Furthermore, it's possible to combine the large forces of local human capital with established services so ideas, effort, and creativity flow up and down and back up again in creative, constant, fluid motion. Solutions grow stronger as they traverse the cycle of plan-do-act-plan in concert with local resources and planners, with true collaboration. Answers to seemingly unsolvable problems become permanent, and everything and everyone progresses.

Our Waves of Evolution

A man for the ages, Winston Churchill, admonished us to study the past to learn at least what not to do. We must learn from our mistakes and vow to do better. We have much to learn from tracing the evolution of public service. Have we thoroughly examined our legacy considering the now dramatic changes in globalization and local authority? Do we know what it teaches and how we can improve ourselves and our service institutions and ideas?

When problems are defined and solutions designed locally with local leadership, it generates ownership.

It's informative to trace how our settlements, towns, and cities were secured by reviewing the eras of some of our first municipal officials. By doing this, we can also discover similarities in how those starting businesses and conducting commerce approached governance. The story of the New Wave arose from the gun smoke and desperation of a land that many times demanded life and limb and also from the careless lawlessness[9] rampant as we formed our new republic and moved westward.

First Wave: Establishment – Confronting Lawlessness
(ca. 1700-1850)

In all of us, even in good men, there is a lawless wild-beast nature,
which peers out in sleep.
– Socrates

As we formed our country by immigration, expansion, revolution, and civil war, circumstances and diminishing virtue invited lawlessness and corruption. People became vigilantes to confront criminals and protect their own. Justice without a courtroom, and sometimes even with a courtroom, was swift and many times meted out with a short length of hemp from a tall tree limb. Let's not forget that the West began on the western outskirts of Philadelphia, our first capitol. There lay wilderness, impenetrable mountains with "eyewitness" reports of monstrous, ravenous beasts lying in wait. The spirit of protecting one's own from both man and beast by any means still survives today.

Instituting Civility

We started as a loose federation of farmers and tradesmen and quickly invented machines to do our work. As the industrial revolution came into full swing, incivility was rampant. To impose order and mutual respect, settlers appointed constables for their municipalities. These constables deputized citizens to help enforce a relatively loose interpretation of the law. No overarching legal system as we know it today maintained order and respect when things got out of hand, so nearly all control over such functions was local.

We needed another 150 years of interpreting the constitution, defining our republic, and establishing legal precedents to arrive at the system we have today.

A Legacy of a Good Moral Compass

In the mid-1800s, New York City and Boston formed full-time law and order operations. Those operations quickly became politicized. Officers had guns, which they were not afraid and were even encouraged to use. How they accomplished their duties depended on the circumstances. Sometimes responses reflected the toughness of the organized crime and gangs they faced, with disregard for individual rights. Public safety had a long way to go because it wasn't regulated; corruption and abuse reigned. Officers largely did whatever they wanted or needed to do to get the job done—or they were told what their job would be and how to do it by the "boss."

The developing country desperately needed organized and regulated governance, so this idea endured, as it had to. Even in the face of corruption of all sorts on the streets and in politics, early 20th-century journalist H. L. Mencken felt most cops were honest fellows. He relates a story of a cop who followed the body of a suicide victim to the coroner's office. The dead man was found with $416 (about $7,580 today) in his pockets, and the officer ordered the coroner in no uncertain terms to ensure that all of it, to the penny, was given to the state. It probably was.

These public-minded servants, except for a very few outliers, have *always* had a good moral compass. But that legacy had to endure an era when politics ruled and "bosses" dominated.

Second Wave: Political Era – Struggle (ca. 1850-1920)

The safety of the people shall be the highest law.
– Marcus Tullius Cicero

Those early days until about 1850 were difficult. Corruption was rampant, politics and politicians controlled city jobs and consequently handled criminal justice. Politicians hired people who helped the politicians stay in office.[10] Citizens had to pay for enforcement, or "protection." Yes, laws existed, but political "machines" held great sway over most local institutions and services. Grease the right hands, promise loyalty, and New York's Tammany Hall under the rule of "Boss" Tweed granted jobs by the thousands. William M. Tweed came to power during the Civil War. He and his machine of associates siphoned off their neighbors' money to the tune of $3.5 billion in today's dollars! He later died in prison but is still remembered for everything that can go horribly wrong with municipal governance. This is another lesson for the learning.

Still, the "flatfoot" on the beat felt a part of and responsible for his neighborhood. (At the time, there were no female police officers.)

A "Flatfoot" for All Seasons

In the mid-19th century, our representatives on the street could be counted on to do much of the following, according to H. L. Mencken:

Many of the multifarious duties now carried out by social workers, statisticians, truant officers, visiting nurses, psychologists, and the vast rabble of inspectors, smellers, spies, and bogus experts of a hundred different faculties either fell to the police or were not discharged at all. . . . An ordinary flatfoot in a quiet residential section had his hands full. In a single day he might have to put out a couple of kitchen fires, arrange for the removal of a dead mule, guard a poor epileptic having a fit on the sidewalk, catch a runaway horse, settle a combat with table knives between husband and wife, . . . shoot a cat for killing pigeons, rescue a dog or a baby from a sewer, bawl out a white-wings [street sweeper] for spilling garbage, keep order on the sidewalk at two or three funerals, and flog a half a dozen bad boys for throwing horse-apples at a blind man.[11]

Look at it through the eyes of the neighbors on this beat. This "flatfoot" was essential to community well-being, such as it was back then. He was doing an excellent job for the times by keeping the neighborhood together and livable. As always, the scenario involved more than meets the eye. This initial experiment in minding our communities included the following:[12]

Often these individuals on the beat were forward thinkers, finding it valuable to gain the respect and trust of those they served.

- *Authorization* – Primarily political. Functional crime control, maintenance of order, and broad social services, which might have included running a soup kitchen.

- *Organizational design* – Decentralized and geographical. This is when a beat was a beat; the officer was on his feet in the neighborhood nearly all day long, with a personal relationship to his environment.

- *Channel* – Centrally controlled. Managed through links between politicians and precinct commanders, and face-to-face contacts between citizens and foot-patrols. The professionals of the day were on their own to mete out justice or at least keep the peace.

- *Tactics and technology* – Walking an assigned location and rudimentary investigations. Largely, the individual gathered hearsay from the street.

- *Outcome* – Political and citizen satisfaction with social order. Even with city hall control, public safety at least provided a modicum of order to hurly-burly 19th-century cities, in which a number of inhabitants were bent on ignoring or outfoxing the law. At least the rudiments of community well-being were forming.

Often these individuals on the beat were forward thinkers, finding it valuable to gain the respect and trust of those they served.

Third Wave: Reform Era and Proliferation (ca. 1920-1970)

*Whenever the people are well informed, they can be trusted
with their own government.*
– Thomas Jefferson

The iPhone of this day was the call box, and cars were considered high tech. So the person on the beat was alone and had to decide and do what he felt was best under the circumstances. Investigation was minimal, and crime prevention was in the form of presence. People were always trying to get around laws, such as saloon owners designating their "establishment" a hotel to continue to sell booze, while the upstairs "hotel" rooms supported a boom in prostitution. In the absence of any substantial prevention, the officer dealt with the *aftermath* of crimes. Even in these rough-and-tumble days, many officers did their best and began to form the traditions of a profession and good governance, which was destined to evolve and still evolves.

> **An arrest was a measure of success, but officials forgot that not having to make an arrest in the first place mattered.**

Understanding and moral demeanor began to guide conduct. At this time, the FBI of Hoover and visionary personnel began shaping our modern community safety and security more by the needs of citizens and less by special interests. Leaders began to remove their agencies from the influence and control of politics. The relationship with the community was about impartiality and evenhandedness. The hodgepodge of duties previously observed was no longer the norm. Walking a beat didn't fit. An arrest was a measure of success, but officials forgot that not having to make an arrest in the first place mattered. The significance and influence of research began to rise. Staff promoted an image that they were the last defense against corruption, violence, and victimization. The reform era was characterized by new definitions:[13]

- *Authorization* – Law and professionalism. Rules prevailed. Roles mainly involved oversight.

- *Function* – Crime control. This meant something had to go wrong before action could be taken. Prevention was yet to be a primary goal.

- *Organizational design* – Centralized, classical. Top-down hierarchy with one-way communication. Individuals obeyed orders rather than discussed appropriate action.

- *Relationship to environment* – Professionally remote. Connection to individuals and community was not established nor maintained. Neighborhoods had little communal involvement in promoting their security and well-being.

- *Channel* – Channeled through central dispatching activities with little thought of connecting to people where they lived before a problem arose. The idea that public governance existed to *work with* the community *not dictate to* the community was not yet well formed.

- *Tactics and technology* – Preventive patrol and rapid response to calls for service. Keeping a community wholesome and secure was still at arm's length—waiting for something to go wrong.

- *Outcome* – Crime control. This was a step up, but at the expense of prevention and connection to the community where the focus could be on promoting well-being. It was yet to be realized that crime could be cut off at the roots by understanding what goes wrong with children and establishing corrective measures such as finding ways to keep them in school.

Public governance continued to professionalize to move beyond politics, but not without distancing from those served.

Loosening Connection with Community

Enter technology, the car, and the radio to fight the first war on drugs against the likes of Al Capone and continue to insulate officers from those served. Officers patrolled in a car, which was abandoned only in extreme cases, as it was easy to call for backup. The neighborhood representative became occasional as the profession, while requiring courage, maintained necessary detachment from the citizenry because of the gravity of "controlling" crime. It was "a war out there." This unremitting mindset thus continued to detach public officials from the community.

Many law enforcement agencies today are small and rural and reflect local values and customs of good governance.

Still, every municipality wanted the promise of order from public safety, so agencies began to proliferate. In fact, many law enforcement agencies today are small and rural and reflect local values and customs of good governance. At the other end of the spectrum, we have statewide agencies such as the highway patrol and national agencies such as the Federal Bureau of Investigation (FBI), Drug Enforcement Administration (DEA), and the Bureau of Alcohol, Tobacco, Firearms and Explosives (ATF), each with a particular law enforcement focus. Private policing, which began with agencies such as Pinkerton, founded as the Pinkerton National Detective Agency by Allan Pinkerton in 1850, also grew. However, at the end of the day, the citizenry and especially those responsible for community well-being knew all was not well.

Isolation – The Price of Reform

Police became isolated in their departmental policies and procedures; regimented practices mattered. Austerity became the new normal. Crime and the fear of crime continued to rise as substance abuse and gang activity rose. Meanwhile, segments of society felt neglected, disenfranchised, or even abused by municipal government. People became better informed and expected much more from their policemen and

> **Governance became guided more and more by a solid moral compass, a critical element that survives and is reflected in today's public practitioner.**

policewomen. Line officers and middle managers conducting roll call were under the rules of command hierarchy, which didn't leave much leeway for line staff to offer comment and suggestions. The generalist in the community concerned with keeping some sort of normalcy became the remote specialist in the unit at headquarters concerned with defined duties and responsibilities.

This necessary reform in response to political control came at a price as the Peelian principles were pushed to the background—but certainly not forgotten. What are the Peelian principles? They harken back to the philosophy of Sir Robert Peel in the 1800s in Great Britain. Peel established a professional, centrally organized police force for Greater London. His principles defined a police force that was ethical and accountable to the public. He measured police effectiveness not by the number of arrests but by the lack of crime.[14] It was quite forward thinking and presaged better governance, both public and private.

We argue that this development of isolation from the public was part of public service evolution and, in retrospect, a sacrifice that was worth the price of reform. Consequently, policing was legitimized and rose in stature. Governance became guided more and more by a solid moral compass, a critical element that survives and is reflected in today's public practitioner.

This profession, essential to our republic, was taking shape and predominance as an example to the world of public service that respects the individual. Law enforcement returned to the community in meaningful ways, armed with research, bent on helping resolve the causes of crime and community dysfunction.

Fourth Wave: Problem-Solving Era – Return to the Community (ca. 1970-2010)

We can easily forgive a child who is afraid of the dark; the real tragedy of life is when men are afraid of the light.
– Plato

The new goal of public service emerged from personal relationships. People wanted to get to know their officers. From the officers' perspective, identifying people as neighbors and getting to know them led to understanding their needs. This, in turn, revealed ways to preserve community safety and security, thus enhancing community well-being.

In other words, when neighborhood problems are defined *by* the people who live there, solutions become more evident and the collective will builds to do something about it. People take more responsibility for solving *their* problems and preserving *their* neighborhood where they can feel safe and secure and be productive and happy. In other words, they can build a community that flourishes.

To that end, some public safety officers formed matrices of local and agency resources to solve what bothered people most—the fact that their quality of life was declining. People often focused on the lower-level crimes that impacted them daily. Public safety services, on the other hand, had been dedicated to high-profile violent crimes to the exclusion of quality-of-life issues. This increased the feeling in the community that their police department was not effective. The willingness to listen to the community, reengage, and evolve improved police community relations because the community had a vested interest in solving their problems.

Law enforcement began delivering Community Policing as their brand of municipal service. Police were marketing ideas and especially practical, realistic solutions.[15]

Personal contact turned out to be a great way to deliver local services. The more time officers spent in their neighborhoods connecting with people, the better they understood their neighbors' needs. This connection created within the official a territorial imperative, the desire to defend the territory, and developed a renewed sense of ownership. With more community contact, the citizenry began to understand their public representatives and what they did, why they did it, and how they did it. New ways of connecting emerged, creating inextricable links between community and those committed to protecting it.

Local agencies broke up headquarters and put substations in malls, public buildings, and neighborhoods. Expectations from both sides grew more realistic. Together, people and public safety officers owned these new ideas. Focus turned more to community wellness, with programs for gang reduction, substance abuse prevention, crisis intervention for mental health, school resource officers, and aftercare programs to reduce recidivism. This Fourth Wave strategy, the era of problem solving, included the following:[16]

> **With more community contact, the citizenry began to understand their public representatives and what they did, why they did it, and how they did it.**

- *Authorization* – Community support (political), law, professionalism. Public safety was gradually legitimized and considered vital to community infrastructure.

- *Function* – Crime control with prevention, plus problem solving. Increased focus on preventing social dysfunction.

- *Organizational design* – Decentralized, with task forces and matrices of resources. Embedding offices within communities aided personal connection within neighborhoods and facilitated problem solving.

- *Relationship to environment* – Consultative: Officials defended values of law and professionalism but listened and addressed community concerns. Individual and communal well-being strengthened.

- *Channel* – Channeled through analysis of underlying problems. More and more, data mattered rather than observation. Problem identification led to problem solving.

- *Tactics and technology* – Foot patrol, problem solving. Being in the neighborhood, nearly door-to-door, exemplified by National Night Out.[17]

- *Outcomes* – Quality of life and citizen satisfaction.

Still, the traditional top-down approach to public governance prevailed. This hindered participative problem solving, which takes advantage of combined resources from the public, private, and private nonprofit sectors. Participants in problem solving did not yet fully understand that the whole is stronger than the sum of the parts. Thus, ideas such as crisis intervention teams combining law enforcement and mental health professionals were tough to establish and costly to sustain, even though the model was proven.

We are now just past the turn of the 21st century in our evolution, which brings us to the New Wave of municipal governance. Before we address the latest developments in public service, however, let's look at the underlying industrial revolutions of our republic. These revolutions provided the backdrop for change.

Our Industrial Revolutions – Where Legends are Made

The New Wave of leadership marks the threshold of our Fifth Industrial Revolution, in which progress is accelerating at warp speed. It's no coincidence that this quantum leap requires a new way of thinking about leadership. Luckily, our republic always produces people who rise to the occasion. Our industrial progress began back when borders were settled and we moved from agriculture to mechanization. Most markedly in this New Wave, we are also entering the age of gene editing, which is both an historic blessing and a curse.[18]

The ability to "edit" the human body is a blessing because it brings the possibility of curing increasing numbers of diseases. Imagine curing many cancers. Likewise, the technology allows "germline enhancements," which means we can improve generations of people by adjusting the first cells of life in an embryo. However, such superhuman ability can be a curse because people will want babies "to order," which is unethical and fraught with danger. What if the editing goes awry and a difficult virus emerges?

Yet with all its potential dangers, the possibilities of gene editing are evident daily. Consider, for example, its impact on creating vaccines. We await what happens when majority sensibility prevails. After all, doom was predicted with the advent of the personal computer. Now nearly everyone who wants one has one, or several in various forms—and we progress. Humans are on a faster, greater, more promising trajectory. Let's trace how we've come to this remarkable time. It's exciting to be alive.

First Industrial Revolution

During the First Industrial Revolution, manufacturing was accomplished largely by steam engine, with supplies delivered by railroad. Imagine! The transcontinental railroad was built in *six years*.[20] It resulted from a collaboration between visionary investors, enlightened politicians, and the engineers, surveyors, and laborers who risked life and limb with brains, brawn, and bravado. The rail bed was hacked out of the wilderness, mostly by hand with black powder, vision, and the grit of immigrants (especially Chinese), freed slaves, and Mormons. They became so good at it, the two builders, the Central and Union Pacific Railroads, bet each other that they could lay *10 miles of track in a single day.*

The bet was on! They had no miraculous machines to prep the gravel ballast, set the 200-pound crossbar sleepers of timber, then lay and fasten the 400 pounds of steel and finish the margins. That 10 miles of railroad required approximately 5,280 rails and 31,680 ties—all moved and set by hand. Imagine blasting tunnels through mountains, suspending trestles over dizzyingly high gorges, and bridging bodies of water. An unimaginable feat!

The same crew of Chinese and Irish immigrant rail setters started and finished the one-day feat. Lunch, by the way, included two liters of beer. The Union Pacific won by laying just over 10 miles of gleaming steel! Nothing stood in their way—not rivers, not mountains, not deserts. Those railroads opened our entire West and presaged the next industrial revolution.[21]

Second Industrial Revolution

The Second Industrial Revolution of mass production was powered by oil, coal, and a new technology—electricity. We moved from the farm to the factory, where efficient production ruled. These innovations fueled more automobile production and manufacturing in general. They also supported an abundant labor market of people willing to work, government policy that backed capital capacity, and of course, innovators and inventors. World-changing inventions such as the steam engine, cotton gin, steamboat, and telegraph were a few of the "magical" creations of the time. Society overall improved exponentially. America became the world's greatest power. But we were just getting started. Next to arrive were computers.

Third and Fourth Industrial Revolutions

In the Third Industrial Revolution, technology, connectivity, and computing automated our manufacturing. Then computing became personal as two young men named Jobs and Wozniak, working from a garage, put wizardry in a box for anyone. Electronics, communications, and computing spread around the world like wildfire after the mind-blowing invention of the internet.

Progress exploded again as we entered the Fourth Industrial Revolution of "smart" technologies, which fused the physical, biological, and digital. Machines were constructed to "think." Robots could make cars by the millions week in and week out. An intricate medical operation could be done remotely, better than directed by the human hand. Computing moved from the desktop to another concept made real—the "cloud." All of this and much, much more alters and continues to improve how we live. "Over the last 25 years, more than a billion people have lifted themselves out of extreme poverty, and the global poverty rate is now lower than it has ever been in recorded history."[22] This speaks of progress we can only marvel at when we contemplate it.

> **In a blindingly short period of time, we've come from farming to the information age of artificial intelligence. Now we're on the cusp of artificial *superintelligence* that can make a machine seem human!**

Taking Flight

In a blindingly short period of time, we've come from farming to the information age of artificial intelligence. Now we're on the cusp of artificial *superintelligence* that can make a machine seem human! It's difficult to believe that a little over one hundred years ago, the greatest minds of the day said that human flight was impossible and we should devote our energies, intellect, and money to more promising ideas. Well, the Wright Brothers disproved *that* belief. Then, only 66 years after the first flight at Kitty Hawk, we accomplished the moon landing—and now we've set our sights on living on Mars!

We're fortunate to live in a republic where we're free to exercise our energies and intelligence to create such advances as well as greatly improve our daily lives. This is indeed a new age of enlightenment.[23] Vast amounts of information are now in the hands of more and more people who care to click on it—and use it for good. We are blasting through the information age to the molecular age and beyond to machines that can make decisions and create cures at the cellular level designed for the individual. We even have a box of blinking lights that can beat the best chess player in the world. And that's just for fun! Imagine the solutions we can discover to our thorniest issues with information building on information. Every institution, whether it's in education, medicine, commerce, banking, the military, social services, or you name it, is evolving to new potentialities.

As our republic winds and weaves and whizzes into the future, so does municipal and private sector governance. Our republic's evolution has much to teach us about how we deliver local services.

Learning from History

What do the previous Waves teach us that we may have forgotten?

- First Wave – *Establishment Era.* We see and establish the need for the sensibility of laws that respect the rights of individuals. *Can we improve on that today?*

- Second Wave – *Political Era.* Keeping order swings to the control of a few for political gain. We see the need for guiding standards. *Can we learn and even be inspired by the truths and wisdom of our Founding Fathers?*

- Third Wave – *Reform Era and Proliferation.* We reformed to define and establish professional public service as a noble calling. *Can we maintain the ancient and rediscovered moral compass?*[24]

- Fourth Wave – *Community Problem-Solving Era.* We learned that collaborating with the recipients of local services is an exceptionally good way to maintain order and wholesome, productive communities. *Can we return to the community in meaningful ways to collaborate and capitalize on our considerable collective resources, especially human capital?*

We believe we can do all of these and more. The times call for us to revisit how we provide public services. Aristotle and Cicero would affirm that concern for common betterment is a natural tendency of the human condition.

Fifth Industrial Revolution

The Fifth Industrial Revolution is emerging and awaits a proper description. It will probably be one in which humans and machines combine with a purpose beyond efficiency, mass production, and drive for profit to make the world safer, better for all, and more beautiful.[25] For example, scientists, the government, and industry are combining to ". . . pioneer a symbiosis between microorganisms, our bodies, the products we consume, and even the buildings we inhabit."[26] This fusion will most likely accelerate improvements in how we live. We will solve many of our most vexing problems. Energy will be sensible and cleaner. We will lurch and lunge toward confronting and resolving disease outbreaks, climate change and environmental issues, race and gender inequality, and poverty as a truly global community working toward these common egalitarian goals.[27]

Remember that we went from the first to second revolutions in about two hundred years. Now we've moved from the Fourth Revolution and entered the fifth in about a decade! As we found our way and grew through each revolution, our systems of governance, public and private, also matured. Leadership had to evolve with each passing era. Enter the leaders of this New Wave.

Fifth Wave: The New Wave MAGNUS–OVÉA Leader (2010 onward)

A man's character is his fate.
– Heraclitus

New Wave individuals continuously strive to be the best they can be—studying, practicing, and developing moral character. The process allows gradual but resolute improvement over a lifetime. The New Wave organization continuously develops all levels of staff to lead ethically, with both intellect and compassion. Today, we find ourselves with both genuine opportunity and grave responsibility. A New Wave MAGNUS–OVÉA Leader understands that giving back is a big part of a life well lived.

> **New Wave MAGNUS-OVÉA individuals take responsibility for their actions, making a lifelong commitment to develop their technical skills, leadership abilities, and especially character.**

The New Wave Leader - Technically Skilled, Morally Grounded

The New Wave of governance is based on leaders developing their minds and *using* them. New Wave MAGNUS-OVÉA individuals take responsibility for their actions, making a lifelong commitment to develop their technical skills, leadership abilities, and especially character.

The public is informed as never before. They have high expectations of those serving their community. The times demand that all leaders be careful stewards of their community's well-being by developing a character-based mindset. Those serving need to understand, even feel, the real needs of those they serve and work *with* them to address those needs and resolve their most urgent problems. Mutual trust and respect are natural byproducts. As we all develop individually, we need to develop collectively as well.

Developing Well-Being with a Range of Both Public and Private Endeavors

Individual and collective progress is first about *all* people focusing on how to live with others for the collective good, learning to collaborate, and living well with virtue and character. We all affect our communal progress, regardless of our life circumstances or career paths. It's the essence of how we survived as a species and will continue to do so.

The private sector stands to grow and benefit most from the emergence of the next wave of leaders in this innovative new era. Consider the potentials of technology, medicine, manufacturing, and all the areas that enrich our lives, including the arts and music, which can uplift our spirits. New Wave Leaders are called upon to help everyone improve their lives and support one another in a growth that will bring the highest good for the greatest number of people. Monumental advancements will affect us in ways we can't imagine. What better if we work together with synergy toward the greater good. People and leaders in all sectors will benefit from adopting the journey of becoming a New Wave Leader.

People employed in businesses of all sizes will see the business sense of understanding how they affect the lives of their neighbors and the impact they have on the future of their communities. In turn, communities will be dramatically redesigned to be friendly and collaborative and to respect the natural world.

The public sector needs to address the causes of social dysfunction from the ground up as we prepare children for school and keep them there. While only a small percentage will finish college, vocational training will gain critical importance. Our youth need to know and feel they have promise and purpose—that they can be productive members of society. In addition, they need to be prepared in mind, body, and character for possible centenarian lives. All must adapt or be trampled by the progress that will alter the evolution of humans.

Lessons to Remember and Relearn – From Surviving to Well-Being

It's been a long journey from near lawlessness to relative calm and order in most neighborhoods. People largely like their neighbors and neighborhoods in spite of media to the contrary. Most of the world looks to the United States for an example of "life, liberty, and the pursuit of happiness." Still, historically, we are a rather new experiment in government and have much work ahead to earn this faith in our example. While we have learned much from the first difficult days of establishing a new country, the following lessons can help inform the New Wave of MAGNUS-OVÉA Leaders.

- *Consent* – Establishing our country taught us that the Ancients were right in that those who govern do so only with the consent of the governed. As Aristotle would say, an essential virtue is unity, that of being connected to those around us and the greater family of people. Thus, we must listen to those we serve, our neighbors.

- *Standards* – Living through the difficulties of political evolution taught us we need standards. Fundamentally, the rule of law prevails. Much depends on getting those laws right and following them.

- *Connection* – Reform detached us from the essence of public service, for example, which is the direct and frequent contact with those served, which generally applies to most municipal services. It would be wise to look at practical ideas that take advantage of collaboration between those served, their public servants, and their local resources. Aristotle, when defining essential virtues, included the virtue of practical wisdom. Modern philosophers make the case that "... practical wisdom is the master virtue essential to solving problems of specificity, relevance and conflict...."[28] Our solutions to promote community well-being must be practical, doable, and sustainable as well as accomplish measurable good for the recipients of the program or service delivered.

- *Decentralization* – Community ownership of the problem and its solution matters. Top-down problem-solving for others to implement has its place, especially for critical actions, but it doesn't work well for most governance. Solutions need to be built from the *bottom-up* to the top and back again, becoming more creative, efficient, and effective with each cycle. Mutual strength multiplies from continuous collaboration, creating buy-in and community ownership. A combination of local resources working to solve locally defined problems is most effective.

History is fascinating—and valuable as it teaches so much. The common theme to progress is communication, including the art of persuasion. To achieve what we wish to do, we must do it *with* people not *to* them, and to do that, we need to not only communicate but do it persuasively.

The Promise of the New Wave

The New Wave marks the rise of the professional, no matter the rank, who is technically competent and leads with intellect and consideration to help build and sustain communities. The new view is those at the bottom matter as much as those at the top because they provide the foundational work and can lead in whatever they do. While we may experience periodic waves of concern for the role of our leaders and those who serve, overall, the quality, qualifications, and character of our new public sector recruits, for example, are impressive. They're eager to serve and do it right.

Even in these exceptional times, we're recruiting a genuinely inspired and talented bunch in the private and public sectors. We know our ranks display ethics, determination, dedication, and pure grit. These people believe in the nobility of their profession. They want to do well and do good, so they are. They're creative and want to build things that last. More and more individuals commit to improving themselves by continuing their skills training, professional education, and especially ethical development. New Wave public officials are focused on legacy that results in a better world.

> Our task is to take our solid foundation in the rule of law, traditions rooted in ancient wisdom, revolutionary spirit, and collective talents and energies to a new level.

Today's managers and leaders have the responsibility to encourage, train, and develop their staff from *pre*-hire to *post*-retirement. This happens through recruitment and assessment throughout a career that focuses on the strengths of well-being and anticipates a productive life long after that career ends. How senior local leadership develops its youngest leaders determines how well our government and governance will perform.

Indeed, we believe that just, wise, courageous, and temperate service is the rock upon which our republic stands and on which it will progress. We have an historic opportunity and grave responsibility to get it right. It will take our solid foundation in the rule of law, traditions rooted in ancient wisdom, revolutionary spirit, and collective talents and energies.

It's an exciting time, and we—you—are smack in the middle of it. Are you ready to do your part? We suspect you are.

Personally Speaking

The Uncommon in Common Hours

James Klopovic

For me, becoming a MAGNUS–OVÉA Leader is about giving back and having fun. One needs to be ready for both! This path for meaning in life inevitably leads to realizing uncommon dreams along the way.

I pushed myself through two careers in the public sector, one with the Air Force and the other with the State of North Carolina. Each career became its own reward and more. With one, I traveled the world, commanded a detachment of instructors, was a college professor, and managed to find myself at Bien Hoa, Viet Nam during the days of the Tet Offensive of '68. With the other, I helped communities put together collaboratives to permanently answer their most difficult social dysfunctions. Along the way, I involved myself in extensive schooling. I didn't know where the pursuit of public service and formal education would take me, but it turned out to be a worthy path. Each educational goal, each degree, led to promotions, new friends, enrichment, travel, and a wider perspective on life.

Education was self-fulfilling; I love to read and write. My learning and experiences inspired me to write this book and others—more ventures into the unknown. Today, I have the unimaginable opportunity to touch and improve many lives. Let me tell you; it just plain feels good.

Who knows beyond that how many lives each one of you will touch in turn? The good perpetuates itself.

I was able to accomplish remarkable things, at least for me, in those careers, but they were largely a matter of duty and obligation. I swore to do my duty to "protect and defend" my country in the Air Force; I even signed a paper that bound me to do so. But it wasn't until recently that I "discovered" (another wonderful, uncommon realization while becoming this new kind of person) that giving back is the unselfish act of heart and fortitude.

Along life's path you, too, may discover that beyond duty and obligation lie dedication, devotion, and even loving what you do and the people with whom you do it.

We both have a chance to make a difference in another's life—and should we be so fortunate, to make a difference in many lives. May we meet with "a success unexpected in common hours."

*If one advances confidently in the direction of his dreams, and endeavors
to live the life which he has imagined, he will meet with a success
unexpected in common hours.*
– Henry David Thoreau

Chapter 2

Introducing the New Wave MAGNUS–OVÉA Leader

In short, being magnanimous means being quietly courageous, self-sufficient, non-sycophantic, polite, discreet, and candid: this is the role model everyone can adopt with enthusiasm and sincerity.[29]
– Edith Hall

You are the New Wave professional. The MAGNUS–OVÉA Leader builds toward permanent excellence in self, others, organization, and community. It's not only about what you do but how you go about directing yourself and influencing the betterment of others for a common good.

Although the lofty goal of becoming and accomplishing more may seem daunting, don't fret. New Wave Leadership is based on practical, daily application. Steady practice, even in small efforts, will build exponentially over your life. Begin with the intent of developing good habits, which is another characteristic of this journey. The sooner you begin the better, as your habits, whether good or bad, form your character.

Good habits give you a strong foundation for when things go bad, and they sometimes will. You need a well of confidence and accomplishment, and an awareness that challenges are how we grow. Pause and think about this. The journey is about learning to live appropriately and well.

A growing core of leaders are building rewarding careers by working to make life worth living by creating the Good Life beyond the scope of work and the term of a career. These New Wave Leaders discover

Although results are important, New Wave Leaders know *how* they achieve goals is more important.

how to influence and inspire others and bring calm during storms. They recognize there's no static formula or checklist for leading and know it's a process that builds gradually. Uniting head and heart, they employ character and talent at the proper time and in the proper framework for leading.[30] Although results are important, New Wave Leaders know how they achieve goals is more important. This goes for all of us as leaders in our own roles and venues.

General Stanley McChrystal is uniquely qualified to explain leadership. He's insightful and even eloquent, especially when discussing how things get done, both large and small. He *earned* his stars and the adoration and respect of all he was privileged to lead. In his book *Leaders: Myth and Reality*, he profiles some of our greatest modern leaders to eliminate misconceptions about leadership and suggest lessons for those who aspire to it. The New Wave Leader must grow and adjust as the times dictate. The following is adapted from McChrystal.[31]

The Myths of Leadership

Successful leadership, General McChrystal asserts, is largely a factor of fate or luck, context, and consideration of the practicalities of putting people and things to work.[32] It's not dependent on a magical, all-encompassing agenda, although many think so. The most unassuming of us rise to the moment and do remarkable things. Following is an excellent example.

> Early in life, Jennifer Doudna, Ph.D. was a gangly preteen, an isolated "misfit" with an insatiable curiosity about the living world. This curiosity eventually led her to become a biochemist. She later collaborated with a French geneticist to co-develop CRISPR, a technology to unlock and edit genes to cure disease and prevent maladies. Thus, she helped usher in the most monumental revolution in history so far.[33]
>
> After nearly a lifetime of staring into a microscope, Dr. Doudna was awarded a Nobel Prize in 2020, just as COVID raged. She assembled 10 teams to attack it head on.[34] Researchers have been able to use the CRISPR gene-editing technology to come up with a COVID test that detects the coronavirus in only five minutes. CRISPR may now enable cures to be more targeted and become available sooner.
>
> Jennifer Doudna's leadership is changing and will continue to change the course of history. With her honed skills to guide her and her curiosity to inspire her, she followed her intuition with an aim to help humanity. She had

no formula for leadership because there isn't one. She captured a moment in history and took charge of defining an unthinkable goal with her vision. There's no telling where gene editing will take us.

> **A deep understanding of the *moment*, the humanistic *system*, and inspirational *symbolism* unite to make the leader.**

With that powerful example, let's begin the discussion of a New Wave Leader by taking an introductory look at what McChrystal considers myths of leadership. We dive deeper into these myths in Chapter 10. After 40 years of leading hundreds of thousands of people, he realized what the essence of leadership success was—and equally important, what it was not.

- The *Formulaic* Myth – There is no formula. Leadership involves circumstances that present themselves to men or women who recognize they are present at a unique moment. They are ready and willing, and they intuitively know what to do.

- The *Attribution* Myth – Successful leadership is not attributed to position, rank, or birthright. This myth describes leadership as involving a project one must finish instead of correctly seeing it as a process to apply. A project is terminal; a process is continuous, which allows creativity, answers, circumstances, and accomplishments to build and evolve.

- The *Results* Myth – This states that objective results, such as winning a war, are paramount. Not so according to General McChrystal. A leader's symbolism, words, appearance, and style are substantial aspects of the leadership package. A leader is a role model—such as Jennifer Doudna.

While we can and must study and practice what goes into leadership, a deep understanding of the *moment*, the humanistic *system*, and inspirational *symbolism* unite to make the leader.

New Wave MAGNUS–OVÉA Leaders recognize that *how* they are perceived and *how* they speak and act matter, *who* they are matters, and *what* they represent matters. Symbolism is about the subtleties of power and the command over the closed impulses of self. An object can become a symbol of a particular leader and thus symbolize leadership itself. For example, General MacArthur's corn cob pipe came to mean "Our leader is here; anything is possible." People like MacArthur *still* lead, even though they are gone.

Legitimacy is About Principles Not Power

We dwell on virtues, values, and character here—but what about principles or a code of conduct to help us carry out virtues with holistic living and embody the character to which we aspire? We need right principles to guide us so we can reject *good* alternatives and pursue *better* ones.[35] For example, principles help us realize the worth of compassion over material possessions. They help us pick associates and especially friends, and measure character and behavior. With principles, the New Wave professional demonstrates character, common sense, and creativity fueled by an intense desire to do well and do good collectively, communally.[36]

Principles are our aspirational goals and supply a code to guide us in how we conduct ourselves. Such is the Air Force code of conduct, which captures essential principles (adapted from USAF 1997):

- *Integrity first* – Integrity is the voice of self-control and the basis of what is just. It encompasses honesty, responsibility, accountability, and humility, for example.

- *Service before self* – This means professional duties come first. It includes, at least, respect for others, discipline, self-control, and faith in the effort of the organization.

- *Excellence in what we do* – This is sustained drive, even passion, for continued improvement, individually and in concert with others.

Why does an exceptionally large operation such as a branch of the military have *only three* core values or principles? It's impossible to draft enough rules, regulations, standard operating procedures, policies, or executive orders to anticipate all instances imposed by fickle reality. Three are enough. Overall, they rely on the convergence of heart, head, and conscience of the individual who faces daily challenges to aspire to become more. Good people know when a thing is right.

Core principles define the individual who becomes a leader and gains the respect and following of those he or she leads. Respect depends on legitimacy, which depends on principles. Whether leading in the public sector or the private sector, in the home or in the community, legitimacy is essential to leadership.

Tyrants, terrorists, and totalitarians try to lead and will continue to try, but the genies of individual freedom and collective will are out of the bottle. Legitimate leaders must sustain a just society that reasonably benefits the many.

> **Legitimacy does not come from position or personality or proclamation; it's earned by principle-centered leaders seeking common good.**

Our communities, organizations, and families are the strength on which society builds. They are microcosms of the whole. The best of our leaders understand that their positions derive from the people of their organization, from humble not arrogant legitimacy—but with a bit of brave audacity. Earning legitimacy is the first step to gaining followership and, let's be practical, a good way to keep a job.

Legitimacy does not come from position or personality or proclamation; it's earned by principle-centered leaders seeking common good. Consider these four suggestions for creating legitimacy in your leadership:

- *Dignity* – Treat all people with dignity and respect. Class, ethnicity, gender, etc. do not matter. We have *all* been endowed with certain inalienable rights as a human being, and that equality demands you treat others as you yourself would like to be treated.

- *Dialogue* – Create opportunities to give people a voice and be attentive to their hearts. Stop delivering monologues and be willing to set ego aside to focus on the thoughts and feelings of others.

- *Real-time decision making* – Base all decisions on real-time evidence, applicable facts, and an understanding of the situation as a dynamic of *human* interaction. Data, research, evidence, experience matter but only so much; eventually people have to take action. Don't make decisions based on who someone is or how someone looks.

- *Demonstrating goodwill* – Show that you care about people and have their best interests at heart and they will trust you.

People who are asked to obey authority must feel as if they have a *voice*—that if they speak up, they will be heard, and if they are heard, they can influence action. That way speaking up intelligently is empowering. A law, policy, or order must be stable, not whimsical to fit the person or moment. People want the rules tomorrow to be roughly the same as the rules today and want them to be fair across the board.

Make a careful list of all things done to you that you abhorred. Don't do them to others. Make another list of things done for you that you loved.
Do them for others, always.
– Dee Hock

The new leader of today and especially tomorrow *understands* and works with institutional strengths by building organizational capacity for meaningful work based on meaningful relationships.[37] This leader musters, organizes, and motivates—better inspires—the many to act as a single force with single purpose.

The job, then, of the New Wave Leader is to leave his or her organization, section, division, agency, community better by having passed through it. This is a considerate way of thinking and acting, essential to long-term success.

A MAGNUS-OVÉA State of Mind

MAGNUS–OVÉA is a way of daily practice that arises from a state of mind. The MAGNUS-OVÉA individual is others and ethics oriented, and virtues and values centric, aiming to accelerate life's worthy pursuits. This leads to a meaningful, satisfying legacy and the respect of respectable people.

In his book *Principles: Life and Work*,[38] philanthropist Ray Dalio recognizes that leadership is a state of mind, which supports the meaning and purpose of MAGNUS–OVÉA Leadership. Dalio explains his personal perspective on how to succeed in life and work. (You'll want this book—a great realistic and relevant read—in your personal library.) He demonstrates that success is based on virtue, the epitome of becoming MAGNUS–OVÉA. He explains through many maxims what virtue-based living and working means to him. His principles are "fundamental truths . . . foundations that get you what you want in life."[39]

Mr. Dalio always wanted to improve the common good. He founded Bridgewater Associates hedge fund from scratch decades ago, and now he makes $100 million value-based grants and shares how to live a rewarding, principled life. His feats include writing bestsellers, lecturing to multitudes, mentoring many, and giving back to society from one of the largest self-made fortunes the world has known. Dalio embraces the very essence of OVÉA in being others centric, living virtuously, and accelerating his accomplishments

Discuss and think with an open mind and flexibility, decide with discernment, plan accordingly, act decisively, analyze results carefully, repeat.

near the end of his career. He offers overarching themes relevant to how we get along and make things happen that capture the spirit of the journey of becoming MAGNUS–OVÉA, of becoming a New Wave Leader:

- *Be radically open minded.* Develop the ability to effectively explore different points of view and different possibilities without letting your ego or your blind spots get in your way. Differentiate between arguing and understanding, and seek to understand others' opinions. If you can acquire this ability—and with practice you can—you will be able to deal with your realities more effectively and radically improve your life.[40]

- *Appreciate the art of thoughtful disagreement.* Approach healthy disagreements as the real opportunities they are, not a chance to nitpick. Listening includes showing respect, talking judiciously and sparsely, and courteously asking for clarification. You are in a discourse to understand and learn. Epictetus observes, "We have one mouth and two ears for a reason."

- *Debate your views with credible people.* Intelligent people are interesting to debate with, not to compete with tooth and nail. Debate with a view to moving processes and ideas to fruition; this is the "how" of it all. So, choose something productive to debate and carefully choose your debate partner—perhaps your well-read fellow colleague who has demonstrated character.

Know when your alternate view causes you to miss something in a discussion. Write down what you missed with its commensurate lessons. Usually those lessons will be a variation on the practice of being objective and open-minded. Be factual and evidence-based, using data whenever you can. Help others be open-minded to good debate. Then decide what to do. Nothing happens without action. Napoleon became emperor of most of ancient Rome's lands with his rallying order of the day: "Activité, activité, vitesse" — Action, action, speed!

In short: Discuss and think with an open mind and flexibility, decide with discernment, plan accordingly, act decisively, analyze results carefully, repeat.

> *Meaningful work and meaningful relationships aren't just nice things*
> *we choose for ourselves—they are genetically programmed into us.*
> – Ray Dalio

Excellence Doesn't Just Happen

Personal excellence is only a means to the ultimate expression of excellence—that which we do together—by being others centric. Accomplishment of any degree does not occur in a vacuum.

In his book *If Aristotle Ran General Motors: The New Soul of Business*, Tom Morris recognizes that collaborative partnership is the ultimate accomplishment of the human condition.[41] Collaboration is how we as a species have progressed, proliferated, and profited. The MAGNUS–OVÉA individual understands this progression from personal to shared excellence. Collaboration is tough. It aligns with the modern New Wave MAGNUS–OVÉA Leadership mindset of seeing challenge as growth—both personal and interpersonal.

We begin the process of getting along a bit warily, but as we strive to agree, we become more. Morris delineates the progression of human relations that describes how we survived as a species.[42]

- Stage 1: *Aggressiveness* – We ready ourselves to freeze, escape, or be combative.

- Stage 2: *Rivalry* – We grow closer but become competitive.

- Stage 3: *Obedience* – We find agreement, and cooperation helps us get more done.

- Stage 4: *Synergism* – Finally, we learn to partner in true collaboration to improve the common good.

Excellence begins with individuals and ends with people in collaboration, from continuous self-improvement to continuous collective progress. Recognize self-defeating antagonism, toxic rivalry, and dull compliance. Move toward the synergy of working well together, in which the whole is greater than its parts.

> **Recognition of excellence can expand and multiply it exponentially. This can be as simple and profound as saying "Thank you" for a job well done—and *meaning* it!**

The role of New Wave Leadership is to define, model, and pave the path to becoming better and better. Motivating. Exciting. Doable.

Your individual and collective motivation is to bring your organization's human capital together in synergy to improve the progress and growing accomplishments of the whole. Recognition of excellence can expand and multiply it exponentially. This can be as simple and profound as saying "Thank you" for a job well done—and *meaning* it!

Pause a moment in your reading to realize the marvels of our collaboration over millennia. Think, for example, of the cell phone, derived from numberless creative minds and determined hands working together. We can talk to the other side of the world, compute the square root of any number, conduct face-to-face meetings online, and even take dance lessons with that small device! Moreover, in little more than a long lifetime, we have come from horse and carriage to cars that drive themselves! Collaboration at its most remarkable.

Setting Sights on Character and Virtue–and Then?

Daily practice. Developing character and virtue takes practice! Always remember, character is perishable unless it's continuously upheld. Aristotle recognized that character is built by ongoing, habitual character-based *action*.

This, in turn, enhances our attitude, which hones our personality and sociability. Virtue, values, character, and holistic living are the building blocks of continuous growth, yet they rely on the quality of your attitude. How you appear to others, what you model, how you connect, and how you make people feel by your presence are vital. You can have all the character in the world and a bad attitude will diminish, most times destroy, your impact.

Everyone leads in some way—from the parent to the president and everyone in between. How you lead matters. Even the uneducated, inexperienced, and untraveled can influence others and are sometimes the most memorable. So, next we turn to temperament, behavior, and disposition to complete the demeanor of the New Wave professional.

The most momentous thing in human life is the art of winning the soul to good or evil.
– Pythagoras

Personality and Temperament in Leaders

We all would love to keep company with our more famous presidents—perhaps especially Abraham Lincoln. He was a truly remarkable and memorable person from early childhood. After he decided to try politics in his twenties, it took him only eight months to gain local support to run for the Illinois state legislature. This is an unheard of accomplishment for anyone—anytime.[43] It takes most politicians many years to run and win statewide office. Lincoln went from a dirt floor cabin to the White House and on to preserving the union of our United States. It was decades before circumstances, experience, and his accrued wisdom led him to write and deliver the Gettysburg Address.

In Doris Goodwin's study of *Leadership in Turbulent Times*,[44] she observes of Lincoln:

> [His success lay in his] *sociability, his "open—candid—obliging & honest" good nature. "Everybody loved him." He would help travelers whose carriages were mired in mud; he volunteered to chop wood for widows; he was ever ready to lend a "spontaneous, unobtrusive" hand. Almost anyone who had contact with him in the little community spoke of his kindness, generosity, intelligence, humor, humility, and his striking, original character. Rather than golden mythmaking tales spun in the wake of Lincoln's historic presidency, these stories told by the score, join into a chorus of the New Salem community to form an authentic portrait of a singular young man.*[45]

Lincoln's virtue, colossal work, and determination to make a mark generated trust in others. His kind, humble, helpful attitude moved them in significant ways.

More striking, his conduct was not contrived. Perhaps it came naturally as a consequence of his hardscrabble childhood, where survival depended on neighbor helping neighbor. He was completely congruent throughout his life.

Mostly, he loved the company of people and loved to help out. He enjoyed seeing neighbors do well and making them happy. In turn, he was happy in the doing of it. That tendency to support others helped Lincoln himself through his unspeakable tragedies and the gloom of writing to the mothers of the Civil War's fallen heroes.

Goodwin studied four of our iconic presidents—Abraham Lincoln (16th president), Theodore Roosevelt (26th), Franklin D. Roosevelt (32nd), and Lyndon B. Johnson (36th). In her book, she captures who they were, how they became great, and the lessons they taught—and still teach us with their legacies. Personality, or temperament, played a big part in their remarkable accomplishments and important place in history.

Lincoln often confessed he didn't know a thing and doggedly pursued answers— many times all night. He did *not* fear failing. He worked on communicating and connecting to people—simply and to the point, and he became profoundly and timelessly remembered. He had the gift of story, usually humorous, to point out the hidden obvious that evaded those listening. With himself as his own best subject, he learned human nature with humility.

True Knowledge exists in knowing that you know nothing.
– Socrates

Theodore Roosevelt was one of our few truly intellectual presidents. He had abundant gifts, which would have been wasted on lesser men but weren't on him because he worked so hard, many times denying even food and sleep. Born to a life of ease, with thoroughbred horses, a fleet of servants, the best food, indulgent parents, and trips to the continent, Teddy was coddled and headed for a life of relative ease. But he had insatiable drive. Not only did he become a statesman, but he was a conservationist, naturalist, historian, and writer.[46] While he's admirable for applying his intellect, talents, and skills and leaving an enduring legacy, Teddy Roosevelt could have developed more life balance—a necessary MAGNUS-OVÉA trait. Balance is vital to respect the demands of both career and family. One must decide when and what to prioritize. The Teddy Roosevelt drive appears to be a family trait as his equally famous cousin soon followed him into history.

Franklin Delano Roosevelt (FDR) exuded ". . . ambition, motivation, resoluteness, language skills, storytelling gifts, sociability."[47] He matched these qualities with ". . . willpower, intellectual vitality, irrepressible liveliness, wide-ranging interests and a growing gratification connecting with people from different backgrounds and stations in life."[48] As a child, he slept with a dictionary!

Personality can have a darker side, and as a man, FDR learned manipulation, agility, and cunning with willful self-preservation.[49] Perhaps he struggled with the morals and ethics of these extremes and justified the means for the common beneficial ends. (The Ancients did make the case that a wrong—perhaps a lie—was justifiable for the greater good. The life of a spy, for example, is one big lie and thus not just. However, spies helped win our Revolutionary War.)

This again recalls the importance of finding the mean between the extremes of our passions, wants, desires, and conduct.

Lyndon Johnson personified a "steam engine in pants" a colleague observed. He could talk to anyone. A study in contradictions, ". . . he would vacillate between security and insecurity, assertiveness and obsequiousness, charm and taunting cruelty, a desire to please and a need for control."[50] He was kind, even generous, but at a cost of demanding total allegiance and 16-hour days. Here was another example of search-ing, struggling, striving for the Golden Mean. Johnson never found that balance; he remained a man of excesses, especially in his political ambition.

What do these men of destiny teach us? Much. Yes, they teach us what to do and what not to do. All these leaders could be gracious and, at times, oppressively demanding. They all worked brutally hard and all were ambitious. They all did their best to be truthful and certainly were courageous and accepted responsibility for their personal actions and their nation. The wisdom of these legendary leaders grew from unending curiosity, grinding study, and a desire to perfect the written and spoken word. In addition, intense personality, natural and practiced, marks all the presidents Goodwin profiles. The truth is, we all have a bit of what these leaders had—and we can bring out the best of it with reasonable diligence and tenacity.

Thus we see that strength of personality is helpful, but it needs to be tempered, aligned with character, and aimed in the right direction. Most important, all great leaders are driven to improve the common good and inspire those around them to be more than they would have been otherwise. These men embodied supererogation—total dedication and devotion to their work and cause.

"No man," Teddy Roosevelt insightfully observed, "is superior unless it was by merit; and no man is inferior unless by his demerit."[51] He turned defeat into a learning experience. Lincoln commanded respect because he respected the commanded.

The attitudes and the natural and sculpted personalities of these leaders overwhelmed situations, circumstances, and people with a common inspiring vision for how things could be, then they set about making it happen.

> *The key is to keep company only with people who uplift you,*
> *whose presence calls forth your best.*
> – Epictetus

MAGNUS-OVÉA Leaders – the New Wave Forward

Leadership evolves! We follow, but in *Leaders: Myth and Reality*, McChrystal asserts we want to know *why* we follow; we want to be *involved* in decisions and outcomes and feel there's *purpose* to our efforts.[52] Desire for involvement is good—and natural, especially to the evolution of private and public governance, which requires *participation* to succeed. A growing symbiosis exists between leader and those led. We are moving from singularly top-down to top-down/bottom-up collaboration in a continuous cycle.[53] As alluded to previously in this chapter, McChrystal presents views of leadership that New Wave Leaders need to understand (italics his):

- Leadership is *contextual and dynamic* and therefore needs to be constantly adapted to the immediate situation.

- Leadership is more of an *emergent* property of a complex system with rich feedback than it is top-down directives by a leader. A New Wave Leader must grasp that *people*, who are unpredictable and multi-talented, make everything work.

- The leader is vitally important to leadership, but not for the reasons we usually ascribe to a leader. The importance of leaders is often more about the *symbolism, meaning, and future potential* that leaders bring to collective action, advancement, and achievement than it is about the results themselves (italics by author).

Thus, we can say that New Wave Leadership aligns with McChrystal's definition in that it's "... a complex *system* of relationships between leaders and followers, in a particular *context*, that provides *meaning* to its members."[54] (His italics.)

Meaning matters. Leaders going forward fulfill our wants and especially needs by helping "... us to make sense of the world, sustain our common indemnitees, and hold hope for a brighter tomorrow."[55] This progression is right and natural.

Yes, being in charge may mean arriving at a particular defined end. But that end is reached as the organizational collaborative of people gains understanding, hope, and identity.[56] This explains why we follow leaders even if they display moral degradation. Because they give us meaning. Leaders matter! But their effectiveness is less and less about command and control than it is about moving people in a certain direction by providing compelling motivation.

Leadership going forward isn't about continually applying a checklist but about understanding how to get things done in an ever-changing context in a certain place and time. Success as a productive member of the community depends on deliberately reaching for your potential. This means having a system for making

> **Leaders matter! But their effectiveness is less and less about command and control than it is about moving people in a certain direction by providing compelling motivation.**

the best decisions, communicating well, cultivating self-knowledge, and having proper intentions.[57]

It is not by muscle, speed, or physical dexterity that great things are achieved,
but by reflection, force of character, and judgment.
– Cicero

Reaching Your Potential – Beginning with a Book by Your Side

No doubt you've heard Yogi Berra's quip, "If you don't know where you are going, you'll end up someplace else." You need a destination and a roadmap. Aristotle knew that planning, done early and often, is fun because the best planning regards what you want and like to do.[58]

It's jaw dropping to realize that despite how far we've come as a species, we have so much intellectual potential that we've barely begun to tap it. For example, every remarkable person has a love affair with books; how much better could we be if we *all* took up the habit of having a stimulating book at hand. When Franklin D. Roosevelt became assistant secretary for the Navy, he amassed 2,500 books and manuscripts on maritime matters. That's an entire library—and that was just *one* of his interests!

It behooves us to take charge of our own development, to buy good books for our personal library, then to *read* them, *learn* from them, and *practice* at least one thing from each book.

If you have a garden and a library, you have everything you need.
– Cicero

Know Your Moral Intentions

Even Benjamin Franklin needed time to correct errata. No doubt he wanted to right his ethical omissions and commissions. Plus, he did not want to avoid doing something because he was cowardly. The trick is to minimize these ethical pitfalls. Mark Twain said, "If you tell the truth, you don't have to remember what you said." This means knowing and being true to yourself.

In her book *Aristotle's Way: How Ancient Wisdom Can Change Your Life*, Edith Hall quotes Aristotle's comments that cut through this important nuance of moral intentions. She writes: "The true-to-themselves have consistent characters, are self-reliant, act in the same way toward everybody, and are not overly concerned with the opinion others hold of them. In this they are like the ideal 'great-souled,' 'who is open about the people whom he likes and dislikes' and 'cares more for truth than for people's opinions.'"[59]

Good intentions defy rules because there are never enough rules to consider every (moral) twist and turn in life. And moral dilemmas, while they can be described and explained in allegory, can't be prescribed individual to individual. We face our unique dilemmas independently. In the end, the respect of respectable people is important—and we must earn it!

The New Wave Stellar Performer

This book describes what it is to be a Stellar Performer—someone who goes beyond the call of duty to dedication, devotion, passion. Becoming MAGNUS–OVÉA is an intensely individual undertaking in its application within specific contexts and times.

Hall à la Aristotle, captures it remarkably well. She says it's about ". . . taking on life's project of becoming a great-souled man or woman—of being magnanimous."[60]

In short, this means being:[61]

- *Quietly courageous* – Assuming challenges because they are right to take on, prepared to sacrifice for a good cause.

- *Self-sufficient* – Well-rounded and competent.

- *Non-sycophantic* – Courteous to the humble as well as the rich and powerful.

- *Candid* – Expressing true thoughts and feelings.

- *Polite* – Giving and earning respect.

- *Discreet* – Avoiding gossip and excessive criticism.

Let's look at other qualities that distinguish a New Wave Stellar Performer.

New Wave Leaders endeavor to become their best selves.

Moving from good to our best selves means considering life not as a project but a *process.* This signifies continuously learning, continuously contributing, and continuously enhancing mutual well-being, while thoroughly enjoying being alive. Those pursuing becoming MAGNUS–OVÉA see life as good yet accept that difficulties are part of it because the tough times make the good times splendid. They're grounded in virtues and morals, which are tested and developed throughout their ever improving and interesting lives.

New Wave Leaders are responsible.

These individuals earn the trust to lead well. Being good stewards of the honor and responsibilities involved in leading sends the message they can be trusted in larger contexts and allows them to be justly proud yet humble in their leadership role.

New Wave Leaders realize that without truth and fairness, little else is effective.

They see truth and fairness as the foundation of living morally. This means accepting the challenge of understanding right from wrong and of doing the right thing even though they are acting on their own. The Asian Ancients understood that one must not even think dishonestly, as this begins a descent into corruption. The New Wave Leader knows that being fair is about building satisfaction and trust among those they lead.

New Wave Leaders have a positive attitude.

Attitude makes the difference in how people are perceived and how well they can lead. These leaders model a positive, can-do attitude. In this, they inspire others to do their best and accomplish what others may think they cannot do. They understand the distinction between cooperation and collaboration to accomplish goals that make a positive difference. They can see a vision and reach it.

New Wave Leaders have grit.

They don't fear challenges that seem beyond what they think they can do. They're especially eager to do those things that contribute to the betterment of those around them, beginning with family. Thus, they choose wisely what they do, because they know in their hearts, they will see tasks, big and small, through to their proper end. As Hall says, "None of us wants to be haunted on our deathbed either by guilt or the knowledge that there was something we didn't achieve simply because we were too scared to try."[62]

New Wave Leaders continually develop themselves.

They love gaining skills and especially knowledge. They continuously read, study, learn, think, and expressly apply lessons learned. They're always aware of their saboteurs and correct themselves through self-evaluation, self-awareness, self-adjustment, and self-development.

New Wave Leaders seek and find what truly matters.

They know life becomes better when the focus is on essentials. Collectively, little things are big things and they matter. Making good memories matters. Earning the respect of honorable people matters. Keeping home and hearth harmonious matters. Doing one's best matters—but self-aggrandizement is not the goal. The New Wave Leader knows the value of exercising restraint, humility, and modesty.

New Wave Leaders know what lies "beyond the beyond."

Although no one is perfect and New Wave Leaders may be the first to accept that fact, they tend to not only go beyond the call of duty but beyond *that*, which is called *supererogation*. How? They are *dedicated* and *devoted* to a common vision, to individual and collective well-being, to becoming more. They have faithfulness, enthusiasm, and platonic *love* for people and a worthy endeavor.

New Wave Leaders seek wellness and well-being.

They strive for health, are generally happy, and want to help those around them be healthy and happy as well. They consider mentoring following generations as a duty *and* a joy, and they're good at it. New Wave Leaders are generally *content* with *who* they are but not content with the way *things* are, and thus they look to craft a brighter future.

Most especially, New Wave Leaders are fun people.

Not only do New Wave Leaders embody virtue, goodness, and wisdom, but they enjoy life and are interesting and fun to be around. Like attracts like, and one is enriched by the company one keeps. When they walk into a room, it brightens. Therefore, they attract people who enrich *their* lives, which is one of the most rewarding aspects of developing these qualities.

New Wave Leaders are MAGNUS–OVÉA.

You are the Next Wave of service evolution. *You* can be one of the New Wave MAGNUS–OVÉA Leaders who work to be their better selves, envision more, and accomplish more—and *you* can inspire others to do the same. Thus, you can build a worthy legacy of improving yourself, those around you, and your community.

A Solemn and Personal Promise

As Immanuel Kant reminds us, "If [we] are to develop into rational, moral adults, [we] must eventually come to see right action as a duty beyond the self." This refers to what lies beyond supererogation, in which dedication and devotion to become our best selves also improves the world around us.

> In this new era, character-based professionals partner with their communities to enhance well-being.

This New Wave creates communities that are welcoming places to live, work, play, and raise children. In this new era, character-based professionals partner with their communities to enhance well-being. *Together*, they manifest permanent solutions to the problems *they* want to solve with *their* resources, *their* social capital, *their* creativity, and *their* determination. Everyone involved has wholesome commitment; everyone thrives.

Making a solemn and personal promise to start the journey to become your better then best self means committing to a disciplined life. We aren't suggesting you become a paragon of virtue—no saint, no mystic, no priest, no captain of industry—just someone you yourself would respect and, in turn, someone who earns the respect of respectable people. It's a matter of trying, failing, analyzing, and doing this again and again in a great virtuous cycle.

When you encounter adversity—and we all have dark days—practice seeing these days as chances to improve. Everyone fails; the best of us resume our upward trajectory. As wise Yoda says: "There is no try; only do." Learning to be MAGNUS–OVÉA means continuously evolving for a lifetime. *It is worth it.*

You are the New Wave. Be *devoted* to becoming a Stellar Performer who is steadfast, constant, committed. *Love* what you do, be loyal, and be enthusiastic for others and for meaningful activity. Know that it's good to be alive.

Thus, we come full circle. New Wave Leaders revere the past because of what it teaches, *recognize* the present because they know how to shape it, and *realize* what the future can be because they can *make it so.*

Personally Speaking

Marty – Seeing More and Doing Much More
James Klopovic

My dear friend Don "Marty" Martin recently passed. We went through basic training together in the Air Force over a half century ago. I tell his story because I consider him a great everyday example of what it is to continuously dream of what can be.

Marty became a middle school shop teacher in a suburb of Houston, although he actually began as a college professor. Most of his students endured difficult home situations, and many left to drift (or careen) into murky futures. He would chuckle, something he did a lot, that he taught "pre-prison." He could have stuck to the usual small engine repair, maybe a little heating-and-air training, welding, and woodworking for his 30+ years at George Middle School in Rosenberg, Texas. Expectations for a shop teacher were not high. It was a class kids took to escape English and math. Marty had chosen a career path which, for others, would certainly lead to obscurity. But Marty saw more—much more—in his young charges.

He taught them manners, he exemplified discipline, he exuded kindness and humor. He taught them to fly model airplanes competitively by flying a very clunky desktop simulator, which he got as a castoff from a flying school—and his students won national titles. He taught them production-line manufacturing, and they hand built fancy, sturdy picnic tables that converted to benches. Those tables were professional works of functional art. The students crafted 104 of them every year for nearly 30 years—and signed them. Those picnic tables are now all over Texas and who knows where else. They were built to last. He taught his students to make baseball bats and pens from exotic woods—more works of art—and they won national titles with those, too. Parents would plead to have their children in Mr. Martin's class because his class was life changing. Imagine that! A middle school shop class—life changing. He guided children to be responsible young men and women who were taught they could do meaningful things. His friends, staff, parents, and especially his students—too many to count—adored him.

Marty imagined and undertook anything. Anything! The four-wheeler path to his deer stand got flooded regularly by the Brazos River. No problem for Marty. He built and installed a suspension bridge to cross that river. It's still there today. He could smoke some of the best deer sausage in Texas; that's a fact confirmed by the many who tried to imitate his recipe.

My friend understood that little things matter—that contributions need not be grand gestures that make the news. They consist of a constant stream of little kindnesses and jobs done superlatively even when no one was watching or ever would. The sum of those little kindnesses toward the many become a centrifugal force when given over a lifetime. Think about Marty's hundreds and hundreds of students who found their way in his classes. Now think of how each of them carries those lessons forward.

Much to his great surprise (and many others), Marty became the *Distinguished Teacher of the Year* for the *entire* state of Texas! An honor he accepted humbly, of course. He could have simply fulfilled his job description. Instead, he followed his talent and heart beyond duty and obligation, way beyond what was expected of an "ol' time" shop teacher. Marty moved from success to significance in everything he touched.

Marty's example and message are to find that thing that's bigger than you are in what you do, whatever that may be. That something will become self-evident as you pursue living well and with purpose—giving back and having fun. Marty epitomized becoming a New Wave MAGNUS–OVÉA Leader, which he did to his very last day.

I sorely miss Marty's Sunday calls and his stories. But more important is his legacy to his students, to his church, to his many communities, and to his numberless friends. He was and is the ideal citizen of whom the Ancients speak.[63]

*. . . [M]any small acts of kindness, generosity, and courage add up
to make a meaningful difference in the lives of others.*
– Patricia Churchland

Chapter 3

New Wave Leadership – A Fundamental Shift

We must get to the point in our lives. What is the point? To become a new kind of man or woman, having inner command and outer excellence.
– Vernon Howard

We are presented with the opportunity for an historic cultural shift in governance—public, private, and nonprofit. Seismic shifts are taking place in this moment of advancing civilizations and evolving humans. In this era of learning to understand and change the human gene at our bidding, we must wisely define how, what, and who we become.

Our global nature forces us to think carefully about how we act locally, as the microcosm affects the macrocosm. What we do can have ramifications in the next neighborhood and on the other side of the planet. Will we use the atom, the information bit, and gene editing to make improvements, solve individual problems, and advance beneficially to what comes next . . . or not? How we create and maintain both family and work communities as places where we can thrive will necessarily evolve. We're moving from what we do *for* or *to* our communities to what we do *with* our communities. We all have a responsibility to strengthen our nation, our neighborhoods, and one another. What we do now will resonate for generations.

This chapter is a brief overview of concepts, science, and themes discussed throughout the book as we make the case for becoming a MAGNUS–OVÉA individual and New Wave Leader.

First and foremost, we are most optimistic about what and who we are as a country. Ours is an incredibly young country in the march of human progress—only about

250 years in the making. This means we're still learning the basics of how our country can function and especially how we use our scientific innovations for progress. Considering the purposes

> We all have a responsibility to strengthen our nation, our neighborhoods, and one another. What we do now will resonate for generations.

of this book, we must address difficulties getting along with one another, which we will. Mainly, we need to learn how to truly collaborate on ideas, projects, and programs that focus on the common good. Doing this will help us all individually and, more important, collectively.

Becoming Legacy Leaders

The current models of training, education, and development no longer work well and haven't kept up with societal advances. They don't address the fundamentals of how we can further the common good and for the most part aren't practical. They teach the why and the what but not the vital how of making all these lessons work—especially when it comes to character development. Such development is a gradual process of continuously learning, growing, failing, and learning again.

Concerning your development as this new promising brand of leader, we are most concerned that you have what it takes to act in a way that's of most benefit to you and all concerned by making good decisions. If a suggestion for good character-based behavior can't be practiced to the point of unconscious habit, the idea is not worthy. Remember, business as usual is not necessarily progress. We wish you to be legacy leaders.

Developing the How

We follow the instruction, consulting, and teaching industries closely, and we see little that's new under the schoolhouse roof so to speak. Career development training focuses largely on policy and the technicalities of the job—the what and maybe the why. However, developing character is paramount because it's the basis of *how* we perform, not *what* we perform. Yes, classes, even courses, on ethics are available, and they're a good start, but only a start. Good character doesn't just happen. Developing it takes constant attention, discipline, and *time* to mature and grow. We have to have a sense of purpose and know the work of becoming our best is worth it—even, and perhaps especially, when we don't feel like doing it. Such individual, personal evolutionary work continues in fits and starts toward maturity and a deep sense of satisfaction.

How do we learn to master ourselves so we thrive with dignity? How do we learn to interact productively by managing our motivational states? How do we learn to collaborate as one? Then, how do we practice these newfound realities and skills so we become good, better, and finally our best at them? How do we become a New Wave Leader who *gets it?* The aim of this book is to help people realize their potential of being their best selves via simple but consistent practices. Thus, we need a fundamental change in how we view staff education and development and how we go about shaping people for a demanding and remarkable future.

> **Good character doesn't just happen. Developing it takes constant attention, discipline, and *time* to mature and grow.**

This book presents a new way of explaining how to thrive. It helps us build on our natural resources to become more aware of our potential to overcome adversity and our fears, and thus become our better selves. This is how we personally evolve.

Reinvigorating the How of Virtuous Living

Only through our awareness and application will the principles of the Ancients and discoveries of modern science reveal themselves to us in all their practicality. Once inculcated, being good and doing good become self-fulfilling.

Following is a brief overview of terms that are more thoroughly explained in following chapters:

- *The Cardinal Virtues* – Understand that all these seemingly lofty traits are simple daily goals. Anyone can strive to be virtuous and thus live a happier life.

  Justice – Fairness. We begin necessarily with Justice, or knowing right from wrong, as without that, little else matters.

  Wisdom – Knowledge. That which comes from intuition and experience. Every day we can learn something significant and apply it.

  Courage – Determination. It takes courage to risk failure. The curious thing is that failure can lead to progress if viewed from the perspective of wisdom.

  Temperance – Restraint. This does not mean to be in a constant state of denying yourself. Temperance is otherwise known as moderation in how we think, behave, and live, always aiming for the mean between extremes. It's avoiding the harmful extremes of excess and deficiency by finding the happy medium of balance and harmony.

- *Character* – So many character traits are written about, taught, and prescribed that confusion may well be the most prominent result. In keeping with simplicity, let's boil it down to two elemental qualities:

  Self-analysis – Socrates declared, "The unexamined life is not worth living." We only progress when we seek to understand ourselves in different times, situations, and stations in life. Through self-examination, knowing who we are in all our strengths and frailties, we can keep what's beneficial and change what's not by learning to know the difference.

  Humility – Our greatest leaders—certainly those who changed civilization for the better—were humble. They understood that from humility comes respect, and from respect comes the mandate to lead. People may follow a tyrant, but not for long. Humility is inspiring. Look for it in the people you lead, for they will inspire you. To be clear, we're not talking about self-deprecation, but the ability to lead from a higher perspective than the ego. It's leading for the greatest good, not for self-aggrandizement.

- *Thriving* – The purpose of natural, noble, character-based thinking and action is to work toward both individual and communal well-being, which is about thriving, not wellness, which largely addresses health. Approaching the matter holistically, we know that true *well-being* results from nurturing body, mind, and inner self, or spirit.

  Body – A nutritionally sound, sensible diet and age-appropriate exercise to condition the body with flexibility, balance, coordination, strength, and endurance.

  Mind – Intellectual stimulation and lifetime learning of worthwhile, enriching information and experiences through whatever modalities best suit the individual.

  Inner self – Uplifting our inner spirit through beauty, laughter, love, and a sense of connection to all life, a vital element of achieving well-being, the capstone of thriving.

There you have it—the wisdom of the ages: Live virtuously with character and achieve greater states of well-being in which you can thrive. We promise to teach if you promise to learn—and practice what you learn.

The Path of Continuous Improvement – Simple, Suitable, Sustainable

Thus, we redefine excellence and how to achieve it: New Wave excellence is realized in lifelong pursuit of character-based personal betterment. It's about how we function to do good in all our relationships—beginning with family—such that the whole reaches its potential.

What is the best way to pursue continuous improvement? Many pursuits, especially of a personal nature, aren't realistic. We need criteria for considering what we undertake. Why? Because once we decide what to do, in the spirit of becoming MAGNUS–OVÉA, we're committed to seeing the endeavor to its natural end.

Consider this formula to represent our basic criteria. We will return to it often.

$$\textbf{Continuous Improvement} = \textbf{S}^3$$

Whether a task is big or small, first ask if it's *simple, suitable,* and *sustainable.* Let's look at each of these criteria in detail.

Simple

A concept or practice must be simple enough to be understood and thus sink into your psyche and, if appropriate, into your physiology so you take right action. The idea or practice may be great but so complex it's counterproductive.

So, to be precise, the essence of leadership is in the practice of the Cardinal Virtues of Justice, Wisdom, Courage, and Temperance. Elegant, exact, simple. To practice a desired behavior and make it a habit, we must be able to learn and do it repeatedly, modeling it to others. Thus, it must be reduced to its simplest form so we can learn its nuances but not made simplistic or frivolous. Being a New Wave Leader must mean something. Repetition is essential to building habits, as that's how we internalize a thought, a word, an action so it becomes instinctual. Aristotle asserted that moral excellence is the result of habit or custom.

Let's look at a few down-to-earth examples of the kinds of actions you can practice on a regular basis:

- Holding your temper, taking a breath, and responding respectfully with the intention of reducing a tense situation and understanding the other person

- Not using the office copier for personal business without paying for it

- Helping your children learn to share (and sharing yourself!)

- Having one beer after work instead of four

- Stretching your skills to try something new, even (perhaps especially) if you're afraid you'll fail

- Bearing in mind the needs of others

- Taking the time to do what you can, considering your time and personal constitution, to get into or stay in good physical condition for health and longevity

- Feeding your mind good thoughts by choosing what you listen to, watch, read, or do with the intention of learning something new or being inspired, encouraged, or uplifted

- Feeding your body with one or two cookies instead of five (and don't forget the broccoli!)

Think of each of your actions as a kata, or form, as it is known in karate, which combines to create a complex ballet of movements when taken as a whole. Every movement counts in this mock battle, but it's taught one tiny movement at a time in the quest for perfection. Even the correct placement of a fingertip matters greatly. Of course, achieving perfection is quite impossible; it's the pursuit that matters. Even Leonardo DaVinci never completed his Mona Lisa, adding a brush stroke at a time for years. The quest for perfection yields a thing of practical beauty—kata movements combined ever more gracefully over time. Along the way, the practitioner gains health, insight, confidence, competence, and more. The rewards greatly exceed even the beauty of the art.

When an undertaking is reduced to its simplest elements, it becomes teachable, learnable, doable, repeatable, then part of us. This is how we approach personal excellence.

Suitable

If something is suitable, it's fit and right for a singular situation or intention and especially for a particular person. If it's flexible, it's widely applicable. Why is this important? Because if an undertaking is so below us that it's uninteresting or so above us that it's unattainable, we won't seek it. For example, physical conditioning for good health and longevity is much different for a youth of 20 than a senior of 70. The long game matters. Excellence has many forms for the attainment of well-being. The excellence we speak of here is how well we live our lives—and lead, because we all lead in some way. Overall goals must be suitable to the individual yet energizing; not impossible, still challenging.

Sustainable

Here, sustainability means that life, leadership, and becoming our best involve a journey over a lifetime. Ask, "Can what I'm considering doing last?" Rather than a one-time or even occasional project to be completed, the journey we suggest is a process that continues from one level to the next, even to the last day. If an effort is so complex it defies continuance, we need to rethink it. That's why we describe and teach the *journey* to *becoming* a New Wave MAGNUS–OVÉA Leader.

Aristotle observed that a man (read person) is not quite ready, not mature enough, to make the most of himself until he nears 50! Only he could explain his reasoning, but it makes sense that one needs to study, think about, and experience life abundantly to learn how to live long and meaningfully. That said, one is never too young to begin that study and build that wisdom.

> **The excellence we speak of here is how well we live our lives—and lead, because we *all* lead in some way.**

Cicero argues that it's not about ending life in gradual decay and regret for lost youth but about living well to the end surrounded by family, friends, reputation, and legacy. Getting old is a privilege denied to multitudes. For the privilege, we must sustain what is worthy. Learning excellence takes a lifetime, as it's a process of realization, refinement, repetition, new realization . . . rinse and repeat.

> *A good life is when you assume nothing, do more, need less, smile often,*
> *dream big, laugh a lot, and realize how blessed you are for what you have.*
> – Unknown

This new millennia demands new ways of thinking locally, acting communally, and collaborating globally. To do that, we need to understand what this next step in our evolution means. Thus, we continue with the vocabulary of the New Wave.

New Terms to Describe New Wave Leadership

Globalization, the COVID-19 pandemic, machines that think and create, the clash between totalitarianism and democracy, CRISPR gene editing, and more demand a new way of approaching life. As with all great progress, it begins with individuals working to realize their potential. We need a new vocabulary to understand the dynamics of leadership required by our rapidly evolving civilization, mainly propelled by two global shifts: collaboration to address our exigent global worries and collaboration to manage the rise of the atom, Artificial Intelligence, and the frightening potential of taming our genes. We're working in complex human-centric systems that require leaders to model character and promote meaningful goals toward a vision that enhances the potential of our civilization.

> **We're working in complex human-centric systems that require leaders to model character and promote meaningful goals toward a vision that enhances the potential of our civilization.**

As a country and as individuals we are remarkably good and generous, *and* we have historically struggled with how to get along with our neighbors next door and oceans away. These realities vex us all, and we are called to address them. It must begin with the individual. How do we refer to our world and define how we prosper in it?

We continue our brief introduction of the new vocabulary for understanding how we must learn to work with our families and our colleagues for a better world.

New Wave Leader

We've arrived at the next step in how we accomplish private, nonprofit, and public governance. Top-down central control is giving way to leaders who understand situational context and how it ties in with values and a vision. For these new leaders, leadership isn't about following a checklist, a prescription, or a formula. They understand that leadership is an honor, not something bestowed by going along to get along. It's about improving individuals who improve others. This New Wave Leader epitomizes introspection and humility. He and she sincerely practice living morally by the Cardinal Virtues. They work hard at the trilogy of the human condition—body, mind, and inner spirit—for well-being then thriving. Thus, they prepare for hard work, conceptualizing a vision, and leading the way to it. New Wave Leaders also work hard at earning respect, modeling the best of behaviors, and leaving a legacy—not to forget making good memories and having fun.

MAGNUS

We have a dire need for a new vocabulary of living with purpose, meaning, and consequence. Hence, the MAGNUS individual who studies and practices virtue, develops values, and builds character. As we have said, this term had its noble beginnings even before Aristotle's Magnanimous Man—the first written description of MAGNUS over 2,300 years ago! Those who commit to continuously becoming their best know the purpose of this lifelong pursuit of the Good Life also aims to improve the common good.

OVÉA

OVÉA is an acronym for Others, Values, Ethics, Acceleration. These activators spark our natural hormonal responses that reinforce good behavior. They are aspirational, not prescriptive. We are *not* advocating we become saintly but that we deal more effectively with being human.

With regard to others, the Golden Rule makes so much sense that "Do unto others as you would have them do unto you" is included in some form in all major religions. Native Americans, for example, advocate to "Live in harmony, for we are all related." Our values and ethics and morals help us stay focused on respect for others. OVÉA is another layer of practical advice for daily conduct.

Yes, we make mistakes, we learn, and we move on, as so aptly stated by this mid-19th-century American philosopher and essayist:

Finish every day and be done with it. You have done what you could.
Some blunders and absurdities, no doubt crept in. Forget them as soon
as you can, tomorrow is a new day; begin it well and serenely, with too high
a spirit to be cumbered with your old nonsense. This new day is too dear,
with its hopes and invitations, to waste a moment on the yesterdays.
– Ralph Waldo Emerson

VUCA

VUCA is not a new term, but it takes on new meaning as we adopt New Wave thinking and doing. The concept originated with students at the U.S. Army War College to describe the volatility, uncertainty, complexity, and ambiguity of the world after the Cold War. However, we experience VUCA, chaos, daily! It's life.

Every day brings its problems, challenges, difficult people. But that's actually the way we want it—challenging and interesting. Living the tenets of the Good Life—virtue, character, well-being—is the best answer to chaos. Still, VUCA helps us understand this reality. We can see it in crisis management, which rarely works, especially for the long term. From this hectic and muddled life, we need predictability so we can prevent problems we know about and anticipate the unexpected. To this end, we can build character in many ways, including reversing our attitude about crisis to see that adversity is an opportunity to grow. While it's not healthy to *seek* chaos, we don't want to fear it. Experiencing and overcoming adversity is how we add to our capabilities and worthy accomplishments, making adversity a tool for growth.

Neurophilosophy

Neurophilosophy, a term coined by Canadian-American philosopher Patricia Churchland in 1986, relates to the development of consciousness and thus conscience.[64] It's based in the science of the brain and body, or neurophysiology.

Over the eons, humans have adapted a hormonal, neurophysiological response to how we behave. We have an extraordinarily strong and positive reaction to doing what is right and beneficial for the survival of our species—thank goodness! We figured out eons ago that collaborating in likeminded collectives was stronger, safer, and smarter than being noncooperative. Indeed, it was logical that we work better together, whether it was in sharing child rearing, hunting and gathering, caring about our neighbors, or keeping predators out of the cave. By being in a collective, our brains grew, then that magical cortex in the brain evolved. With language, there was no stopping our development.

Think about it: Prehistoric Europe was peopled by an estimated 2,000 souls, who survived an ice age of thousands of years,[65] and now we are headed to 10 billion souls on our blue orb while solving our most intractable concerns. By living with a conscience, living well and with purpose, and living with respect for and the betterment of others, we grow our brains to do more of the same. As we practice more optimal behavior and indulge in fewer practices that are less productive and beneficial, our brain physically changes to support our new behavior. That is how we continuously grow.

Later in the book, we discuss neurophilosophy with a bit more specificity as it relates to evolving the brain and, with that, enlightened leadership.

Reversal

In the mid-1970s, British psychologist Dr. Michael Apter and psychiatrist Dr. Ken Smith developed the idea of Reversal Theory. In his book *Zigzag: Reversal and Paradox in Human Personality*, Apter explains that we can *zigzag*, or *reverse*, between *motivational states* or *mindsets* depending on the moment.[66] We can influence how productive our interpersonal interactions are when we learn to reverse from one state to the other efficiently. An improper orientation negatively impacts our performance. Know we have resources to reverse our *motivational state* or mindset appropriately to continually strengthen our approach to others and our surroundings. We present an overview of Apter's helpful theory in Chapter 6.

Resiliency

Resiliency is the degree to which we can easily and quickly recover from stress. It's our natural propensity to seek balance—or resiliency—from extremes of emotion and chaos. We can learn to be more resilient using our own physical, physiological, and mental resources. With resiliency, or balance, we can begin to work on being antifragile, which is another facet of building inner strength.

Antifragility

Antifragility is our ability to actually gain from disorder. Here we put to work the views of Nassim Nicholas Taleb in his book *Antifragile: Things That Gain from Disorder*.[67] When we are antifragile, we can better prepare for and confront the chaotic nature of living and prosper *because* of the experience. As we bolster our defense systems, we learn to flourish during chaos, and our perspective changes from confronting or battling crises to learning from them. Resiliency and antifragility are both natural survival techniques of the wider work of developing a MAGNUS-OVÉA lifestyle, which can be taught, learned, practiced, and strengthened with continuous application.

Leadership Defined by the Realities of Context, Systems, and Symbolism

Leadership evolves, as it must. It has taken us two and a half centuries of learning how to govern ourselves, from establishment, through politics, reform, and lately problem-solving, both locally and globally. The new millennium marks a turning. Now we are in the next wave, the New Wave, of leadership and governance—public, corporate, and nonprofit. We are on the cusp of learning how to get things done by correctly perceiving what the moment means relative to taking leadership action, how people can best collaborate on a vision, and how this demonstrates New Wave Leadership. In other words, we are relearning what it is to lead and follow in modern organizational systems.

> **People must *want* to follow, not be *made* to follow. This is the age of the willing follower born of a noble purpose of people doing good work.**

We notice the rise of the following as observed by Stanley McChrystal in *Leaders: Myth and Reality:*[68]

- *Complexity* – We need to understand chaos as normal, expected, and a genuine occasion to make things work well permanently. It's thus to our advantage to automatically, instinctually learn to read the immediate situation, which is in constant flux, and more important, understand what it means. Surely there's more than meets the eye.

- *Human systems* – We all exist in systems dominated by human nature and thus unpredictable and surprising. Our most successful leaders, good and bad, even from antiquity, recognize that they needed hearts and minds to win. In the New Wave, we learn how to truly collaborate to realize important goals for bettering communal well-being. Consider a colloquial understanding of working in the average human system as like "trying to clap with one hand." Without a collaboration of people who understand their roles, getting things done is indeed tough. These roles need to be defined by a common vision and led by the personification of that vision. Every decision in the New Wave must be couched in how people will act or react to what is said and done and modeled. People must want to follow, not be made to follow. This is the age of the willing follower born of a noble purpose of people doing good work.

- *Symbolism* – New Wave Leaders demonstrate, symbolize, and are the living embodiment of a vision. They turn inward to understand their frailties and thus understand the frailties of others. Their humility is one major way they earn respect.

It's all about learning to thrive, not just get to the end of the project and clock another day toward retirement. It's about modeling how to flourish and teaching those around us to do the same. This involves a complete change of attitude and behavior from complacency to actively pursuing how we can do better physically, mentally, and morally.

Moral conduct is fortified in two ways: character building and physical brain building. Building character is about learning to behave in productive and right ways. As fantastic as it sounds, moral conduct is also supported by neuroscience, which we'll explain in a little more detail in Chapter 5. Behavioral and neurophysiological forces are mutually reinforcing and create a sum greater than its parts. This natural symbiosis is part of being human and what helps us advance.

A Trifecta of Resources to Aid Our Progress

To neurophilosophy,[69] and Reversal Theory,[70] we add the science of well-being, supported by American psychology professor Sonja Lyubomirsky in *The How of Happiness: A New Approach to Getting the Life You Want.*[71] We combine these three approaches in a unique way: one to understand conscience, two to be in command of our behavior situationally, and three to bring it all together in the realistic pursuit of well-being, which even transcends happiness. Thus we are combining: the neuro-physiologic reality that practicing moral conduct strengthens with time; the practicality of self-managing our human interactions for optimal outcomes; and the introduction of balance and well-being into the chaos in our day. We can be in command of our capacity to be our best and more consistently and continuously relate to others more effectively.

Lastly, ancient philosophy and decades of science tell us very credibly how to achieve well-being. This isn't about happiness per se, although happiness is likely to result. It isn't about becoming rich but being wealthy and secure, which we all can achieve. Science tells us that pursuing riches and position, more money, more beauty, a bigger house, and plenty of garage space for a few cars gets old rather quickly. The pursuit of that kind of happiness is out of our control. The more we pursue it, the more futile and frustrating life becomes. However, we can pursue well-being, which is realistic no matter who we are. It's a matter of a healthy attitude and being content with life . . . even without the Bentley.

We also know we have resources to call upon when we experience crises or have emotional swings. Resiliency is a matter of strengthening such common resources as religion, family, and friendships. With that, we find self-value in our virtues, self-respect, self-maintenance, and contributions to others. It all works together and we find ourselves solidly wholesome.

> **Few make the changes necessary to improve a lifestyle geared to being energetic, creative, enthused, and filled with promise. Intentions re good, but practice is wanting.**

As we train our brains in the direction of virtuous living, we quickly move from mere physical wellness to the holistic well-being of a healthy body and mind made complete by an uplifted spirit, along with being productive in society for the grand satisfaction of it.

Learning to Thrive Beyond Wellness

Let's consider what and how it is to thrive instead of just survive. The current thinking about how to live concerns mainly physical and mental wellness, which is a good base for general health but only a start. Few make the changes necessary to improve a lifestyle geared to being energetic, creative, enthused, and filled with promise. Intentions are good, but practice is wanting. Look at the numbers of us who are obese, sick, addicted, and living a life that's short not only in years but in accomplishment, fun, and satisfaction.

For well-being, we need to move from the relative inertia of simple wellness (which is a good start) to flourishing. Let's discover what it is to prosper in this New Wave, this new era of advancement as a people living and working in a global reality. It's a new day, a new millennium, with more potential for good than ever before. Most notably, we look for *conceptual shifts* that help us better conduct our work and our lives, from . . .

- stagnation to productive activation;
- a fixed mindset to a growth mindset;
- technical skills training to human capacity development;
- vicious cycles to virtuous cycles; and
- extremes to moderation.

We become aware that health is not just a matter of wellness but much more. It's also about actively pursuing well-being. Such a journey results in a reasonable legacy such that later in life, on reflection, we can say: *Perhaps I wasn't great, but I did my best, and that's okay. I developed character expressed as introspection and humility. I benefited others. I lived within the mean between the extremes of vice and virtue. I learned it's okay to err, given I learn and correct my ways. I was and still am a New Wave MAGNUS–OVÉA individual, leading in my own way, redefining distinction.*

We learn to lead with *heart* and *head* from the perspective of communal well-being.

The New Legitimacy of Principles Over Power

Power does not lead, principles do. Legitimacy does not derive from position, personality, or proclamation; it is earned and willingly given to those with character, humility, and virtue. Principles help guide us. Policies and procedures are encumbrances without core principles. The new era, the New Wave, demands we lead by a code we inculcate over time. Thus, we learn and practice integrity, service, and excellence in their finest sense. New Wave Leadership is about character first, *then* business. We learn to lead with *heart* and *head* from the perspective of communal well-being. Notice that heart comes first.

Educating the mind without educating the heart is no education at all.
– Aristotle

Personally Speaking

What About Those Amish?

James Klopovic

I grew up on a small Ohio truck farm. It helped make me who I am—and still does. After World War II, Dad and Uncle Ed pooled their benefits from the GI Bill and bought 56 acres in Huntsburg, a farming community east of Cleveland. Yes, I can milk a cow and blast a stump, though it's been a few years and dynamite is hard to come by.

The farm came with an historic barn built before the Civil War. Listing precariously on its arthritic hand-hewn oak beams and trusses, it was threatening to keel over any day. No problem for these Croatian brothers. They got railroad jacks and positioned them with beams poked under the eaves, which were jacked a click a day till that ol' barn stood again. Uncle Ed reinforced every joint and it still stands decades later. Oh, if that barn could speak.

The men planted 750 fruit trees and 3,000 broccoli plants another year. They raised beef and dairy cows and hogs, and grew massive gardens. I began doing what I could to help at five years old. We put up chest freezers brimming with veggies and meat for seven. We even butchered a hog . . . once. How in the world did the pioneers do this every year? The work was brutal, as only a farmer understands. Sometimes I went to bed too tired to eat after a day of putting up hay. I hand hoed acres of row crops under a sun bigger and hotter than it's licensed to be. I could put out matches with hands and fingers tough as boot heels. This instilled in me persistence and discipline, both needed as I later pursued family, education, and two careers. I left the dynamite behind, though.

Some of my fondest memories are the times spent with our Amish neighbors, who taught us so much with their genuine company, industry, modesty, friendliness, and humor. Dad paid for hay each summer by farming me and the tractor out to Dan Miller. I remember one of his daughters bringing me a jug of my favorite flavor of Kool Aid. There she came, in bare feet, long dress, bonnet and glistening smile, at just the right moment while I was cutting hay at the back of the farm. It was strawberry season so lunch was a huge bowl of bananas and strawberries with freshly baked warm bread with butter and more Kool Aid. Nothing better. The table groaned under the bucket-sized bowl of berries and piles of bread for about 10 hay-makers' appetites.

When we were in the hay mow stacking the day's bales, here came the daughters—after tidying up the kitchen, of course—in their long dresses, whispers, smiles, and lacey head pieces. Without a word, they picked up bails and stacked 'em shoulder to shoulder with us without a note of fuss. It was as natural as breathing. We were happy to be together in good but sweaty work. Few things are as gratifying as seeing a barn full of beautiful fragrant bales, evidence of the day's work and your part in it.

A recent happy memory is being invited to neighbor Joel Miller's sugar house to boil sap for maple syrup. He taps about 1,800 maple trees on three farms, most connected by plastic tubing. Years earlier, he gathered sap with a horse and sledge, bucket by bucket, but now he uses a Bobcat, a concession to efficiency and effectiveness.

The evaporator pan is 14 feet long, and he can run off a gallon of syrup from about 50 gallons of sap every 20 minutes! Enter the sugar house and you can't see for the dense fog of maple steam. Oh, the aroma of it! The sap traverses the troughs of the pan and jumps eight inches high with the boil. The ever industrious and frugal Amish salvage wood from old construction or slashings of downed trees after the woods are logged.

Through the delicious fog, I spot at least 10 family members and friends just enjoying community and comradery—and the sweet, sweet scent. No one asks for the fire to be stoked. Joel Junior just steps up, and his little brother and a friend do the last splitting of planks, formerly part of a dock into Lake Erie.

Lunch time. A daughter steps up with a sieve brimming with eggs to set in the boil. Why not? Then the wieners go in as well. Is that why the syrup is award winning? When the first gallon of sap is filtered through a felt cap into the barrel, Joel passes out shot-sized paper cups to sample the warm elixir. Now that's the way to enjoy shots—nothing like it!

Farm folks, and especially our Amish neighbors, epitomize the spirit of community, collaboration, and cooperation, not to mention humor. Many willing and skilled hands dispense with endless work, and the spirited balance of family, fun, and collective effort is passed down through the generations. No one asks what's to be done; they just do it. Even a two-year-old child is given an ear of corn to shuck. I know now it's a display of love.

It takes work to engender true friendships, but the results are enjoyable and well worth the effort. When someone says, "Y'all come down," do it—and bring a jug of maple syrup from the farm (or your personal equivalent). You'll earn respect, attract friends, and meet interesting people who add significantly to the quality of your life.

If you admire our faith—strengthen yours.
If you admire our sense of commitment—deepen yours.
If you admire our community spirit—build your own.
If you admire the simple life—cut back.
If you admire deep character and enduring values—live them yourself.
– Amish Challenge[72]

Chapter 4

Ben Franklin –
Our First New Wave Leader

What more valuable than Gold? Than Diamonds? Virtue.
– Benjamin Franklin, *Poor Richard's Almanack,* 1751

We return now to take a closer look at Benjamin Franklin, an excellent example of a New Wave Leader—and arguably our country's first. *Why Ben?* He was one of our Founding Fathers and one of the most significant people in the tortured and glorious trudge of civilizations. We would be wise to take his counsel and example as he is rooted in the wisdom of the ages.

It seems that everything he attempted he took to remarkable success, even more remarkable because he had no formal education. He had humble beginnings as a printer's apprentice born to revolution. While he was gifted as few have been or will be, his accomplishments were as much due to brawn and sweat as they were to inspiration and a good brain. He would *not* quit; he didn't take *no* well, and he cut to the core of every task. What might he teach us? How can we act on his guidance?

In one basic way, our tasks and challenges are no different from Ben's moment in history and little different from that of the Ancients. That is: Each age struggles with the issues, trials, and triumphs of what it is to be human and humane.

Franklin understood that ideas, thought, contemplation, and endless analysis are nothing without action.

Let's take a look at what we can learn from this New Wave MAGNUS–OVÉA 18th-century writer, printer, political philosopher, politician, postmaster, scientist, inventor, humorist, civic activist, statesman, and diplomat.[73]

Ben's Journey of Becoming His Best

Inspired by the ancients, Ben Franklin pursued his own 13 Virtues,[74] writing them on a grid in a journal. Franklin understood that ideas, thought, contemplation, and endless analysis are nothing without action. His problem was determining how he could tell quantitatively if he was developing better character, which is highly qualitative. Even he could not track all 13 virtues at once, so the ever-so-practical Franklin worked on only one virtue at a time so he could focus one day at a time, almost hourly, for seven days, cycling each five times during a year. He epitomized persistence and continuous growth. Every time an infraction of a virtue, say Temperance, occurred, he put a dot by it. That way he could monitor the dots and watch them (hopefully) diminish in frequency when he tracked the virtue again.

This mechanical method kept track of his improvements in bearing, behavior, and character. More important, it forced character improvement to be ever present in his conscious thoughts and actions. Therefore, good character could gradually became habitual, instinctual as much as possible. He also knew full well that he was his own worst enemy and could develop bad habits as well. Thus he was compelled to fight these urges with virtue. Further, he was aware that less than the best of good habits and behavior are insidious and he needed a conscious, consistent, and committed effort to keep them at bay. This self-analysis and introspection were more to expose his foibles, weaknesses, and negative character traits than good ones. Bringing them to light, he could correct them, ever improving his good character. This he did for years, even to his end.

The process is synergistic, so improvement in one area helps foster improvement in another. Franklin also understood the value of persistence. Our weakest point of character is its limit. As with everything he did, he worked on self-improvement intensely. This gave him appropriate pause and valued instruction and engendered intuitively good decisions the rest of his long, monumentally productive life. He was never idle, even when it seemed he was. During one of his long and usually boring trans-Atlantic voyages (even with fair winds it took at least six weeks), he was the first to chart the clockwise Gulf Stream current, which whalers knew of but didn't understand. His little "amusement" to pass the time was instrumental in the colonization of our country and others of the Americas.

Do not squander time for that is the stuff life is made of.
– Benjamin Franklin

Yes, Franklin was a genius, but it was this simple, practical action of monitoring his pursuit of virtuous living that helped him become one of the most significant people in history and made our world a much better place.

Consider reading his autobiography, which he wrote at age 83, the year before he died. Perhaps you can start your own grid of virtues today, track your dots, and work to become what you were meant to be.

Now, in a flight of fancy, let's let Ben tell a bit of his own story.

* * *

Ben's Own Story

Having just turned 50 in this year of 1756, I've decided to undertake what I see as a duty—being the chief justice of the peace of Philadelphia. *The Pennsylvania Gazette, Poor Richard's Almanack*, and other efforts of mine are popular and useful; thus I gratefully prosper. My belief in personal improvement and industriousness allow me leisure time in which I might wander whence my mind, spirit, and energies take me. This also fits my philosophy to never be idle; so it is that I have done much while enjoying the company of my fellows, the love of my good wife, and a few amusements.

Understanding how we use time gives me a moment to consider and take on the challenges of bettering the welfare of my hometown in my leisure, which is most productive, as it should be. As a case in point, recently on a muggy day fit only for frogs, my inventive muse sparked the idea for a rocking chair that fans the occupant. The neighbors love to give it a go. Now on to other considerations for enhancing my community.

Our system of night watchmen is inferior at best, considering the rapid growth of Philadelphia.[75] So I now have taken on the privileges, promises, and privations of being our first constable. I do this simply because it is a noble, worthy pursuit as this community is where Deborah and I live, work, recreate, raise our children, and serve.

Civic duty consumes much of my days as I've developed an automatic sense of accountability and responsibility in my public endeavors. I find by working for the general purpose and giving back, I inevitably gain and am the main benefactor of any kindnesses I may do to improve things. It is with this philosophy that I thrive with my fellow man in body, mind, and disposition. Living thusly, that is seeking the Good

Life as described and practiced by my good friend Aristotle, whom I know well through his books, I am up to challenges even though they are daunting. I suspect there are many more to come if I am blessed with growing old.

This leads me to ponder further about lessons learned from the ancient philosophers. I ask, or have had friends ask in so many words, "What's it all about?"

Persistence at purpose matters.

To me, it's about studying rational, respectable, realistic living and taking subsequent right action to become the best person my talents allow me to be. From a very young age, I have tried to be always gainfully employed, especially in mind and purpose. I blush at accolades; they say I am intelligent, even brilliant, creative, friendly, adventurous, charming, and the like. Dear me, my cheeks redden even at the writing of it, but it is to make this point: My chief characteristic, I would say, is that I am determined. Persistence at purpose matters. Thus, I have always kept an accounting of my words, deeds, and contributions to the general good. I do earnestly work to mind every minute of the day.

I know that to progress we must learn to live and work as a community. Thus, I trust to be careful in my dealing with people so as not to offend—but not to be taken advantage of either. Dignity has been and always will be important to me. Keep it carefully, I say. And a little true wit and humor go a long way to pave healthy, bonded relationships. Even as a young man, I loved a pun and told them almost to distraction. Thus I learned to laugh at my mistakes and meter the punning.

To me, living well means taking challenges and doing well while we are young to lay the ground for a graceful life later. I do try to live the Good Life of strengthening virtues and lessening vices. *Moderation is the goal*—most sensible and very American. By doing so, I aim to have a lengthy life and a good death, as dying well is about living well by correcting errata in one's longevity. It seems that those who grow old with increasing terror have missed the example set by those peacefully progressing to a serene end. It's no secret how this latter group does it. If one lives tranquilly with some accomplishment to calm the heart, the end is equally peaceful, even sought after.[76] It is with this intention of living well, giving back, and leaving a legacy that I assume the duties of our chief justice of the peace.

> *Be at war with your vices, at peace with your neighbors,*
> *and let every new year find you a better man.*
> – Benjamin Franklin

Early on, I realized that to do significant things, one must put even more directed intention and action into continuously building strong, virtuous character. This is founded on personal struggle with what it is to be truthful—a struggle taken up by our ancient philosophers, whose works I read religiously. I was doing thus even before I began the Junto nearly 30 years ago to discuss morals, politics, and philosophy guided by probing questions.[77] I look forward to our Friday evening meetings.

> **One cannot consider the good in us without the reality that we all can be difficult, if not wicked. Correcting our vices is equal in effort and intent to bolstering our virtues in becoming our best selves.**

This gives me an opportune moment in this discourse to comment about virtuous living. Pundits wrongly focus nearly exclusively on good character. One cannot consider the good in us without the reality that we all can be difficult, if not wicked. Correcting our vices is equal in effort and intent to bolstering our virtues in becoming our best selves.

In my own way, I sought to improve by charting what I thought to be my better qualities as I sought to know Ben Franklin. I began by charting 13 virtues that comprise character as I see it to arrive at ". . . moral perfection."[78] I present my chart here for your edification.

Benjamin Franklin's 13 Virtues[79]

1. **Temperance.** Eat not to dullness. Drink not to elevation.

2. **Silence.** Speak not but what may benefit others or yourself.

3. **Order.** Let all your things have their places. Let each part of your business have its time.

4. **Resolution.** Resolve to perform what you ought. Perform without fail what you resolve.

5. **Frugality.** Make no expense but to do good to others or yourself. Waste nothing.

6. **Industry.** Lose no time, be always employed in something useful. Cut off all unnecessary actions.

7. **Sincerity.** Use no hurtful deceit. Think innocently and justly. Speak accordingly.

8. **Justice.** Wrong none by doing injuries or omitting the benefits that are your duty.

9. **Moderation.** Avoid extremes. Forebear resenting injuries so much as you think they deserve.

10. **Cleanliness.** Tolerate no uncleanliness in body, clothes, or habituation.

11. **Tranquility.** Be not disturbed at trifles, or at accidents common or unavoidable.

12. **Chastity.** Rarely use venery but for health or offspring; never to dullness, weakness, or the injury of your own or another's peace or reputation.

13. **Humility.** Imitate Jesus and Socrates.

It remains one of my most worthy and most vexing challenges, this self-introspection. I expose my weaknesses, much to my chagrin, and pray to the Divine for improvement. I observe that the pursuit of virtue brings character with it.[80] The result is the strength to endure trials and tribulations and at day's end realize a happy life! What follows are lessons on attaining virtue that I, Ben Franklin, have come to agree upon:

- *Make character a habit.* Hold your personal character to be *the* example. Do not even *think* dishonestly, as thinking leads to actions.

- *Seek ideas.* Be creative. Creativity comes from reading, writing, speaking, thinking, conversing, and especially doing. Be a student of the human condition and development. Learn from other professions.

- *Champion the less fortunate.* I have heard it said that one should recognize the doorman on your way up as he will be there on your way down. Everyone matters and can instruct. Be courteous in the same way you would wish to be treated.

- *Use time wisely. Lose no time; be always employed in something useful; cut off all unnecessary actions.*[81] Waste nothing, especially time. I am always with a book, pen and paper, and an idea to occupy a stolen moment.

- *Be early to bed and early to rise.* And rise with purpose: Ask, "What good shall I do today?" Waste neither your evenings nor mornings.

- *Hone your public image.* You are always on stage even when not before others. Act appropriately—especially when a child is watching.

- *Fear not risk.* Neither should you be foolhardy with risk. Remarkable things will be accomplished by venturing into uncomfortable yet worthy endeavors—but wisely.

- *Make connections.* Establish friendships wherever you go. Don't be shy but neither arrogant nor abusive. Make sure to be remembered well. You can do thusly with a word or gesture; study the art of this diligently. Study and develop good punning, wit, which when judiciously and kindly played, lubricates conversation.

- *Be frugal.* Learn to be parsimonious as a matter of course. Frugality to me is second only to Justice, king of the Cardinal Virtues.

Ben Presents Aristotle's Golden Mean

To do this thing of becoming better and being good, we must heed the ancient Greek maxim "Know thyself." Knowing ourselves requires we give a fair estimation of our virtues *and* corresponding vices to find what Aristotle called the Golden Mean, the middle ground, of good conduct, encompassing thought, word, and deed. Thank goodness great thinkers discussed this natural juxtaposition with suggestions on how to balance the two. I do admire profound brevity, which stands throughout the ages. Thus, I present Aristotle's ethics table delineating the mean between virtues and vices, for which we aim.

SPHERE OF ACTION OR FEELING	EXCESS	MEAN	DEFICIENCY
Fear and Confidence	Rashness	*Courage*	Cowardice
Pleasure and Pain	Licentiousness/ Self-indulgence	*Temperance*	Insensibility
Getting and Spending (minor)	Prodigality	Liberality	Illiberality/Meanness
Getting and Spending (major)	Vulgarity/ Tastelessness	Magnificence	Pettiness/Stinginess
Honour and Dishonour (major)	Vanity	Magnanimity	Pusillanimity
Honour and Dishonour (minor)	Ambition/ empty vanity	Proper ambition/pride	Unambitiousness/ undue humility
Anger	Irascibility	Patience/ good temper	Lack of spirit/ unirascibility
Self-expression	Boastfulness	Truthfulness	Understatement/ mock modesty
Conversation	Buffoonery	Wittiness	Boorishness
Social Conduct	Obsequiousness	Friendliness	Cantankerousness
Shame	Shyness	Modesty	Shamelessness
Indignation	Envy	Righteous indignation	Malicious enjoyment/ spitefulness

Figure 1: Aristotle's Golden Mean[82]

Aristotle's comprehensive categories of virtues and vices allow us to discover our own best and worst characteristics. Note that expanding our virtues and minimizing our vices will not only make other people around us happier but we will be happier as well.[83] In addition, as we become better, we bring out the best in others.

The Greats observe we are best able to manage ourselves when we reach middle age, which for them was 49! It takes time to become self-controlled—to tame our emotions. Therefore, adhere to the mean with these remarkable insights from the Grand Master of the Lyceum, Aristotle:[84]

- *Virtue in the extreme is a problem.* Virtue can tip to being a vice. For example, too much duty to a parent could lead you to sacrifice your life for that parent and thus forsake your own children. This would be the vice of misplaced fealty.

- *Vices are not equal, so know the difference.* For each virtue there's more than one expression of its corresponding vice—most often in a hierarchy. We need to look to the least harmful to decide the middle ground of better behavior. Too little courage can lead to cowardice, yet too much courage can make us rash.

- *Work on taming your worst vices to enhance your virtues.* For example, do not allow frustration and anger to sabotage your self-control, which can allow other vices to run rampant. Thus, your effort in taming vices eclipses enhancing your virtues. Beware because the slippery slope of cascading into vice is steep and direct.

- *Understand the downside of too much pleasure.* Many things we enjoy are harmful in the extreme. A good stew ceases to be good after the third helping, and we know what too many pints of ale will do to us. We can ask ourselves if a behavior or desire is an impediment to good behavior and consequently to our balance in word and deed.

The goal is not to be a paragon of virtue but to be reasonable.

Achieving the mean between *excess* and *deficiency* in our thoughts and behavior keeps us on the journey of being our best, of being a good person, ultimately content with life. The goal is not to be a paragon of virtue but to be reasonable.

Consider the domain of *self-expression*: Aristotle defines it as being truthful, which falls under the category of Justice, the king of virtues, without which exploring virtue isn't possible. Note that when we express ourselves boastfully, we are most likely going overboard to an excess. Conversely, if we are overly modest, we are still being less than honest, tending toward a deficiency. This, then, is Aristotle's suggestion for how we work on being truthful. I think about this from time to time, even now.

Every excess causes a defect; every defect an excess.
– Ralph Waldo Emerson

The Cardinal Virtues

Knowing right from wrong takes continuous, serious contemplation and practice, as sometimes truth is complex. Thus, I must expound upon the four Cardinal Virtues, which were distilled from many virtues proposed by Plato.

Justice – The King of All Virtues

Justice is considered the king of all the Cardinal virtues because it means fairness. The other virtues cannot exist without first knowing the difference between right and wrong. It takes a lifetime of study and discipline to make just choices automatically, correctly. I should know. The Eastern Asian Ancients caution us to never even *think* dishonestly. It takes a lifetime to build a good reputation, which is fragile. One misstep, one ill thought, word, or deed and a life can unravel. Then we are lost, no matter how wise, courageous, and temperate we may be. I take heart in knowing the Ancients assure us that being *just* is a natural part of being human.

Wisdom

Wisdom is basically knowledge gained from both experience and continuously reading, studying, learning, and applying the lessons learned. I do love learning. I am most curious, thus this is no chore for me.

Reading helps us become more interesting people, so I heartily recommend reading meaningful books. It's the key to communicating, and by communicating well, we can teach and lead. It's the key to persuasive oratory. Build a library of a few books of interest (mine contains more than a few!) on topics such as ancient philosophy, health, building and managing your wealth, biographies, travel, your hobbies—both nonfiction and fiction. Read the notables so you know you're imbibing and imbuing quality. (See Major Resources.)

> **It takes a lifetime to build a good reputation, which is fragile. One misstep, one ill thought, word, or deed and a life can unravel.**

We can absorb wisdom on three levels.[85] First, we may hear wisdom from others who impart a truth, perhaps in a conversation. Then, we can absorb intellectual wisdom, whereby we go deeper into learning by reading or taking instruction, for example. Lastly, we gain insight and truth through experience, which the Ancients prescribe as the most beneficial to our growth. Confucius resonates here: "I *hear* and

I forget. I *see* and I remember. I *do* and I understand." (Author's italics) Wisdom causes curiosity. Curiosity piques investigation. Investigation makes life fascinating!

Courage

It often takes fortitude—courage—to work hard, sometimes beyond endurance, at doing what is right and good, even if it is a bit unsettling. I must say it took courage and mighty restraint to sit through the debates of the Continental Congress. My Lord! We must plan well (as I am fond of doing), aim well, then take confident action.

Certainly, of the many expressions of courage, the ultimate is to face mortal danger. Yet, daily living requires continuous resilience, strength, and stamina. It takes courage to voluntarily assume or be given a worthy task that is just beyond us. However, if we accept the challenge and work to figure it out, we are extremely gratified to succeed—beyond what we expected that challenge to yield. We become more than if we did not try. Even an "out and out failure" usually (many say inevitably) results in personal growth and progress way beyond the initial disappointment. Often failures shape future successes, which push those failures well into the background of time and memory. I marvel at my failures, at the continuous failures of my accomplished neighbors, and of so many greats. I smile and humbly observe to others, *I didn't fail the test, I just found 100 ways to do it wrong.*

Having the courage to accept a challenge just beyond our reach, risking collapse or catastrophe, is the main way in which we wend our way through life. It is indeed the natural way of things and is to be seen for what it is—progress.

> *"Courage is not something that you already have that makes you brave when the tough times start. Courage is what you earn when you've been through the tough times and you discover they aren't so tough after all."*
> – Malcolm Gladwell
> *David and Goliath: Underdogs, Misfits, and the Art of Battling Giants*

Risk, when considering character, is the price we pay for growth and accomplishment. Growth takes risk but not foolhardy risk; risk is best served by the fourth Cardinal Virtue—Temperance.

Temperance

This virtue means prudence, or self-control. Exercise restraint in sensible behavior and modest living.[86] Indeed, I thought it the height of extravagance when my wife bought me a pewter dinner plate to replace my perfectly good clay one. I take pride in my frugality. Over the years, it has allowed me to grow my businesses, be free from worry about paying my way, and save a little money to invest in research and ideas, not to mention enjoy a few wholesome pleasures. It is my fond hope that my investments in good works such as the University of Pennsylvania, our public libraries, the U.S. mail system, our fire stations and hospitals, and my inventions will serve generations to come.

This leads to the question of appropriateness or the correct intention. I note that Aristotle advises us to consider our reaction to others in terms of what is right.[87] Consider:

- *The right person* – Ask, is a person worthy? Someone who criticizes another as a reaction without thinking can be forgiven; but not when criticism is repeated or meant to be malicious.

- *The right extent* – Not to extreme. If you are generous to a fault and give beyond what you can afford, that's wrong, because if you impoverish yourself, you are little good for much else. In fact, in being overly generous, you can become a burden.

- *The right time* – Helping a worthy person with a house payment after the foreclosure does little.

- *The right purpose* – Is the purpose worthy? Few things are better than investing in a child with potential.

- *The right way* – Do you hold being virtuous over someone by expressing conceit or superiority? Or do you set an example by living to the mean?

And finally, the true heart of the matter is that we have been discussing how to achieve well-being, and thus to be *happy!*

This leads me to a discussion of how I spend my time . . . judiciously, of course.

Spending "Leisure" Time

I do try to make waking hours productive. I am involved in paving, cleaning, and lighting our streets, for one. Meanwhile, the fire department I helped establish, Philadelphia's Union Fire Company, does its vital work. My idea of the Philadelphia Contribution for Insurance Against Loss by Fire helps those suffering from the fires that plague our city. The Library Company I formed has been loaning good books to good people for nearly 20 years now; I am thankful for every book by which it grows. Many appreciate my eponymous stove—as do I on many a cold Philadelphia night.

I am considering forming a hospital, and something must be done to educate the many; it will be our strength as our country grows, which it does and will. Goodness, I hear Connecticut has nearly 200 miles of roads already. What a wonder! Everything fascinates me. I am most interested in lightning—yes, lightning. Could it be electricity?

(Yet I am distracted by the grumbling I hear from my Junto Club[88] compatriots about our dear king, his lieutenants, and their policies. A tax stamp is egregious.)

St. Thomas Aquinas knew that ". . . leisure is more important than work and that people misuse it if they are not educated in constructive pastimes."[89] The Greats understood that boredom is not peaceful, nor does it make us happy. Using time well determines who we become and what we create.

Time well used, balanced, and thoughtful multiplies my energies, creativity, and wit. I have always slept well and eaten frugally, which sustained my endeavors. Printing was dawn to dusk, six days a week or more; and it rewarded my resolve. Even then, in my earliest most youthfully ambitious days, I took time to simply stop, read a good book, and take things slowly compared to the day's labors. I did not know at the time that these habits would lead me to my most valuable time spent— my leisure.

To use our leisure time well, we must be prepared in body, mind, and disposition. In fact, I must say to make the best use of our leisure, we must give it even more effort and thought than we do the regular work of our lives.[90] Further, I issue a caution: The people with whom we spend our leisure are as important as how we spend it—or more so. For leisure time is when we come to better know ourselves and how we can become content with life. The unworthy waste our greatest most limited gift, our time.

Next, I treat the subject of simplicity, which I consider akin to temperance.

The Virtue of Simplicity

I am determined to bring the simplest of philosophies to the job. *Little strokes fell great oaks*, I say. Some observe I am accomplished. If so, it is only because I have had good company and guidance and I diligently applied myself to the task at hand. While I have leisure now, still I employ the daily schedule ingrained in me since youth as it is apropos to my duties to my neighbors, to my Philadelphia. My day begins at 5 a.m. and comes in six parcels.[91]

- *Rising* – Three hours. Getting ready for the day: bathing, breakfast, personal study,[92] and preparation for work. I like to ask a morning question such as, "What good shall I do this day?"

- *Morning work* – Four hours.

- *Review* – Three hours. Review of current projects or business and eat lunch.

- *Afternoon work* – Four hours.

- *Relaxing/recreation* – Four hours. Dinner, rest, and wrapping up the day. Putting things in their proper order, music, diversion, or conversation. I ask myself, "What good *have* I done this day?"

- *Sleep* – Six hours

Thus organized and scheduled, I have done much; I do not fritter away my time. Let me hasten to say that while I hew to this regimen, I don't do so rigidly. If I must deviate, at least my alterations are guided by my concern for doing things well. I always seek to strengthen my moral fiber and the good I can do for my friends, family, and fellow Americans. Contrary to what people say about the illusiveness of creativity and inspiration, I find my best ideas come when time is thus spent. Those ideas benefit me and mine and energize me.

The Skill of Working with People

My aim has always been to ask as much of myself, or more, as I would ask of others. Thus, I always ask myself: What comes first in the establishment of character—an internal sense of right and wrong? Or behavior—acting rightly? Experience tells me it is not a case of either/or. It is the duality of study and practice together. One begets the other and vice versa. We can't know what living virtuously is unless we study it intently so we can internalize it. Yet we can't be respected for living well if we simply *intend* to do right without *displaying* just behavior. Therefore, it's best to practice being just even with trifles so we are most likely to act well when it's most important. I am aware so many are watching. Then, I have found, people will trust you, especially at critical moments. In other words, if you *intend* good, you will more likely *do* good and thus earn respect, followership, and legacy. This takes much study, introspection, and practice as working with people is never this or that; it's a matter of degrees. If we start early, we won't have as many errata to correct later in life.

To make no mistakes is not in the power of man; but from their errors
and mistakes the wise and good learn wisdom for the future.
– Plutarch

I have always been motivated to make Philadelphia a place where our neighbors can have the opportunity to be industrious, prosperous, safe, and happy. As the Ancient Greeks observe, people are naturally virtuous, industrious, and civic minded. I plan to nurture what is natural and good in our municipal services and, in turn, encourage our neighbors and thus their communities to do and be the same.

The first question is how to manage people, politics, and processes and give each its due. I always consider people first because working with people is also to manage the politics and process of getting things done. I aim to be flexible yet firm and fair. My approach is to do as follows:

- *Rise above.* First, I always remind people of possibilities, goals, and the dream of what can be accomplished together. People will rally when inspired. Reaching the mountaintop of a worthy goal affords us better perspective of the next and yet the next worthy goal, and thus we progress. Then we can focus on the essential details to get there.

- *Make allies.* I find it an extremely rewarding pursuit to make friends. In fact, one of my guiding principles is to earn the respect of honorable people. My ultimate achievement is to make a friend of an enemy.

- *Don't engage when incited.* Agitation is never a good counsel and an indication of wickedness. It is exceedingly difficult to recover from a verbal barb delivered in haste. Ill words remain while the good we speak fades in their wake.

- *Don't speak ill of people who may disagree with you.* Speak *to* not *of* people who disagree with you.[93] One must get to know people and learn of their strengths, weaknesses, and moral fiber. We cannot shoulder communal endeavors alone. Collaboration is best when bettering community well-being; it has the quality of continually improving. And it is simply harder for people to say no when you look them in the eye.

There are those who *play* politics for personal gain and those who *do* politics for general betterment. The latter are the ones who, in the end, win the day, win the battle, and win the war of life.

I turn briefly now to the managing of political affairs.

Politics—the bane, bungling, and blessing of it all. It's the art of managing people, simply said—quite complex and frankly devilish at times. I have noted there are those who *play* politics for personal gain and those who *do* politics for general betterment. The latter are the ones who, in the end, win the day, win the battle, and win the war of life. Thus, I seek those who do politics and study those who play politics; I befriend both—the former more openly, the latter more circumspectly. My job is consensus.

I have always enjoyed a good relationship with our leaders. Again, I do it by knowing myself first. I am still learning about this fellow Ben Franklin, a wily personage.

My Work as Chief Keeper of Our Community Harmony

I am *always* planning, as I have said. With that, a plan can be successfully followed only with extreme focus, ". . . cutting off all amusements or other employment that would divert attention, [which] makes the execution of that same plan the sole study and business."[94] Decide well what you will do as you must see it to its logical and realistic end. Yes, even to letting it go when the endeavor ceases to breathe if a goal proves to be unrealistic. Conserve your limited resources. There's little time to travel a road to nowhere. In my experience, when a task, job, or goal comes to its natural conclusion, though that may not be the envisioned goal, the work of it fades quickly, but the immense satisfaction of the road traveled remains. And if that work is for good and general well-being, that accomplishment unceasingly grows in proportion to the work. Always be industrious about that which is worthy.

*I have always thought that one man of tolerable abilities may work great changes,
and accomplish great affairs among mankind, if he first forms a good plan.*
– Ben Franklin

While I'm new to the work of keeping our neighborhoods whole, well, and
welcoming, I'm not new to the study of people put to action. My first task will be to
learn mainly through my own eyes and the council of others. I will structure my day
to allow time to meet people, organize them, and motivate if not inspire them. I must
start with our assigned charges, of course. I will do it seriously most of the time and
jovially when the moment is right. My goal will be to know, really know, each of my
followers so I can recall meaningful, personal, purposeful details even on a chance
meeting. Let me flesh out my goals:

- *Know people.* I would begin to get to know people who have direct effect on
  our services and goals. I must visit everyone in the organization; listen much,
  talk less. My neighbors will see me frequently, and I will become even better
  friends with our elected and appointed officials. Each has much to teach;
  I have much to learn.

- *Do not let character go unnoticed.* Praise in public when dually earned.
  Admonish in private; never let faults of character go uncorrected—
  expeditiously, fairly, and firmly.

- *Assess the direction of the agency.* I will investigate the mood of our staff
  individually and collectively, assessing if it is divisive or cohesive, and
  build cohesion where necessary. I will see that staff are aligned with our
  goals, and if goals are not clear, restate them to do the greatest good for
  the greatest number.

- *Redirect the agency if needed.* I will start with *Make the community safe,
  secure, resilient, and productive.* Such a goal, simply stated, is suitable to the
  capacities of our professionals, amenable to the community, and sustainable.
  Naturally, this purpose when vetted by all may vary by a word or two but
  will inform our direction forward. The leader must be the standard-bearer
  of the agency's purpose.

- *Make processes efficient and the agency effective.* The community must
  know and support the results of the efforts made.

> **We can each be great in our own way. It is in knowing the difference between activity for activity's sake and productivity and in actualizing our individual capacities to be the best we were meant to be.**

Note I haven't dwelt upon being the man in charge. Rightly, I feel it necessary to dwell on how to get those under my hand to espouse and realize their potential, thereby taking this organization upward with them. I believe we can each be great in our own way. It is in knowing the difference between activity for activity's sake and productivity and in actualizing our individual capacities to be the best we were meant to be.

Final Reflections

In short: Be industrious. Be frugal in word and deed.[95] Speak ill of no one. Endeavor to speak the truth. Learn to gain wisdom. Dare to take worthy challenges. Strive to be someone you admire.

Personally Speaking

Faded Jeans

James Klopovic

I think of Franklin's temperance, or prudence, and realize that one doesn't need much to be fulfilled. We lose sight of that when we see the latest bigger-than-life flat-screen TV being delivered next door. It's a different reality for much of the world.

I found myself in Moscow back in the late 70s. I was in the "uniform" of the day—a leather jacket, faded denim shirt, Frye boots, and my trusty Levi's, all to which I gave no passing thought. A young Russian boy joined me in the elevator of the Moscow Hotel. He was cruising the tourists to trade military bric-a-brac. In a flash, he offered me $125 for my old, faded jeans, the ones with the orange tag on the right back pocket. Remember, this was over 40 years ago. Turns out he could have sold those shabby old taken-for-granted jeans for much more on the underground market. As I recall, a goodly privileged salary back then was the cost of those jeans.

It occurred to me much later, it probably wasn't the jeans the young lad was after. They were, and still are, a symbol of freedom he couldn't have—and still doesn't have if he's yet on Russian soil. We are most fortunate to live where a simple pair of faded jeans is commonplace. The New Wave MAGNUS–OVÉA spirit does not take these things for granted and is humbled by the simple yet significant all around us.

What we see depends mainly on what we look for.
– John Lubbock

THE SCIENCE AND THEORY OF NEW WAVE LEADERSHIP

Be sure to love . . . and you can love anything and anyone.
Just put yourself in the place of the person you wish to love.

– Wanda O. Klopson

Section Overview

The idea of New Wave Leadership is anchored in character-based development, for which we have an exceptionally large and rapidly expanding body of supporting literature in both science and theory. We only touch on some of this evidence, data, study, and experience, thus keeping our approach simple, suitable, and sustainable. It's gratifying, however, that our approach to teaching New Wave Leadership is validated by brain science employing the technical ability to peer into our brains. Thus scientists are able to observe how brains react to moral behavior for the good of the collective. In addition, our approach is strengthened by one of the techniques of this journey. Reversal Theory[96] is well established in the literature and scientific journals. We now know we can optimize our human "footprint" of collective impact by understanding and employing the principles of continuously becoming our best. Section II presents the evidence and how to use it.

Chapter 5: The Neuroscience of New Wave Leadership – A Quick Look establishes that our bodily systems, especially our autonomic hormonal system, support moral character and action. Science shows we have *conscience*,[97] which is the basis of MAGNUS–OVÉA development and conduct.

Chapter 6: Reversal Theory – Zigzagging Through Life introduces a way to benefit from our human interactions. We can intentionally match our mindset to the moment to achieve balance and better outcomes. This harmony is a basic drive of the human condition as explained by Reversal Theory.

Chapter 7: Putting the Theory and Science of Becoming Our Best to Work elaborates on how to enlist our neurophysiology and natural ability to be moral and contribute to our collective communities. Together, these factors help optimize and balance our human interactions and improve our well-being.

All three chapters emphasize the practicality of specific behaviors, actions, and techniques to continually strengthen our ability to thrive.

Chapter 5

The Neuroscience of New Wave Leadership – A Quick Look

There is no scientific study more vital to man than the study of his own brain.
Our entire view of the universe depends on it.
– Francis Crick

Patricia Churchland, a Canadian-American philosopher noted for her contributions to the relatively new field of neurophilosophy, claims there's a neurobiological basis for our natural propensity to be good and do good by being moral.[98]

It's fascinating that over two millennia ago our ancient philosophers and scientists knew it was natural to be concerned for the betterment of our family, friends, and by extension, the wider neighborhood. Today, growing areas of research confirm the reality of conscience and the value of improving ourselves then doing what we can to better what is beyond our immediate reach. We have an emotional, physical, and chemical response to being with others. More than that, we're neurologically and emotionally geared to, and even bettered by, doing good for and with others. We're inexorably driven to be and do things with immediate and extended family and fellow co-workers, friends, and even casual acquaintances, where we tend to display our better selves.

Humans are unique among mammalians. We're capable of being ethical and moral; we tend to protect those who need protection; we value virtue; we're drawn to collaborate out of instinct and by will; and we can empathize deeply. Other mammals may exhibit some of these traits of collective survival, but most are instinctual. They don't come in a bipedal bundle like a human who can think abstractly, intuit, and build the unimaginable. More than any other living creature, we can determine our individual and collective destinies.

What the Ancients, occidental and oriental, intuited is now proven by science with ever increasing surety and evidence. We encourage you to read *Conscience: The Origins of Moral Intuition* by Patricia Churchland for an illuminating review of the science of living morally with character. Her book is quite understandable and pleasant to read as it is written for the layperson. Its message is simply to aim to do good in life; you *will* get better and better at it; and along the way, contentment then happiness will arise. With that, we can individually and collectively make good and right decisions. Our collective potential is yet to be realized.

Redefining New Wave Governance with Conscience

Conscience underpins the next evolution of character-based individuals and organizations that have the potential to redefine governance—whether running a family or a Fortune 500 conglomerate. Two arguments are posed for developing New Wave governance: one, to reaffirm *moral obligation* and two, to rework how we *collaborate* in groups.

Moral Obligation

First, let's address moral obligation. In the confusion of galloping progress, at times there seems to be a loosening hold on morality. Personal benefit, even if it harms others, can rule over the common good or the rights of others. Oh yes, we can overrule our natural, neurological propensity to be our better selves and be wrong and do wrong. For example, an employee of a big box store mentioned a rush for the latest and truly spectacular TVs just before the Super Bowl, only to have many of them returned *after* the big game! Many apparently considered "borrowing" a TV they could not afford appropriate. These "borrowers" are well down the slippery slope of deceit. The cure is prevention by knowing what is wrong and not doing it. It's not always easy to discern, and some people's culture and upbringing may have influenced them otherwise. Perhaps the best place to start is with the Golden Rule of *Do unto others as you would have them do unto you.* Doing the right thing is always meaningful and gratifying.

The first priority of a New Wave individual is to act responsibly and honestly and attempt to behave rightly. By extension, we need to model and teach those we connect with, especially children, to be and do the same. We hope to educate as many individuals as possible to be role models so the tried-and-true Good Life can spread.

> **The New Wave theory of behavior recognizes the difficulty of our rising to high standards and teaches that moral development is *worth the work but needs constant attention*.**

The gift of natural conscientiousness is fragile. Conscience can be misused to rationalize bad or even immoral actions. The realm of politics provides a stark example. Most politicians think they have the proper, shall we say, enlightened, view of what is right for the taxpayer, or the voter, which can be at odds with the data, experiences, and record of history, not to mention the opposing party. Perhaps noble in its statement, factually the view can be various degrees of harmful. We can and do act in opposition to our natural tendencies for our own aims, to appease others, or simply because we've convinced ourselves it's for the best even though we haven't thought it through.

Science evidences physiological and psychological growth when we act correctly for communal well-being; but science cannot help us decide a moral dilemma. *Enter conscience.* The New Wave theory of behavior recognizes the difficulty of our rising to high standards and teaches that moral development is worth the work but needs constant attention. That's why becoming a New Wave MAGNUS–OVÉA Leader is an uninterrupted, focused journey. It's not within human nature to get life perfectly right without guidance, but working toward acting with character causes us to grow morally in beneficial ways. A moral lapse is an insidious slippery slope in the opposite direction with unappealing consequences sooner or later. Life will teach us what was wrong—sometimes most bitterly.

> *In truth, whatever is worth doing at all, is worth doing well;*
> *and nothing can be done well without attention.*
> – Philip Dormer Stanhope, 18th-century British statesman

Collaboration

The second argument for New Wave governance concerns collaboration in small groups or between agencies, which is a major theme of this New Wave theory of behavior as it impacts leadership. What does this have to do with science? Well, humans are unique to the animal world in that we feel a general collective direction to take then combine that with judgment, which determines appropriate action to follow that direction.[99] It's a matter of employing that which makes us human and humane, melding the physiological and neurophilosophical in all of us.

However, don't confuse collaboration with cooperation as they are distinctly different. Cooperation, for example, is working with others to finish a report. That teamwork is completed when the group submits the report. Collaboration, on the other hand, is a collective effort that's often perpetual. It can involve alliances with individuals and agencies outside a particular organization on a continuing program to answer an ongoing concern or need.

Cooperation is good, of course, but it has a beginning and an end. Collaboration consists of continuous effort to address a permanent need for community well-being with the goal of helping individuals and communities thrive. In the private sector, for example, many businesses depend on supplies or services from other businesses and/or subcontractors to do their work. The public sector is used to doing things as individuals, singular agencies, or defined services. While we need agencies that specialize in, say, education, city planning, or transportation, they can no longer stand alone. Agency resources aren't adequate to maintain these insular specialties. These services can be redundant, for one thing. For another, they may need economies of scale that require the parts of a solution to work together, in which case the sum becomes greater than the individual specialties. In this New Wave, people work to find linkages of talent and resources rather than remain isolated in their areas of expertise. Evidence the partnership between private sector immunologists, drug companies, the medical community, and public sector support to combat and win the COVID "war" and prepare to face threats yet to come. Necessity demands both our communal cooperation and our collaboration. What a dramatic example of conscientiousness.

The solution to combining forces is twofold. First, we need to learn how to collaborate more between *individuals* to achieve organizational purposes. Concurrently, we need to learn to function with *other agencies or organizations* when we need more global solutions to problems and needs. There's truth in the maxim

Communities of the future will demand more and better services, which will require interagency or interorganizational collaboratives.

"strength in numbers." What more can we achieve if those many are grounded in virtue and character *and* have a singular purpose? We'd be unstoppable, really.

This is not to say that agencies designed to provide a specific service, such as a state department of education, must completely refocus and reorganize. No; providing educational services is a specialty best served by experts. But classroom education is not that simple. A productive learning environment requires social service, counselors, public safety, public health, and more. Communities of the future will demand more and better services, which will require interagency or interorganizational collaboratives. We can specialize where we need to and collaborate when it's beneficial to all.

By continuously developing our sense of conscience, of what is morally right or wrong, and combining that with a communal sense of purpose and collaboration, good things happen—and we want *more* of it. So, let's see how some of the most notable science supports us in continuously becoming our better then best selves.

The Neurobiological Basis for Being Our Best

Our natural propensity to be good and do good by being moral has a neurobiological basis. Several key micro-players encourage communal attachment. They are stimulated when we do good, especially for others. Four of these are the "... *neurohormones oxytocin and vasopressin, opioids* and *cannabinoids* that your brain makes naturally to make you feel good." In addition, "... it (is) highly likely that the basic motivation for sharing and cooperation, and for learning social norms, (is) fundamentally owed to the genes that build brain wiring."[100] Thus, we experience a physical difference between insular independence and collective interdependence, which when taken as integral parts of each condition, strengthens the former and expands the latter. A crucial part of this natural blending is empathy.

Empathy is functional and feels good. It's habit forming. When nurtured, empathy and trust engender more empathy and trust in a virtuous cycle throughout our lives. Our feel-good neurohormones encourage us to *do it again*. Within our lifetime, we can expect this character- and conscience-based neurological growth to continue if we know how to foster it. Basically, it's about looking for opportunities to collaborate successfully so sharing skills, work, and achievement becomes ingrained. Thus, the brain grows in a healthy way. Furthermore, we can probably expect this neurological improvement to continue incrementally within the population, thus contributing to the positive evolution of us all. The better we get individually, the better we get collectively.

We bond neurologically and socially. That's how we develop norms and values.[101] These, in turn, construct our moral compass, which is a guide to expressing ourselves with integrity, kindness, responsibility, fairness, and collaboration.[102] It even guides us to see the humor and goodness in and around us.

. . . [T]o have no sense of humor is to be a seriously flawed human being.
It's not a minor shortcoming: it shuts you off from humanity.
– Alan Bennett

Advances in biology and neuroscience gather more and more data on our propensity to live by moral standards and behavior. When we build habits of behaving morally, our brain rewires itself in the direction of moral action. The science of *neuroplasticity* tells us that, with *synaptic pruning*, we learn behaviors that build character and improve the common good. Less than optimal synapses are lopped off, and the good-leaning ones are strengthened. We can and *do* grow our brains for a lifetime! The better behavior we "wire in," the better we will survive—and even thrive. And the sooner we start the better!

Thus, we can make a strong case that neurobiology explains our natural tendency to steer away from vices toward virtues. Our huge mammalian cortex with its 86 billion neurons[103] all working together helps us survive by collaborating socially. Remarkably, scientists observe that neuronal development is exponential, not linear; so creativity, progress, and accomplishment likewise expand exponentially. Pause in your reading and think about this.

This brain action is also the basis of moral conduct. Our brains developed and learned that acting for the benefit of the whole is a good thing. First it was about survival, then it became the basis of progress, and it remains the way forward.

We need to pay attention to the development of conscience because the opposite, lack of conscience, does happen. If we begin down an amoral path and are unable to feel remorse, our brains will develop to help us along that path, too. Remember our Superbowl TV borrowers? Have they gone too far? Can their minds and brains still be changed? Or, in the extreme, might they end up in prison some day? It's their choice.

When we build habits of behaving morally, our brain rewires itself in the direction of moral action.

History is littered with narcissists, sociopaths, and psychopaths who destroyed civilizations. Think what they could have built if they had been compelled in the opposite direction for good through proper nurturing, awareness, and training. The brain does not choose our path for us but will support the path we choose—conscientious or not. Conscience is the reason we survived as a species, and the lack of it in some cases is doubtless a reason many experiments in empire building and individual lives failed.

We are blessed with brains that support and increase thinking and acting morally *if we are aware and choose that path.* We can't take that for granted. Growing in the right direction requires vigilance. Thankfully, acting morally for personal and communal well-being can quickly become a habit. Even more justification for committing to the journey of becoming this new brand of leader.

More poetically put:

> *Our mind is a garden,*
> *Thoughts are seeds.*
> *You can grow flowers or*
> *You can grow weeds.*
> – Unknown

Activating Harmony and Balance Through Body Chemistry

Our brains get a hormonal reward from approval and a negative hormonal hit for disapproval, which is how our conscience is built.[104] Our hormones are constantly fluctuating. Thus, our entire being—physical, spiritual, emotional, societal, and psychological—constantly looks for balance between approval and disapproval.[105] This constant straining to gain approval and avoid disapproval is the height of distress, and it debilitates the whole person. Our natural propensity to seek equilibrium is nothing less than Aristotle's search for the Golden Mean—the most virtuous behavior *between* excess and deficiency. (Refer to Aristotle's table of the Golden Mean in Chapter 4.) The Greats hypothesized that we had chemistry driving our behavior and sensed we are compelled toward harmony, which they called *sophrosyne.*

Thus, we all have a part in general human progress as there is strength in numbers, even though tragedies occur along the way. This more than justifies our personal study of how to live well, in balance. Great benefit comes of it, not the least of which is legacy and the realization that life overall is good.

The wisdom of one of our great philosophers comes to mind:

Step with care and great tact and remember that Life's a Great Balancing Act.
– Theodore "Dr. Seuss" Geisel

Let's continue this discussion with how each hormone acts within us and actually affects who we are and what we become.

Hormones – Overview of What They Are and How They Function

Hormones and neurotransmitters, the means by which brain cells communicate, are a marvel of evolution, survival, and life. They're chemical signals released in the body from many causes, from stress to a sense of accomplishment. Directing and synchronizing our numerous functions, they control our sexual health, growth, disposition, procreation, and metabolic processes—and scientists are investigating further functions. Our hormones and neurotransmitters lead to specific beneficial or deleterious effects, such as pleasure and good health or pain, ill health, and addictions. In addition, they support our moral growth.

Depending on the types and number of hormones and transmitters released, the effects can vary greatly. Their magic is they all work together in a delicate synchronization to direct how we think, function, and develop. Not so surprising, we have more control than we may think over our hormones through our thoughts, emotions, and choices.

It's important to discuss the effects of hormones and transmitters as they relate to New Wave Leadership and MAGNUS–OVÉA character development. Simply put, our neurophysiology helps us make better, even moral, decisions, and our decision making improves over time with continued attention. Principled living continually strengthens synaptic connections related to moral behavior in a virtuous cycle. By understanding how the body reacts chemically in certain situations, we can know ourselves better and improve the connections between our mind, body, and emotions for well-being as well as the quality of our character. With this knowledge, we can avoid or limit harmful actions. When we learn, for example, that alcohol's chemical components trigger serotonin, which can lead to addiction, we're less likely to drink to excess. We already know addictions make us lose control of ourselves. In turn, loss of control may lead to actions that don't reflect well on our character and may even threaten our survival. Why go there?

By knowing our neurobiology, we can avoid harmful behaviors and strengthen opposing, protective good behaviors. For example, certain positive, feel-good hormones such as dopamine are released when we do good things for others, which encourages those behaviors. This exemplifies and justifies our behavioral decisions toward the good and away from the detrimental or destructive. Awareness also provides insight into the actions and reactions of others as we interrelate. It helps us optimally balance behavior *and* decision making for ourselves and improves our social interactions. A remarkable aspect of our hormones is that they have physiological *and* psychological effects because they affect our physical selves and our personalities.

The table in Figure 2 provides a brief summary of some of our major hormones and their functions.[106]

Note that a *neurotransmitter* is "a chemical that is released from a nerve cell which thereby transmits an impulse from a nerve cell to another nerve, muscle, organ, or other tissue."[107] It's therefore a neurological messenger, relaying information between cells.

NAME	A.K.A.	TYPE	FUNCTION	EXAMPLE
ENDORPHIN	**"The Internal Morphine"** **"Pain & Pleasure"**	Neuro-transmitter & hormone	Binds to opiod receptors to: • Increase pleasure • Decrease pain	• "Runner's High" • Released with good food, sex, music, chocolate, exercise
DOPAMINE	**"Chasing the High"** **"Feel Good Hormone"**	Neuro-transmitter & hormone	• Released during good behavior, which leads to more good behavior • Regulates electrolytes	• Schizophrenia from high dopamine • Parkinson's from low dopamine (Rx: levodopa/carbidopa) • Drugs that raise dopamine: meth, cocaine, heroin, nicotine
SEROTONIN	**"Mood Stabilizer"**	Neuro-transmitter	• Efffects: happy, calm, focused, balanced • Low levels: anxiety, aggression, insomnia, sweet cravings	• Serotonin syndrome from high serotonin • Drugs that affect serotonin levels: LSD, ecstasy, anti-depressants
OXYTOCIN	**"Cuddle/ Snuggle Drug"**	Posterior pituitary hormone	• Released with touch, loving thoughts, actions • Good for social bonding/trust • Strong association with empathy	• Pet therapy • Allows social species to survive
CORTISOL	**"Stress Hormone"**	Steroid hormone	• <u>Short term:</u> raises BG for muscle/brain, inflammation, immunity, fight or flight response • <u>Long term:</u> raises anxiety, depression, aggression, weight. Lowers learning, recall, immunity	• <u>Short-term:</u> Helps for split-decisions, "life or death" situations • <u>Long-term:</u> Cardiovascular risks • Cushing's Disease from high cortisol

Figure 2: A Brief Review of Major Hormones and Their Functions

It's amazing how much being human, and even alive, depends on hormones. For example, oxytocin, the social bonding hormone, is a basis for intimacy, among many other effects and physiological results. At this time, scientists know of 50 hormones and counting that work to regulate who we are, what we are, and how we behave.

A Closer Look at Five Major Hormones and Neurotransmitters

Following is an expanded explanation of the five hormones listed in Figure 2. Think about the effects of these hormones on *you*.

Endorphin is known as "internal morphine." It's a neurotransmitter and hormone. When it's released, it binds to special opioid receptors (called mu receptors) located in the body (brain, spinal column, peripheral nervous system, and digestive tract). As it binds to the receptors, it inhibits the neurotransmitter gamma aminobutyric acid (GABA), which then delays the uptake of another hormone in the body called dopamine. With dopamine lingering longer in the body, the person experiences increased pleasure.

Endorphins also inhibit a hormone called substance P, which regulates pain. When substance P is inhibited, pain is decreased. In this way, endorphins increase pleasure and decrease pain—the same effect morphine has in the body, which is why morphine has been a desirable drug for centuries.

Example: Endorphins are released during physical activity such as running. The effects are commonly referred to as "runner's high." They're also released with good foods, music, chocolate, experiences in nature, and sex. So, some things can be equal to or even better than sex, which we may discover if we prepare for longevity and age gracefully. Aging well, facilitated by self-managing our hormones, is an important theme of this book.

Dopamine, like endorphins, also acts as a neurotransmitter and a hormone. This is the "feel-good" hormone responsible for people "chasing the high." It's released when we have a positive outcome to an action. With regard to evolution, this is advantageous because it reinforces specific behaviors that lead to favorable outcomes. It also acts in the rest of the body by causing narrowing of blood vessels (vasoconstriction), increased heart rate, increased blood flow through the kidneys (renal vasodilation), and increased sodium output in urine. Certain levels of dopamine are beneficial to our health, but extreme levels can lead to problems such as aggressiveness and addictive behaviors such as gambling.

Too much dopamine in the body promotes schizophrenia, which characteristically leads to being out of touch with reality. Too little dopamine gives rise to Parkinson's disease, a disorder affecting motor skills with symptoms such as tremors, stiffness, and difficulties with coordinating smooth movements.

> **Oxytocin is multifaceted: It helps us sleep, improves social understanding, enhances intimacy, eases anxiety, and aids in strengthening relationships and attachments.**

Example: Many drugs, such as methamphetamines, cocaine, heroin, and nicotine, increase dopamine release. It's easy to become addicted to these drugs because they derive from natural chemicals. Their effects encourage their use, reinforcing this addictive and destructive behavior.

Serotonin is considered a mood stabilizer neurotransmitter. The effects of serotonin are feelings of happiness, calmness, more focus, and a sense of balance. With insufficient serotonin in the body, the feelings change to anxiety, aggression, insomnia, low self-esteem, depression, and sweet cravings. These negative effects of low serotonin are counteracted with SSRIs, selective serotonin reuptake inhibitors. These medications impede the reabsorption of serotonin, allowing it to send more messages between nerve cells, thus harmonizing and balancing our system.

Substances such as LSD, ecstasy, and MDMA increase the amount of serotonin circulating in the body. The surplus leads to a sense of euphoria, which becomes a highly addictive, albeit disorienting, state of being.

Example: If you're depressed, your serotonin levels are probably low. Exercise, natural light, and dietary measures are ways to increase serotonin.

Oxytocin, better known as the "cuddle" or "snuggle" hormone, is stored in the posterior pituitary of the brain and is released upon affectionate physical touch as well as loving thoughts and actions. This hormone, like dopamine, has an evolutionary advantage for developing social bonding and trust. It also has a strong association with empathy. This effect allows species to survive by encouraging collaboration and differentiating friend from foe.

Example: Oxytocin is multifaceted: It helps us sleep, improves social understanding, enhances intimacy, eases anxiety, and aids in strengthening relationships and attachments. Pet therapy is one method of increasing the release of oxytocin. Sharing a meal, giving a gift, using social media (no wonder it's addictive), telling people you love them, and hugs also work to raise oxytocin levels.[108]

Cortisol, the "stress hormone" is a natural steroid released during times of tension. When released for a short period of time, it increases levels of sugar in the blood to aid in muscle and brain function. It also decreases any inflammation in the body and suppresses the immune system. These effects are part of the sympathetic nervous system responsible for "freeze, fight, or flight" responses. When the body is subjected to situational stressors such as confronting a wild bear in the woods (experienced by this author without event—thankfully), cortisol is released to prepare the body to stand stock still, confront the bear, or flee. Ideally, stressors only present themselves sporadically and for short periods of time, allowing for quick thinking and fast action. Unfortunately, stress can be much more frequent and sometimes nearly continuous in this day and age.

> **Stress management using such measures as a simple, daily guided meditation induces positive hormonal responses in a virtuous cycle.**

When cortisol is released for long periods of time, it leads to increased anxiety, depression, aggression, difficulties learning, decreased memory recall, decreased immunity, increased weight gain, and increased blood sugar levels among other dysfunctions. Ultimately, cardiovascular risks result. A condition in which the adrenal gland releases high levels of cortisol for long periods is called Cushing's disease. Although this disease is rare and most often caused by either too much corticosteroid medication or a benign tumor in the adrenal or pituitary gland, people can contract the disease due to long-term stressors in their daily lives and consequently suffer from increased cardiovascular and other problems.

Example: If you have symptoms such as weight gain with fatty deposits around your midsection and upper back, face, and between the shoulders, pink or purple stretch marks, fragile skin, or slow healing of cuts, see your doctor. If you have none of these symptoms and your blood pressure is under control, your cortisol production is probably working well. If your stress level is high, take natural measures to reduce it such as meditation or more exercise or relaxing activities.

It behooves us to understand how hormones work and how we can work with them. A takeaway from this brief discussion on a few of the main hormones is that stress management using such measures as a simple, daily guided meditation induces positive hormonal responses in a virtuous cycle.

Balancing Our Human Interactions

As we practice virtuous living while striving for well-being, we also become increasingly better at human interactions. This improvement is enhanced by understanding how to manage our motivational mindsets to minimize conflict and foster collaboration.

Reversal Theory, which we discuss in more detail in the next chapter, basically deals with balancing our human interactions more effectively. While we need more scientific research into how hormones guide and react to each motivational state, we can be certain a significant interplay exists between hormones and this balancing process. Hormones are individually and collectively geared to supporting us when we do good for others, seeking the balance of well-being and having optimal person-to-person interactions. When we balance our conversations, we are evoking a primal response, the original goal of which was to *collaborate to survive*. It worked then, and it works now—but now we know enough to harness hormonal responses to our advantage. Instead of just surviving, we have a way to thrive.

The Importance of Balance

When our systems sense we are out of balance, we can recalibrate ourselves in two ways: physiologically by working toward well-being and psychologically by engaging techniques and tools such as reversing our mindsets as needed. Life can be stressful, and it's best to prepare for stress *before* it becomes distracting or debilitating. This fits with the MAGNUS–OVÉA philosophy of learning to be prepared with an optimistic perspective to face down any problems and disappointments that arise.

We *learn* to stay in a state of stress from family, work, bills, an endless to-do list, missed goals, and disappointments. Likewise, we can *unlearn* stressful living by training and retraining our systems to be more robust. We have neurophysiology, innate values, and social relationships to bring to bear on stressors. Thus, we can direct our neuroplastic brains and nervous systems toward being and doing good.

Valence and Well-Being

Our hormonal networks are extremely sophisticated and based on the concept of valence, or activators, of our autonomic endocrine system.[109] Such activators are described in the scientific studies of eudaimonics and hedonics. *Eudaimonic* happiness involves meaning and purpose, and *hedonic* happiness involves pleasure and enjoyment.[110] Both relate to the pursuit of individual excellence. We can experience *eudaimonic* happiness, for example, when we lose ourselves in the work of overcoming adversity or accepting a challenge at the risk of failure. It's the spark that lights the promise of accomplishment and growth.

Hedonics is the study of how we are activated to seek pleasure and avoid pain. In short, it's the study of well-being and how to achieve it. (Note that Yale University offers an online course anyone can audit for free called "The Science of Well-Being"—the school's most popular course *ever.[111]*) Relative to becoming our best, studies of eudaimonics and hedonics provide rationale for our propensity to be and do good and avoid that which is not.

The cultivation of virtue is another way of describing valence, the activator of being who we were meant to be. We can actually feel the valence, the spark of OVÉA, in that ". . . feelings of 'oughtness' (positive valence) or 'ought-not-ness' (negative valence) typically accompany social habits that emerge from reinforcement learning, as well as from imitation, which also engages components of the reward system."[112]

By extension, valence is also a factor of neurobiology. "Conformity to social norms meets with approval (positive valence) . . . transgressions meet with disapproval . . . (negative valence)."[113] The brain's reward system (positive and negative valence) is known to play a powerful role in what we think we ought to do, morally and otherwise."[114] Again, this means we have a hormonal reaction to doing what is good and right. A whole-brain function directs the whole-person function, which builds well-being with the goal of personal, interpersonal, and communal thriving.

According to Aristotle, a state of well-being is achieved through the following hierarchy of self-development:[115]

- *Self-acceptance* – Liking who is in your skin.

- *Personal growth* – Living into your potential.

- *Autonomy* – Developing and using your own moral standards to measure yourself.

- *Mastery* – Feeling up to life's challenges and seeing obstacles as opportunities for accomplishment and growth.

- *Satisfying relationships* – Being loved and loving, which also applies to friendships in a healthy give and take.

- *Life purpose* – Having a long-term reason to get up and get going in the morning.

These factors don't just describe happiness; they are most practical. Plus, anyone who works at each state of well-being synergistically can achieve them with commitment, persistence, and determination.

Well-being concerns developing awareness, connection, self-esteem, and purpose. Those qualities are based on resilience, outlook, attention, and generosity.[116] All characteristics of becoming MAGNUS–OVÉA. The related science involves our hormonal system as well as neuroplasticity, genomics, the interconnectedness of brain and body, and the fact that we are innately good.[117] Note these themes also wend their way throughout New Wave individual development and leadership style.

It's all about seeking sophrosyne, the Golden Mean, the moderate middle between extremes by which we achieve the Good Life.

A Compelling Case for Conscience

We can describe the journey of becoming a new brand of forward-thinking leader in yet another way: It's a process of self-analysis for self-discovery. It's a natural and personal evolution that bears explanation and description more than it needs justification. Simply put, the more moral we are, the more moral we become, which bolsters all the other justifications for the work of the journey. Character is built by ongoing habitual action that we consciously choose, and our evolution is

> **Well-being concerns developing awareness, connection, self-esteem, and purpose. Those qualities are based on resilience, outlook, attention, and generosity.[116]**

supported by our biology. In *Conscience: The Origins of Moral Intuition*, Patricia Churchland explains that ". . . undergirding moral judgement as it actually functions in humans are instinct, habits, norms, social skills, values, and context-sensitive problem solving."[118] These traits are either passed down in our DNA (nature, biology, psychology) or learned over time and experience (nurture, sociology). Despite factors that may militate against the moral development of conscience (it's tough to learn and sustain moral action), reason and efficacy keep us moving in the right direction. Simply put, moral grounding feels good and our lives work better, which reinforces our efforts. Naturally, arguments against the neurobiology of conscience are raised.

For one, philosophers ask if we will ever understand the mind. How could a lump of grey tissue allow us to write a poem, fall in love, invent a cotton gin or a computer, paint the Mona Lisa, build a transcontinental railroad or a F-35 Lightning fighter aircraft, or run into a hail of bullets for a friend? We may never know, but neuroscience makes a compelling case for conscience.

Let's take a couple of concerns we may get from skeptics arguing that acting morally can't be explained scientifically—or at all.

How can one explain wrongdoing?

In truth, neuroscience is not yet able to provide a scientific answer to why some people succumb to varying degrees of immoral or illegal acts. We see it every day via the media and within our personal circumstance to reinforce the above state-ment and ask, is there a neurobiological motivation to act *badly*? So far, the connection hasn't been emphatically made. But just because wickedness can't be explained, do we abandon conscience? Certainly not, as at the very least, we can model better humanity born of conscience. Plus, moral conscience is the best, completely explicable, bulwark against those who *don't* act for the common good. History is a brutal testimony to evil, but over time, the strength of conscience overcomes aberrations. That counter-action is to be the example for how to live well, meaning to live the Golden Mean, which is to live with common sense—neither erring to excess or defect. Balance matters. Any other path than that of developing a conscience seems to lead to a bad end.

Some say humans haven't learned much, considering people can be quite atrocious and treacherous. We believe that through science and experience, the overall trajectory of human development, both personally and communally, seems quite positive and encouraging. But what about a suggested weakness in the research because it has to involve a most unpredictable subject, people?

Isn't studying human subjects restrictive and a matter of interpretation?

It's prohibitively difficult, one might say, to justify clinically probing a live human brain. We believe that soon ways will become available to conduct ethical human trials. These experiments will most likely confirm and relate more than what we've learned from promising mammalian trials. For example, Kenneth Kishida ethically worked with Parkinson's patients to ". . . couple dopamine release—up for positive reward, down for negative reward."[119] This study proved that these types of experiments can be done on human subjects as the technology, science, research, and subsequent inquisitiveness advance.

Doing Our Best

Know thyself. Churchland points out that Socrates warned us of the temptation to fool ourselves, to not be honest with ourselves or admit our mistakes, which can result in disaster.[120] We need to practice introspection and be realistic about our strengths and weaknesses. When things go wrong, we need to ask ourselves, "What did *I* do to cause this circumstance?" Then we can correct. Also ask this question when things go *right* and continue that path. When we confront challenges, even extreme adversity, we grow—though it may not seem so at the time. This isn't mystical pap. Reflect on your difficulties when you persevere (which you will), and you'll perceive what it means and how it leads to better days or unexpected gifts. Thus, you will grow. With that growth will come the confidence that you're ready for the next challenge by seeing its opportunities through the maddening fog of things going wrong. This is life—and a healthy part of thriving.

As Churchland wisely suggests, ". . . the best advice is perhaps to allow yourself broad life experience and exposure to the human condition in all its beauty and horror. Do your best, but even then, you will make mistakes."[121]

We can surely strive to do what's right, to be kind, honest, and trustworthy. Thus, we develop a growth mindset. Bonding between people enhances our life capacities as well-being strengthens.

Being engaged in some way for the good of the community, whatever that community, is a factor in a meaningful life. We long to belong and belonging and caring anchors our sense of place in the universe.
– Patricia Churchland

Personally Speaking

The Perfect Skeet Shot – Relaxing?

James Klopovic

When I spend just 10 minutes a day, every morning, relaxing and clearing my mind from thoughts, I realize benefits all day long!

Why do I need this time of relaxation? Stress is insidious, sneaky, and counterproductive. I don't notice getting wound up till it's too late. The stress in my body is hot and distracting after staring at my computer screen for hours, driving long distances, or simply attacking my endless to-do list. I feel bands of pain across my back, or I realize my forehead is screwed up in tense wrinkles, and usually both. When I practice relaxing tension mentally and physically regularly—daily is optimal—I feel a wave of relief to any afflicted body parts. Furthermore, experiencing deep relaxation even for a few minutes helps my concentration and even endurance with sustained work, mental and physical. Knowing how to truly relax, I can feel the relaxation ooze naturally and nicely into activities of the day.

Believe it or not, shooting skeet well is mastering the dynamic opposition of focused concentration and whole-body relaxation. Even world champions work extremely hard on making that perfect shot. It's a lifetime pursuit. The goal is to shut down conscious thought of the shot and let the unconscious take over. Why? We can't consciously calculate how a target will fly. The brain can't take in all the variables such as wind, distractions, variations in speed, and unpredictable flight patterns. Only our unconscious is quick enough to make the minute calculations necessary to break the target with a shot.

Even before I step onto a skeet station, I breathe rhythmically and deeply and evoke full-body relaxation. Then I imagine the clay target breaking. I sense a release of tension wash over me. Believe it or not, I can feel the pull of gravity on my face as my unconscious "computer" takes over. It's the proper preparation for a shot. My game improves. Not only that, but I know that anytime I pursue doing something well, the lessons I learn migrate to just about anything else I may undertake. This skeet-shooting journey is very much akin to continuously improving as a whole person.

A regular practice of relaxation helps me realize that when things aren't going right, they will pass. It's okay to miss a shot—because one day, I'll hit that clay pigeon full on and blast it to smithereens. Bullseye!

A man can never have too much red wine, too many books
or too much ammunition.
– Rudyard Kipling

Chapter 6

Reversal Theory – Zigzagging Through Life

. . . [T]he philosophers warn us not to be satisfied with mere learning, but to add practice and then training. For as time passes, we forget what we learned and end up doing the opposite, and hold opinions the opposite of what we should.
– Epictetus

As mentioned earlier in Chapter 3, psychologist Dr. Michael Apter and psychiatrist Dr. Ken Smith developed the idea of Reversal Theory. Of all the theories explaining human interaction, why do we turn to Reversal Theory when teaching New Wave Leadership? Because this theory and its process can be simply explained, learned, and most important, practiced as one way to cope with the day. By doing so, we seek to prosper from good, productive, and mutually beneficial human interaction.

Reversal Theory depicts how we view the world in basic motivational mindsets and how we can think and interact more harmoniously by reversing these mindsets at will. Reversal recognizes that our mental states exist in four opposing pairs, which is uncomfortable, and thus we seek to balance them. For example, we seek the middle ground between being playful and serious. We can apply tools to reverse and balance the appropriate motivational state for the situation at hand. Furthermore, the techniques of reversing can be habituated rather quickly, a wonderful situation for near instinctual, more appropriate interactions with our environments and the people in them. Thus we have another method to gradually and surely increase our well-being and thus grow our abilities to thrive.

Consider our mindset when we're thrust into a potentially difficult situation at work. We're prepared ahead of time for achievement, which is a *serious* state of mind necessary to remain focused and productive. The inherent stressors of staying in this state for significant portions of our day impact each of us, often in more ways than we recognize. While remaining in this state is necessary for success in our jobs, dwelling in it may not be appropriate to our wider circles of human contact. What about when we go home and interact with our significant others, especially our children? Reversal teaches us that being respectfully, appropriately *playful* counters this imbalance.

One of the many unique and beneficial aspects of learning to reverse is that it promotes a growth mindset, which can be increased with consistent effort, confirming that habitual and targeted practice works.[122] It can make the difference between seeing difficulties as roadblocks to be avoided and seeing them as opportunities to improve and accomplish worthy endeavors. People with a positive attitude toward life, a growth mindset versus a fixed mindset, accomplish more and are more satisfied with how they've done.

Reversal Theory depicts how we view the world in basic motivational mindsets and how we can think and interact more harmoniously by reversing these mindsets at will.

With a growth mindset, our brains develop in positive ways to increase our capacity to accept rational risk as positive; thus our stress levels reduce, and so do despair and unease. We work better in groups with increased individual and collective capacity. Work becomes less like drudgery, more enjoyable. The growth mindset is always learning, creating, progressing, achieving. Mindset theory drives reversals. Science supports the obvious; it's good to be positive and be competent in reversing. Now let's connect reversal theory to its physiology.

Each of the four motivational states are opposed, in a state of tension, discomfort, or stress, and thus produce an emotional state that correlates with the neurophysiology of our hormones as they respond to stress. As presented in Chapter 5, hormones in general are an extremely complex and sophisticated self-alerting, self-regulating system that helps us balance stressors and thus balance our entire organism. More pertinent is that hormones are activators themselves. They come into play as we continuously react to the external stimuli that bombard our five senses. This is how we survived as a species and will continue to survive . . . and prosper.

Know yourself to improve yourself
– Auguste Comte

A Practical Theory to Support New Wave Leadership

Reversal Theory recognizes that not everything we do is defined, static, and predictable, so we need to be flexible with our interactions. Being able to balance our conversations to the mean as the situation demands makes us more capable socially. We're stronger, more adept, and more successful at engaging our world. In other words, we're much better at not just surviving but prospering. This fits with a major theme of becoming a New Wave MAGNUS–OVÉA Leader—that of moving beyond wellness to well-being then flourishing.

Now that we know the *why* of this psychology, let's consider the *what* of it before we get into the *how:*[123]

- *Structure* – Our minds function in four pairs of opposing mindsets, or motivational states, for the purposes of reversal theory: serious vs. playful; conforming vs. rebellious; mastery vs. sympathetic; and others-oriented vs. self-oriented. This structure is universally applicable and thus can be used to describe behavior and summon appropriate responses to circumstances.

  Each of the four pairs of states is called a *domain.*

  Two of the domains relate to *Activities* and two relate to *Relationships.*

  The two Activities domains are *Means-Ends* (Serious–Playful) and *Rules* (Conforming–Rebellious).

  The two Relationship domains are *Transaction* (Mastery–Sympathy) and *Relationships* (Others–Self).

The configuration of reversing is compatible with the Cardinal Virtues of a New Wave Leader, which also provides structure for moment-to-moment behavior, accruing improvements in living over time.

- *Motivational states* – Each of four motivational states has an opposite. Both are appropriate for certain circumstances, and each are situationally fluid. These states not only describe how we behave but are flexible to fit the context of the moment for preferred human interaction. This dovetails with the essential character of a New Wave Leader, which is based on introspection and humility—preferred ways to approach interacting with others.

- *Styles* – Each motivational state describes a unique style of experiencing our environments. We learn to recognize which state we are in, if it's appropriate to the situation, and how to reverse it to balance its opposite. This describes a New Wave Leader, who responds to context instead of applying a formula for leading.

Understanding how we and others behave allows us to take full advantage of our strengths and modify our weaknesses.

- *Opposition* – Each motivational state stands in opposition to another. Thus, the practitioner must seek balance in a modern interpretation of ancient sophrosyne or seeking the mean (per Aristotle) between deficiencies versus excesses. So, for example, courage lies between timidity (a deficiency) and recklessness (an excess).

- *Human dynamics* – Reversal does not relegate people to various types of personalities. It puts us in charge of modifying our behaviors rather than having to conform to any specific idea of who and what we are and how we should be "fixed." This fits with the theme of continuous personal betterment.

- *Fluidity* – Circumstances (and thus states) change, but another factor is that people can change a motivational state moment to moment. With practice and insight, they reverse unconsciously, quickly, and even randomly. It's human nature. Knowing the fluidity of reversing and how to use it to correct, constructive advantage (not manipulating it for unfair advantage), is congruent with the New Wave imperative that we grow and improve for a lifetime.

- *Focus* – We are in one motivational state at a time. Thus, we can focus on that state to intuit its appropriateness and modify it accordingly. This is only one mechanical way we can improve that fits with our development as New Wave Leaders. Reversal encourages our psychological growth as we grow in well-being with morality and integrity.

- *Biases* – Biases can be good or not so good. Reversal Theory favors a balance of each pair of mindsets. We might lean one way or another—say toward being serious, conforming, mastery, and others-oriented as opposed to playful, rebellious, sympathetic, and self-oriented. The theory helps us understand how we behave, not how we are labeled—as having a "dominating" personality, for example. Understanding how we and others behave allows us to take full advantage of our strengths and modify our weaknesses.

- *Essentiality* – Each state is vital to our discovering how to live well, how to live the Good Life, which the ancient Greeks and Romans preached and practiced. This is the essence of the MAGNUS individual as an expression of Aristotle's Magnanimous Man, the ideal man defined nearly 2,400 years ago and practiced even long before that.

- *Misuse* – Apter offers a caution: When a motivational state is stuck in an extreme or a reversal is blocked, it can lead to inappropriate behavior.[124] Reversal offers a toolbox of appropriate practices, resources, and behaviors to prevent this misuse of a state.

Reversal Theory offers a simple, optimistic way to understand ourselves and others in the context of various situations of being human.

As an example of reversing, let's look at learning, accumulating wisdom, from the perspective of three of the pairs of opposite motivational states, as the process of learning is central to becoming a New Wave Leader.[125] It's a *joy (playfulness)* to learn new things, yet *seriousness* facilitates building new skills, accumulating a library of knowledge, and expanding what we can do. We learn from the accomplished, respectable, and worthy among us, past and present, as we *conform* to their experiences. Yet when we are rebellious, questioning not being fractious, we think creatively, critically, confidently—beyond conformity. Resolving problems strengthens *mastery* for confronting the next problem and the next, thus plotting a better way forward. Collaboration for the greater good is cooperation with *sympathy* between those given a task, a goal, a vision. Without sympathy, even empathy, we wouldn't accomplish nearly as much.

Self-education is often the most valuable form of instruction. It begins the moment we leave the classroom for the "school of hard knocks." Balancing our human interactions, then, can be a tool for personal growth.

Reversal Theory offers a simple, optimistic way to understand ourselves and others in the context of various situations of being human. Learning to reverse according to current demands and circumstances gives you ". . . different 'ways of being' . . . [and thus better] chances of being able to adapt to changes in that environment—and as a result to survive and thrive."[126]

Tools for Balanced Living

As you review each state and see how it applies to your interpersonal interactions, ask yourself, *How will this state help me achieve a mutually beneficial goal of the moment?*

Reversals Between Opposite Motivational States		
Motivational State	**Domain of Experience**	**Motivational State**
	Activities	
Serious	Means Ends	Playful
Conforming	Rules	Rebellious
	Relationships	
Mastery	Transactions	Sympathy
Self-Oriented	Relationships	Others-Oriented

Figure 3: Motivational States: Activities and Relationships

Let us pursue this chart by briefly examining the four pairs of motivational states as shown above.[127] The top two consist of the Activities domain, and the bottom two of the Relationships domain. Now we have a visual through which we can understand how our minds work as we reverse motivational states. Our *activities* determine how we affect our *relationships*. We can see how to guide our neural networks to do what is natural, that is, seek the middle ground of a successful approach to our dialogue with others. We seek productive means and ends with rules, transactions, and relationships. As a simple way to understand reality, we can access each state as the situation and players dictate.[128] For example, Apter points out that during an evening with friends we can choose to be playful and laugh and dance to fun music, or we can be serious and judge people and consider those activities a waste of time.[129]

Before we explain the chart more fully, it's helpful to review some of what the chart does

> **An individual response that balances a human interaction depends on those involved; the methods and outcomes are just that, individual.**

and does not imply. It's an attempt to visualize complex human actions, reactions, and motivations.[130] With that, the motivational states are wants, not what one gets. No graphic will ever depict what goes on in the brain and psyche; the graphic speaks of possibilities of behaviors. In fact, an individual response that balances a human interaction depends on those involved; the methods and outcomes are just that, individual. Also, we can be in more than one motivational state at one time. Apter points out that when we are self- or other-oriented, we may also be in a sympathy or mastery state.[131] Finally, the states are not iron-clad, this or that, but rather variations of relevant or not. The chart is, however, a teaching tool by which we can "see" a reversal and, with practice, effect it. Now to consider each essential part of a reversal.

Activities

- *Seriousness* – To the person in the serious state, achievement or a goal is the basic value. Ends justify means; delayed satisfaction is okay. We may conform with a sense of duty or we may rebel with a sense of freedom. The tension is between rules and feeling the restraint of them. When we're in a serious state, we can concentrate on the task at hand with efficiency and effectiveness, so we progress. We can delay immediate indulgence because we envision good conclusions; all obstacles fall away. There's significance, purpose, meaning in what we do.

- *Playfulness* – Enjoyment or doing something for its inherent pleasure is the basic value of playfulness. The moment matters. The playful state is nearly self-explanatory; in its essence, we have fun, good fun. We can see and count our many blessings and appreciate being with family, a friend's guitar playing, a great movie. We exercise our imagination in play, which can result in creative endeavors. It's also good practice for survival because we persist by being spontaneous and inquisitive; we experiment, imagine, dream. Napoleon said, "Imagination governs the world." We use it to create new realities.

- *Conformity* – The basic value for conformity is belonging. Here, duty and virtue matter as they're part of acting justly, doing the right thing, even being a good follower. When we conform to a specific social system, we become better employees, better friends, and better leaders. We can learn from a mentor—better yet, become a mentor. When we conform, we learn to adapt to our social factions and truly collaborate to accomplish only what the collective can accomplish together. "… [R]ules, roles, and rituals …" help us,[132] and our matrices of human capacity accomplish tasks, projects, goals, and lifelong legacy.

- *Rebelliousness* – The basic value of rebelliousness is freedom. Think questioning, not anarchy. This state provides feelings that accompany freedom from restrictions. When we're rebellious, going against convention, we tend to think acutely; we feel sharp. When we rebel, we take the brave step beyond planning to meaningful action, then get things done. We're willing to question conventions to provide necessary checks and balances and ensure we don't fall prey to group think or some other cognitive bias that hinders our progress. We don't see limits; we see only possibilities. We take a chance on innovation, which may be daunting, but we plow on with confidence anyway. It's fun being rebellious in a productive way.

Relationships

- *Mastery* – Personal responsibility is the important value here. We achieve via self-mastery, influence, and personal intensity. In the mastery state, we feel the collective capacity of all our strengths. We know we can and do problem solve. We have a sense of command over obstacles, which are viewed as opportunities (a major theme of this book). It's being determined and confident without arrogance. We take the initiative to develop a range of skills—for the job, for our roles as family members, for living with value.

- *Sympathy* – Belonging ultimately expressed in love is the basic value of being in the sympathetic state. Sympathy allows us to recognize we are surrounded by love—the platonic love of friends, the intimacy of a significant other, and the love of familial connections. Being sympathetic allows us to see the good in others, to be compassionate, to demonstrate empathy, and to be kind to others and ourselves. When sympathetic, we cooperate then collaborate with great effect and meaning. The sympathetic motivational state allows us to develop strong and lasting relationships. Being sympathetic helps us see that friends won't *make* us happy but are *part* of a happy life.

> *We live in a time when science is validating what humans have known*
> *throughout the ages: that compassion is not a luxury;*
> *it is a necessity for our well-being, resilience, and survival.*
> – Joan Halifax

- *Self* – Individual identity is important to this motivational state, with the basic value being self-care. When we are self-oriented, we can fully grasp the importance of honoring ourselves with self-respect and well-being. Things make sense, they are possible, and we are the spark that makes them happen. We know as well as others that we can be relied on to do what's right, the intelligent thing to do. It may take a little daring, but we do it with modesty. All our talents are actualized, and we muster those talents to learn more of what counts. This could be when we tap our hidden resources to become resilient, even antifragile. Taking time to recharge is not only desirable but necessary to enhance our well-being.

- *Others* – The basic value for the others-oriented state is empowerment. Apter suggests that an others orientation is a transcendent state in which we selflessly help out; we realize true giving without expecting anything in return is most rewarding. When we are others-oriented, we know we are part of the larger community. Through others, we realize it's good to be alive in a new age, with a New Wave of opportunities. We're in the others-oriented mindset when we can face danger for the sake of another or be involved in acts of kindness, including philanthropy. Even the least of us can be a philanthropist. In this state of mind, we can improve a life, a neighborhood, a community.

In combined subtlety, the motivational states work together to form our personality and how we fit in the scheme of our day. For example, we may be others-focused in a simple gesture of kindness to another without expectation of any return. Or, in self-orientation, we may visit a spa for relaxation or enjoy reading for pleasure. Both are who we are and how we function. Reversing is also a factor in achieving health—physical and especially psychological.

Reversal is a theory about how to conduct and enjoy life. It's a path to meaningful living and significant accomplishment, which results in contentment, another major thrust of this book.

Proposed by Michael Apter in 1970, Reversal Theory has survived extensive research, refinement, and practical application, affirming his insights ever more strongly. The theory has wide application because it makes human behavior understandable by describing personality and human motivation. With that, we can develop our individual style, our repertoire of appropriate life skills, for each state. Hence, we become better at being who we are and creating the life we imagine.

Apter's insight about behavior is that we can and frequently do reverse from one state of being to the other depending on our *attitude* to the situation. We need to have facility in moving between all eight of the motivational states, depending on timing, purposes, and situation.[133] This practiced ability is most helpful in choosing preferred behavior. Because we can be in only one state at a time, we learn to reverse to the other when we choose or when it is mutually advantageous. In fact, to be emotionally healthy, we need to be adept at reversing our motivational states. Hence, we zigzag throughout our day.

Much is at stake here, as balancing our mindsets, our motivational styles, is a significant step to achieving overall well-being.

Strategies for Balancing Our Ways of Being

Balancing our day is a matter of understanding the dominant parts of our personality and balancing them with their opposite mindset. Reversal is the epitome of seeking the Golden Mean, the middle of extreme behaviors that Aristotle deduced so long ago. Reversal is particularly useful to balancing our mental states because it's practical and eminently doable. We can learn the techniques of reversal because they're simple common sense. Reversing is universally suitable because it's based on universal human tendencies. Best of all, they're sustainable because, as we use them, we find that reversing techniques increase in applicability and value.

That said, we don't want to *over*simplify learning to reverse. Developing any new habits, especially the good ones, takes awareness of who we are and the situation we're in and dogged persistence. We need to employ a new technique until it's imbedded in our psyche and can be recalled as a normal reaction to the situation at hand. Much is at stake here, as balancing our mindsets, our motivational styles, is a significant step to achieving overall well-being.

Employing reversal can look like everyday behavior, a mean between selfishness and self-sacrifice; it's about taking care of yourself as you give to others. You're neither tyrant nor doormat. You may volunteer to read to children, visit a shut-in, or leave a nice tip for wait staff. This is neither too much nor too little. It's the happy middle ground of the behavior of a good person—one whose company we would all enjoy.

Well-being cannot exist just in your own head. Well-being is a combination of feeling good as well as actually having meaning, good relationships and accomplishment.
– Martin Seligman

Well-Being – The Purpose of It All

The discussion of well-being began at least as far back as the fourth century BC and is now supported by growing volumes of science.[134] This matter of optimal psychological and physiological functioning is basic to our pursuit of becoming a New Wave Leader. Reversal fits well with this worthwhile work of a lifetime.

Becoming adept with reversing allows us to change our motivational states to balance our mental, emotional, and thus physiological systems. Our thoughts and emotions affect our physical state, which affects our overall health and happiness. Remember that happiness is the occasional feeling that comes as a bit of a surprise when life's accomplishments accumulate and we realize the good outweighs the bad. When all is in balance, we're in a state of well-being.[135] It's intuitive that the physiological response of hormones confirms a good and acceptable interplay of actions and emotions. When things are going well, positive emotions result, and oxytocin and dopamine are likely to rise to reinforce them. Conversely, when our motivational states are out of balance, plummeting serotonin will likely signal a problem.

The bottom line: Our choice of mindset has positive and negative effects that shape us neurologically and physiologically. More important, it shapes our character development. With practice of staying within the mean and balancing the pairs within a domain, good character is reinforced and, conversely, bad character is illuminated. When we feel bad as a result of a choice, we tend to avoid that behavior. So good character develops—or not—according to how wisely we choose between mindsets and value-driven action. As we progress on our journey of developing our character, we leap from well*ness* to well-*being*. The insight of reversal is that if we grasp at happiness directly, we never achieve it. But it becomes a reality for us as we experience the satisfactions resulting from multiple wise choices.

We see life as a wonderful challenge, full of bumps, if not pitfalls, but also of blessings. As our facility with our motivational states continuously improves, we gradually learn to appreciate the little things, the beauty in life, the warmth of human connection. As we experience affection and realize a comfortable balance within the eight motivational states, we begin to understand what happiness means to us. It's about the way, not the arrival. We are always arriving, thank goodness.

> **Our choice of mindset has positive and negative effects that shape us neurologically and physiologically. More important, it shapes our character development.**

Personally Speaking

To Conflict or Not to Conflict: That Is the Question

James Klopovic

Ah, conflict. Attitude is everything. Easy to say, tough to adjust, worth the work.

I have observed that one-on-one conflict is nearly always due to a miscommunication. Someone heard something other than what was said, even though the communication was face to face, not wildly interpreted by a third party. Here's where you can benefit from reversing a potentially harmful state of mind.

Of my numerous conflicts, I recall a particular one in the office that could have had a far different outcome. . . .

I was waiting in line at the office copier, wondering with frustration when those in front of me with multiple copies would be done so I could copy my one page. My mind drifted.

I remembered getting picked in grade school to run the mimeograph machine with the blue copies. I could almost smell the fumes. We couldn't wait to be picked. It's a wonder we survived primary school, never mind life. That little rotating cylinder made a *voobah, voobah* grinding noise. . . . So I asked my colleague on the copier how her copying was going and if it was making that grinding noise, as that was innocently on my mind. My colleague heard a slur, which was not even close to what I said. Almost overnight, the incident grew to harmful proportions, and my colleague became remarkably distracted by it, to say the least. Certainly, we could accomplish no work, let alone the collaborative work required for the job. I needed to do something—and quickly.

I decided not to go through an intermediary—the boss—and risk further inflaming the conflict with inevitable diversions from the truth. Experience had taught me that the result would be a false accusation that remained as fact—guilty never to be proven innocent. I elected instead to talk to the offended person directly, respectfully, thoughtfully, truthfully. Even before I could offer an apology, my coworker understood—and it was no longer a problem.

The lesson? I learned to address conflict at its roots as quickly as fairness, wisdom, and prudence allowed. I could have chosen to say nothing, detached and determined. After all, it really wasn't my fault. Instead, I chose to be sensitive to my colleague's feelings and address the misunderstanding openly and directly. Result? Resolution. Work could then resume, which it did.

Your silence will not protect you.
– Audre Lorde

Chapter 7

Putting the Theory and Science of Becoming Our Best to Work

Morality is the set of shared attitudes and practices that regulate individual behavior to facilitate cohesion and well-being among individuals in the group.
– Patricia Churchland

The purpose of becoming a New Wave individual is reflected in individual and collective betterment. Our physiology, our psychology, our sociology all have been primed over the millennia for us to achieve the overall goal of becoming our good selves, our better selves, our best selves. We're primed in body, mind, and will to do more of the same.

We've just hinted at our inexplicably complex and marvelously efficient neural systems fueled by hormones. Further, we've discussed how we naturally seek balance with life and our fellow humans by managing our motivational states, which helps us interact harmoniously. Let's review the science and theory that we are naturally equipped from a neurophysiological standpoint to be moral. Then we'll consider how to put it all to work.

Moral Conscience – The Foundation of Living the Good Life

Conscientious collaboration leads to well-being—individually, socially, and communally. We learn to optimize with goal-directed behavior balanced by a well-conceived plan. Our neurobiological impetus is to seek harmony between extremes. Thus we have more justification for understanding how to be, how to associate with others, how to lead, and how to progress from a basis of character and values in a rapidly advancing civilization. More and more people want to belong to something worthwhile, to associate with like-minded people, to leave a legacy.

If we're grounded with an appreciation of the realities of life, when we experience a setback, we self-analyze and perhaps get advice from honest friends and learn when life goes a little, or a lot, sideways. We learn and are wiser for the experience, growing our moral conscience, our self-examiner, which is self-regulating.

> **It matters not that you can master the techniques of Reversal Theory, build your social and personal resources, and become resilient and antifragile if you don't have a conscience.**

"Resilience, hope, and determination are *biological adaptations* that keep us going when times are tough."[137]

We evolved socially, we're wired socially, and we behave socially so we can survive individually and as a species. We do it with conscience, which "is a uniquely human brain construct . . . in our neural circuitry."[138]

Thus, science alone justifies that the work of becoming MAGNUS–OVÉA, of living well with intention, is worthy. That said, it matters not that you can master the techniques of Reversal Theory, build your social and personal resources, and become resilient and antifragile if you don't have a conscience. Then and only then will employing the practices of living well work. Moral living is driven by conscience.

Morally directed New Wave Leaders are steeped in the Cardinal Virtues, practice virtue daily, and build character through ongoing habitual action. They also appreciate, even embrace, the work of learning to thrive via whole-body well-being. We *know* when a gesture is worthy, even noble, because it feels good, and that is the only reward necessary. Giving more than may be expected is an ancient Latin concept. Yes, doing something beyond duty and obligation and then beyond supererogation is difficult—but worthy and within reach.

What lies beyond supererogation? We suggest it is love. Supererogation is dedication to do something good and do it well. It's devotion to a cause—that clear and inspiring vision lived by a dynamic leader. *Beyond* that, it's about love of what you're doing and platonic love of your compatriots and leader. Therefore, what lies beyond supererogation is realization of the potential of the human spirit. We see it every day in our first-class, world-class, epochal industries, and in the best aspirations of our military. We see it in some of our most notable companies inspired by a leader who embodies a vision, such as Steve Jobs, who aimed to put "a ding in the universe." We see it in General Stanley McChrystal leading a branch of the military through turbulent times.

And yes, we can even see it in a humble but superlative enterprise. At La Farm,[139] for example, the bakery just a few minutes away from where this is being scribed,

Lionel the Master Baker from Cordon Bleu France strives *"For The Love of Bread."* Lionel faithfully and lovingly follows a vision and has won awards and fame for his baking expertise. This kind of love beyond duty and obligation is an expression of the journey of becoming a New Wave individual—a journey of becoming one's best.

If we *intend* to do good and *practice* doing good, we *will* do good, if not great, things for ourselves, our relationships, and our organizations. We maintain that such actions make for meaning, good memories, and legacy. Our conscience is the key, and it takes constant care.

Putting Science and Theory to Work – One Example

As we learn how to enhance our well-being, we can use our knowledge and tools to counter VUCA, or chaos, as explained earlier. How we anticipate it, confront it, and make it work for us is the task of counter-VUCA. Note that chaos can come out of good and not-so-good circumstances, from inter- and intra-personal dynamics, and from external and internal organizational friction. All can disrupt or unhinge a conversation, a group collaboration, a plan, a mission, or a vision. This isn't about resigning to the reality of ever-present chaos with an attitude that complications happen so just let them happen and deal with it. Management by crisis is a poor tactic. We can mitigate, even prevent, chaos using skills to tame it when it does happen.

Prepare for the unknown by studying how others in the past have coped
with the unforeseeable and the unpredictable.
– General George S. Patton

Don't forget the success of any technique of daily living must be built on character, the development of which is the task of daily living. But VUCA is relevant. It characterizes what New Wave Leaders must learn to navigate successfully. Naturally, attitude matters. Rather than fear VUCA, the MAGNUS–OVÉA individuals among us see it for what it offers. Challenges, adversity, obstacles, and problems are part of life and exactly what we need to learn, grow, and progress. We don't innovate, change, or grow much without challenges and obstacles.

> **If we *intend* to do good and *practice* doing good, we *will* do good, if not great, things for ourselves, our relationships, and our organizations.**

Pause and reflect on this a moment. Consider an event that, at the time, seemed troubling or even devastating. With a bit of grit and belief in yourself, you can turn adversity into advantage—and you can end up being better off because it happened. Repeat this philosophy of resurrection from chaos and you build confidence and experience for the next growth opportunity. Being positive and realistic is a state that's natural to you and to us all, especially if it's encouraged and practiced.

Resilience – Important and Essential

Here we are talking about personal toughness, the ability to cope with a crisis mentally and emotionally and return quickly to pre-crisis normalcy, or homeostasis and balance. Notice how the theme of searching for the Golden Mean between extremes applies here. In the case of countering crises this means returning to the calm waters of daily progress but much informed and improved by the experience. Consider those who may be injured on the job. They must demonstrate resilience to return to pre-crisis normalcy to function effectively.

This quality of toughness is also the capacity to maintain core functions and values during chaos.[140] In simpler terms, hardiness exists in people who develop psychological and behavioral capabilities *prior to* a crisis. This flexibility allows them to remain calm during crises/chaos and move on without long-term negative consequences. More than that, hardy MAGNUS–OVÉA individuals learn and strengthen themselves beyond just recovery. They become better for the experience. Being able to view the inevitable problem or obstacle to progress as a chance to learn, a chance to improve, is another definition of the New Wave Leadership approach. Let's explore the nature of personal toughness a bit further.

Our ability to be calm during disruptions to the day considers our resources, our ability to be optimistic, and our wells of social relationships. It also depends on our natural ability to engage in strengthening pursuits such as a hobby or reading. These attributes tend to maintain a certain level, a set point that varies from individual to individual. It's yet another aspect of our physiological and psychological tendency to get used to things, which reflects our natural ability to seek and establish stability. For example, we acclimate to, or get used to, routine exercise, that new dream car, even our pool of resources.[141] This set point, or resiliency, is a baseline, a point of departure for becoming tough and actually *improving* with our command over chaos. This is also why a little disruption, a problem, the unexpected shake us out of possible malaise, challenge us, and point the way to improvement. Now back to developing hardiness.

Hardiness has two unique aspects. First, some people are genetically more robust than others. They inherit the tendency. Second, we seek to balance our resources, so taking a hit of bad news depletes that well, requiring us to refill it. This explains why resiliency is only a launching pad for how we become less emotionally fragile. Most important, this aspect helps define what we can do to achieve well-being and points us in a positive direction. That is, we can control how we develop friendships, and whether or not we take up a hobby or develop a strategy to become more optimistic, savor the many joys around us, and forgive.[142]

Individual improvement is interdependent on that of teammates.

Considering building hardiness as the ability to bounce back from adversity,[143] General McChrystal aptly affirms "Individual resilience is important – team resilience is essential."[144] How apropos that he also quotes a fellow historical leader, General Patton, who observed that "The test of success is not what you do when you are on top. Success is how high you bounce when you hit the bottom." This concept proves much more powerful when *a group* collectively bounces back high with every test. It also provides insight into personal development, leadership, and organizational effectiveness. It's simple because anyone can realize that individual improvement is interdependent on that of teammates. It's suitable in that anyone can understand and support the group. It's sustainable because lessons learned are self-fulfilling. Most important of all, it leads to action. We learn how to confront, learn from, and recover from everything from mistakes to unforeseen tragedy. Such has been the collective learning and recovery from the COVID-19 pandemic. Collaboration has permanently improved the world of epidemiology. What lessons has this situation provided for organizational resilience?

In his *Field Manual: Team Resilience,* General McChrystal has equally elegant suggestions for building New Wave organizations. Build mutual and organizational trust with stability, connection, and agility:

- *Stability* – Have a common purpose that's just a little out of reach but worthy. Move from a survival mentality to a growth/accomplishment individual and organizational mentality.

- *Connection* – Ensure that communication is functional, action oriented, and helps build emotional connections so people learn to trust leadership and one another.

- *Agility* – Build a learning environment in which staff don't fear failure but treat it as a calculated, worthwhile risk to improve individually and organizationally and reach goals. Thus, people learn to deal effectively with failure.

New Wave Leadership is based on empowering staff to execute what they do in a trusting environment. The key, according to McChrystal, is make the lowest level in the organization as capable as possible because things get done next to front line action. Communicating *how* is more important than *why*. Interaction is harmonious, a mutual give and take. Natural, normal chaos is tamed with simplicity.

Building a trusting organization is foundational to New Wave Leadership. It has always been, but it's been forgotten as efficiency and hierarchy became an obsession. Trust, says McChrystal, is about benevolence, thinking of and acting for the good of others. It's about also trusting in the competence and reliability of people and processes. Leaders consciously build trust and maintain it over time. The message is that building a trusting organization takes sustained focus and work. Such effort helps us become antifragile.

> **True hardiness is not about simply getting through adversity but about *thriving because of it.***

Fragility to Hardiness

If we have a difficult time recovering from adversity, we are fragile. Signs of fragility may include but aren't limited to: feeling overwhelmed, having a short fuse, feeling empty, being unable to dial down our reaction to stress, being cynical, apathetic, and the like.

As individual hardiness grows, so does team and organizational hardiness. This is way more than just coping moment to moment to the end of the day or end of our working lives. In another virtuous versus vicious cycle, the gradual strengthening becomes self-fulfilling and grows organically within an agency or company. This points to a major feature of the New Wave organization; MAGNUS staff and leadership recognize people can and do make mistakes, even with the best of intentions. They know mistakes and corrections are part of the creative process of experimentation, which is how staff, and thus the organization, become resilient and strong.

True hardiness is not about simply getting through adversity but about thriving because of it. Nassim Nicholas Taleb says it best in his book *Antifragile: Things That Gain from Disorder:*

*"Some things benefit from shocks; they thrive and grow when exposed to volatility, randomness, disorder, and stressors and love adventure, risk, and uncertainty. Yet, in spite of the ubiquity of the phenomenon, there is no word for the exact opposite of fragile. Let us call it antifragile. . . . **The resilient resists shocks and stays the same; the antifragile gets better.**"[145]* (Bold in original)

Note the distinct difference between being resilient and antifragile. Gaining resiliency is a step toward becoming antifragile, just a start, which is a state of continuously improving.

Learning the skills and tools of becoming antifragile is most important for the success of a New Wave Leader. How do we achieve the fortitude to meet challenges productively, persevere, remain inquisitive, and have confidence to get the job done come what may? We need an activator, or valence, to energize us.

The Valence of It All – OVÉA as Our Activator

In Chapter 5, we explained that our behaviors are normally guided by activators (valences) that either reinforce positive behavior or discourage negative behavior. These activators can be hormonal as well as social approval or disapproval and the good or bad feelings we get associated with certain behaviors. We've pointed out that wanting to flourish, to be well and do well, is natural to us as sentient beings based on our hormonal motivations and responses. We also seek pleasure and wish to avoid pain. These natural tendencies can be augmented by understanding how to reverse and balance our motivational states. We can also call on the strengths of our reserves of living virtuously with value and meaning. All of this, however, requires an activator or a collective of many activators, which parallels the concept of OVÉA as the spark, the energy, that activates leadership.

OVÉA, meaning Others, Values, Ethics, Acceleration, are those things that ignite us, excite us, and spur us on as New Wave Leaders. It begins with pursuing virtue, morals, and character to engage our neurophysiological motivation and responses sparked by hormones. The perils of not being good make living morally with character worthy.

Then, when we are sparked by the discomfort of certain human interactions, we seek harmony. This, in turn, urges us to control our emotional responses to our interpersonal dealings by employing one of two opposing approaches to enhance mutual, productive human interactions.

Third, when we confront the ups and downs of our day, we are sparked by our many resources—social, nonsocial, and those of deeper meaning such as duty and the desire to help—which strengthen us. A resource can be as simple as a quick dose of calm from meditation, humor, hugs, or playing with a pet.

> **OVÉA, meaning Others, Values, Ethics, Acceleration, are those things that ignite us, excite us, and spur us on as New Wave Leaders.**

It may seem odd, but one accelerator is chaos. Why? Because it brings variety, challenge, progress, growth. The more we accomplish and the more we're challenged in the process, the more we become energized. Said another way, easy results are rather ho hum to the individual and especially to collaboratives. We're fond of saying, "Man, I'm dying of boredom." Literally, it's true; ennui impairs our health by putting us at risk of mood disorders, addictions, and poor human interactions, and we can be more accident prone.

When we continuously practice using these tools and resources of constantly improving, we evoke positive emotions and one day happily discover what it is to thrive—because we are *doing* it. It doesn't come with a thunderclap, no matter how we wish for it; one day we quietly realize we're quite lucky and it's good to be alive.

Building Our Reserves to Thrive

As our journey is about positivity, let's now turn to the "broaden and build theory of positive emotions" proposed by renowned psychology researcher Barbara Fredrickson.[146] She asserts that "positive emotions broaden an individual's thought-action repertoire: joy sparks the urge to play and interest sparks the urge to explore."[147]

Notice how these broadened mindsets, or positive valences, parallel positive motivational states. Our instinctual response to danger is to freeze, fight, or flee, any of which tend to activate negative emotions and behavior, or negative valence as we observe our responses to daily crises. Chronic hypertension, hyperactivity, and hypervigilance from constant anxiety about self-preservation are debilitating, even life threatening. Someone with this propensity to negative valence might experience, for example, a suppressed immune system, heart damage, and an inability to establish and maintain healthy relationships. Longevity suffers, and the person receives diminished reward from what could have been enjoyable.

According to Fredrickson, positive emotions—those characteristic of the MAGNUS-OVÉA individual—promote ". . . discovery of novel and creative actions . . . ," which are ideas and social bonds that, in turn, build the individual's personal resources to prosper.[148] On the other hand, someone with a negative approach to daily stressors can be tense, nervous, upset, sad, depressed, lethargic, and fatigued. Contrast that with someone who trains him/herself to be positive. This individual is likely to be alert, excited, elated, happy, content, serene, relaxed, and calm as a rule, and even during chaos, constantly activated to be creative, motivated, and cheerful. Those resources, physical and intellectual, build situational toughness. Fredrickson is saying that a positive outlook alone improves the chance of not just survival but successful coping and even happiness. This way of thinking is how we can maintain or improve our set point, or baseline, of flexibility and constantly move toward becoming better at life by surmounting obstacles and savoring that which helps us be content.

Numerous studies support the fact observed by the Ancients that a good attitude augments one's personal resources—physical, social, intellectual, and psychological. Fredrickson notes that people can ". . . transform themselves, becoming more creative, knowledgeable, resilient, socially integrated and healthy individuals."[149] We can't describe the benefit of pursuing the journey of becoming A New Wave Leader better than that!

Just what do Fredrickson's decades of research relate about broadening and building your reserves of positive emotions? And what does her investigation suggest for how to build and evoke your natural reserves?

According to Fredrickson, positive emotions can do the following for you:[150]

- *Broaden thought-action repertoires* – Positive patterns of thought are creative, integrative, open to information, and efficient, thus broadening your reasoning. Conversely, negative emotions, such as anxiety, depression, and fear of failure, narrow your ability to think well. Maintaining a positive outlook, training yourself to notice and experience joy, and building your social and personal resources all improve your ability to think and act well. Learning to focus on what's good and worthy supports this growth.

- *Undo lingering negative emotions* – As you broaden your positive emotions, your negative emotions narrow. Positivity is self-fulfilling; the more you're optimistic, the more you're capable of being so. You recover from adversity faster and better due to your increased positivity. This decreases negativity, and we become increasingly, consistently buoyant. The lesson is to practice being positive and bouncing back from adversity by realizing, properly, that a challenge promotes personal growth and accomplishment. It helps to continuously remind yourself that you have much to be grateful for in your life.

- *Fuel psychological resiliency* – Data suggest that positivity increases our psychological *and* physical well-being incrementally. People can and do learn to cope if they practice learning how to thrive. We can use humor, good wit, creativity, and exploration to our advantage. We can practice relaxation and look for good wherever we can find it. We can remind ourselves and learn to feel that "the future's so bright, I gotta wear shades!" Because we're confident we can make it so.

- *Build personal resources* – Psychological toughness is enduring and compounds as it builds like a brick wall on a good foundation of healthful, helpful practices. It can be as simple as a daily practice of finding *one* thing that's positive. One then leads to another until your resources are a real stockpile of positive outlook and energy. Positivity predicts and builds mental well-being and physical recovery. Being able to move beyond just coping, then, is a result of *intention* and *practice.*

- *Fuel psychological and physical well-being* – Positivity is the how of learning to prosper. Use an unfortunate life event, say losing a job, to plan next moves, yes with normal concern, but know you will figure it out and be the better for it. Tap your resources to broaden possibilities. You have discipline, skills, creativity, education, experience, networks, family, friends, perhaps a little garden, and certainly a good book. Employ all obstacle-crushing mechanisms at your disposal; they're formidable. It's part of the virtuous cycle, the upward trajectory of being principled and having an expanding view of your possibilities.

Overall, what does this research in theory, science, and experiential data suggest? That the journey to becoming a New Wave Leader with its focus on how to live well is a route to much better cognitive capacity and productivity. Even the pursuit of positive emotions induces more contentment with how our life is progressing. With that, happiness in its fleeting, illusive nature, sneaks up on us as we construct our fortress of well-being. As our ability to be positive grows, negativity diminishes, and we recover from adversity more quickly. We don't fear what comes next; we see it as a productive challenge whereby we grow, improve, and accomplish.

> **We can be smarter than our given talents allow by taking on challenges and not fearing failure.**

Will our lives be perfect? No—and believe it or not, we wouldn't want everything to be perfect because we crave a little good excitement, a bit of "wrestling" now and then. But as our coping skills compound, positive emotions remake us with better health, better social interconnectedness, more intellectual capability, more effectiveness and resilience. We live longer with zest for what's next. What we do is a matter of choice; we can languish or develop.

Continuing with the science of becoming a New Wave Leader, let's look more closely at how the inevitable failures and struggles of life benefit us.

Growing Our Brains with Failure

Consider the assertion of Stanford professor Jo Boaler that struggle, especially when we fail, causes our brains to grow![151] Her illuminating thesis in *Limitless Mind: Learn, Lead, and Live Without Barriers* sums up the science of becoming our best. She claims we can be smarter than our given talents allow by taking on challenges and not fearing failure, which describes one of the four Cardinal Virtues of a New Wave Leader—Courage. It's brave to accept what's a bit beyond us and somewhat frightening. We learn by lumpy, bumpy, hurly-burly experience that we have what it takes to figure things out to a good, if not extremely rewarding, end.

Boaler makes the following six points around scientific research that help describe the making of a New Wave Leader:

- *Neuroplasticity changes everything.*[152] Learning is not fixed. Our brain is a muscle, albeit a sophisticated one, which responds to a workout. It seeks challenges in physiological, intellectual, and sociological stimulation. Living with virtue, value, and character and growing the whole person—body, mind, and disposition—is like bench presses for the mind.

- *Mistakes, struggle, and failure can be beneficial.*[153] This doesn't mean we should go looking for trouble; don't worry, it will find us. But we can meet it, get it behind us, and be better for it. Two of the main benefits of challenge are we grow more capable and become more confident.

- *Changing our mind changes our reality.*[154] If we believe we can, we *can.* Developing a growth mindset improves our brains. Optimism and gratitude open both mental and actual doors. Again, a massive amount of continuing research based on the study of well-being, the science of hedonics, supports the fact that we are all capable of achieving well-being, an endeavor we *can* control.

- *The connected brain optimizes multidimensional thinking.*[155] Here we are talking about connecting to others in mutual pursuits. When working in creative groups, we are stimulated by different points of view and various ways to tackle the work of a program. Little is out of reach when accomplished collectively in a spirit of creative destruction in which we tear down obstacles and rebuild, especially for an exciting, collective, collaborative vision. This also describes the strengthening of indispensable group resilience. The more we can achieve together, the more that is possible.

- *Speed is out and flexibility is in.*[156] We don't need to think fast. Learning optimizes when we approach ideas and life with creativity and flexibility. Being pressured to think and do things fast is stressful and unproductive. Relax. Being calm matters. Try to practice daily relaxation even for a few minutes. This practice then finds its way into what you do throughout the day.

- *Collaboration multiplies effectiveness.*[157] Collaborating, not just assisting with a task, geometrically multiplies the work produced and the sense of accomplishment and satisfaction with the work and its results. This is another way of saying we are at our best when working with others in a matrix of talents to answer personal and communal needs. Working with people beyond simple cooperation grows our brain and enhances learning. Human collaboration is the original, fundamental force multiplier and why we survived and dominate as a species.

If we can learn from our mistakes and keep pushing ourselves to accomplish the difficult, especially in collaboration with others, we can enjoy greater self-confidence, resilience, and satisfaction in work and social relationships.[158]

Failure is the true test of greatness.
– Herman Melville

Ah, Happiness—Or Is It Well-Being? Which Do You Prefer?

If you answered well-being, you're getting the message of pursuing the New Wave MAGNUS–OVÉA Journey. Let's make a distinction between happiness and well-being. The Declaration of Independence gave us the right to *pursue* happiness. The Founding Fathers knew that nothing can *guarantee* our happiness, as that state is fleeting and up to the individual. Just when we think we have it—*poof*—it could be gone. Yes, we have the conditions to be happy; it's up to us to construct them and realize when they exist. It doesn't take much to be happy, yet we're obsessed with happiness as if it's something we can grab and hold, like the classic desires of more wealth, beauty, money, and possessions. Such desires are endless, and the results of achieving them are unsatisfying in the end. This fact is proven by binders full of research on what makes us happy. When we realize that only the *pursuit* of happiness can be promised, we're on the right track.

Contrast that with well-being, which we construct, and therefore can be under our command. When we refer to the pursuit of happiness, we're actually talking about the development of well-being, and the measure of that is how well we're thriving. In this process, we consider our motives and become someone who is curious, enthusiastic, and wise; we plan and understand what matters.[159]

An essential book for your library is Sonja Lyubomirsky's *The How of Happiness: A New Approach to Getting the Life You Want*, which suggests how to be in command of your day and your life. It offers encouragement, voluminous research, and practical advice about how to be happier, continuously grow your well-being, and have a satisfying, even remarkable, life. Read it prepared to take notes as it will lead you to many insights about yourself and your potential. The very act of studying such books and putting the simple ideas to work is a substantial step toward being okay with your life.

> **Is the extended, difficult work to achieve well-being worth it? Yes, it's the most important work you can do.**

Why Work on Your Well-Being?

Before beginning work on this book, we knew we would find research to support well-being as one of life's great quests. We were pleasantly surprised, overwhelmed in fact, to realize that very many studies about living the Good Life are decades old. They evidence hundreds of methodologically sound experiments involving thousands of subjects. So, what we propose works—but is the extended, difficult work to achieve well-being worth it? Yes, it's the most important work you can do.

Let's go to Lyubomirsky for the why of this objective of happiness as an expression of doing well and being satisfied with ourselves.[160] Our goal is fulfillment beyond just feeling good. As it turns out, people who strive for happiness are more ". . . sociable and energetic, more charitable and cooperative, and better liked by others" than those (control groups) who don't.[161] They stay contentedly married longer, have various networks of acquaintances and friends, are better leaders and negotiators, and make more money, even without an original "silver-spoon" childhood. And another thing: As a group, they're healthier and live longer! It gets better: These well-adjusted people experience more joy, love, pride, and awe.[162] They have more energy overall, especially at work, where they collaborate better than other (experimental control) groups. They have more self-esteem, self-worth, and respect. All this spills over to their partners, families, and the wider community. Being content is infectious; we all win.

Now let's reflect on a few practicalities of how to get these results for yourself.

The How of Well-Being then Thriving – Proven Strategies

When it comes to the how of working to achieve well-being, the fundamental principles remain discipline and practice. While those words may not exactly exude joy because of the prospect of more work in an overworked day, they simply mean we need to develop habits so our actions and reactions become habitual then instinctual. Then, when a moment of choice arises, we'll make the choice that enhances our life and brings us closer to well-being because we've studied and practiced the steps in the journey. Beyond resolving to do something worthy, we will have established nearly immutable routines that drive us in the right direction. For example, health is one of our basic goals, so we involve ourselves in a conditioning routine and eat wisely. This requires establishing habits, which takes practice—but, yes, also leads to the joy of feeling strong and energetic.

> **We feel as if we're "in the flow" when we have it right. We lose ourselves in our work such that creativity and innovation seem to come automatically.**

Practice must always pass the New Wave Leadership test of being simple, suitable, and sustainable. In pursuing contentedness, for example, we can use the research-based strategies of regularly cultivating optimism, savoring joy, and learning to forgive.[163]

We have many ways to confirm we're on the right track. We increase our capacities, we're better able to go beyond just coping, and we're generally pleased with how our day goes. We feel as if we're "in the flow" when we have it right. We lose ourselves in our work such that creativity and innovation seem to come automatically. Mihaly Csikszentmihalyi studied flow and observed that when we experience flow, we are clearer, in control, and balanced about goals. We can concentrate better and our relationships with others are more harmonious. Time seems to stand still.[164] Work is no longer "work." Flow is common when pursuing well-being.

In Dr. Lyubomirsky's book *The How of Happiness*, she presents activities she's researched extensively for their effectiveness in realizing happiness and well-being. While they seem "soft," such as expressing gratitude and kindness, they're far from it. She explains the activities with easily applied proven actions that guide the practitioner to achieving the desired results.

This book is bright and useful for many reasons. It includes questionnaires to determine your strengths and weaknesses in this pursuit, which reveal your preferred strategy. This strategy then offers only a few activities tailored to your personality and propensities. Thus, the tool fits our requirements that any recommendation for the New Wave MAGNUS–OVÉA Journey be simple, suitable, and sustainable. You supply the can-do discipline and determination.

Strategies for Optimism

For an example, let's look at *Activity No. 2: Cultivating Optimism*, completed by combining it with strategies for learning to forgive and savoring life's joys.[165]

All these attributes of well-being are about attitude and doing what it takes to develop a proper attitude. What we think and what we believe determine how we get there, wherever *there* may be for us. Naturally, Lyubomirsky gives general disclaimers and observations to define the parameters of the activity. It's a great beginning to understand what optimism is and, more important, what it is not. Let's consider its various aspects:

- *Extension over time* – Optimism is more than getting through the day; it's about celebrating positive past, present, and future prospects. This is a superior expression of our criteria for what we do: simplicity, suitability, and sustainability.

- *Flexibility* – Optimism can fit the situation, large or exceedingly small.

Big optimism – We live in the most exciting age of the Fourth Industrial Revolution.[166] The age of the New Wave Leader. So much is possible.

Small optimism – Confidence that the day will be good helps us be creative and constructive as we move through it.

Very small optimism – We know each day will hold its share of the good, the bad, and the ugly, but we believe things will work out. This helps us be graceful, pragmatic, and perhaps meet challenges with wit and a smile.

- *Realism* – Being optimistic doesn't mean we're unrealistic Pollyannas. We know we'll have challenges and some dark times, but we feel sure that life is good and positive outcomes will cumulatively outweigh even the most tragic. (An acquaintance shoots skeet from a wheelchair and beams when he crushes those small targets, scooting across the range at 44 mph at the whim of winds. He takes joy in what he *can* do rather than bemoan what he can't do.)

Maintaining a proper attitude is critical to how we act in prosperity and, especially, in adversity. Envisioning our goals as already accomplished tends to be self-fulfilling. If we believe they're possible, good things happen—many times in unexpected ways. Imagining is first, but nothing happens without commitment, discipline, and determination aimed at a worthy goal.

Picture your desired life, work, education, relationships, hobbies, realistic and lengthy retirement, and some version of all those situations will happen. However, it's good to leave room for something better than we can imagine, follow our intuition as we go forward, and be flexible. Certain things may matter less and less as time goes on. For example, our dreams of a vacation log cabin complete with a creek sparkling in the sun and a view of an insanely picturesque valley may not come to fruition. However, we may realize we'd rather use our limited funds for travel and see the many wonders of the world. Besides, the vision of that vacation home may become blurred by the prospect of an exhausting and expensive to-do list, a second mortgage, bats in the rafters, and a dried-up creek bed in the summer.

> **Envisioning our goals as already accomplished tends to be self-fulfilling. If we believe they're possible, good things happen—many times in unexpected ways.**

Betterment is the overall goal of living well with purpose, but we need the tools to improve. Let's return to the topic of strengthening optimism.[167] Having a bright disposition for the day and life in general is self-fulfilling. We flow around obstacles like a mountain stream around boulders. If we pause for a moment and reflect on the problems of last week, even yesterday, we probably can't remember many of them and are thus not vexed by them.

By practicing optimism, we cope better no matter the task, job, or career. Optimism allows us a realistic yet confident mastery over what we do, and *we live longer and better for it!* We've given a few characteristics of optimism and strategies to achieve it. Now for three scientifically and experientially based activities to enhance it that are simple, suitable, sustainable:

> **Envisioning and writing goals help you know your efforts are leading to something good, productive, even lasting.**

- *Keep a best-possible-self diary.* Writing your vision for yourself is the first step toward taking your dream to practicality.

- *Keep a goals and sub-goals diary.* There's something concrete about writing down how you want things to be as well as your strategies and tasking, right down to a daily to-do/activities list. Writing compels action, if only because it helps you see where to start and the order of activities: #1–A, B, C, #2–A, B, C, etc.

- *Identify barrier thoughts.* Pessimism is natural, self-preserving caution; we tend to consider possible downsides, conditioned by evolutionary survival. Optimism is not letting negative thoughts get in the way of your betterment. You can train yourself to see possible good, opportunities, and lessons, and how you can learn from them and thereby strengthen yourself.

Plan all you wish; but you must act, so start with small daily actions. Envisioning and writing goals help you know your efforts are leading to something good, productive, even lasting. Small actions are very doable and create little successes. Cumulatively, they amount to life accomplishments. This book began with a word on a page. The confidence you gain helps you feel capable of achieving your next life goal. Ultimately, your actions build to a life well lived.

Lyubomirsky describes a study done with fifth and sixth graders, who were given optimism lessons for only 12 weeks.[168] They were measurably less depressed than the control group, *even two years after the training.* If 10- and 11-year-olds can enhance their well-being, some no doubt permanently, what does that mean for us?

Strategies for Forgiveness

Combine the strategies for optimism with these strategies for forgiveness:

- *Learn to forgive.*[169] Forgiving is learning to bolster our self-worth despite any tendency to spiral downward when we are slighted in either big or small ways. The Asian Ancients claimed that hatred or revenge is like grasping a hot coal intending to throw it at the person who hurt us. However, we are hurting ourselves emotionally and physically by all aspects of retribution. This approach is not soft spirituality; it's practical science confirmed by millennia of observation. Lyubomirsky reminds us we can learn forgiveness through the following practices:[170]

  Appreciate being forgiven and forgive yourself. We all screw up. Forgive yourself, learn, move on. Be the example.

  Write a letter of forgiveness. Many offenses can be traced back to miscommunication! A simple airing of a difference clears up things that can fester for years or may have already done so. It usually melts the offender, and the act alone soothes your ill feelings. You just may restore a valuable, especially rewarding connection.

  Practice empathy. Analyze a toxic situation from the other person's perspective. Why did the person behave that way? With this practice, you become automatically empathetic.

  Write an apology. Send it to the person you offended. Besides being a learning tool, this is a way to humanize the situation. You can learn the strength of empathy and thus how resilient you are.

  Ruminate less. Today's worry is tomorrow's "What in the world was all that about anyway?!" All that brooding over what you or someone else has done is of no help. Better to develop the habit of experiencing disappointment then turning from its negativity to a positive outlook.

  Make forgiveness a habit. Practice forgiveness until you do it automatically. Dwelling in retribution, recrimination, or retaliation only diminishes you and impedes or halts your progress toward well-being.

Strategies for Savoring Your Joys

Simply savoring the many joys of life can increase our optimism and move us toward more well-being. We return to a theme of this book—that we are among the most fortunate of peoples. First, if we are on the New Wave MAGNUS–OVÉA Journey, life is increasingly productive, rewarding, and good. Second, we are most fortunate to live in a remarkable country. Remember, remind yourself, and relish the thought of these realities and their possibilities. Find joy in living in the present, as this heightens and preserves pleasure in addition to lessening mental and physical illness. Savoring positive experiences is one of the most important practices of well-being. Savor what is good by developing this state of mind:[171]

- *Relish the ordinary.* Learn to perceive how simple things are individually and collectively uplifting. That is, understand that the mundane is an endless source of bits and pieces that provide you with something good, and there's a lot that's mundane in a day. What about a stove or microwave that heats your food? Or a freezer that creates ice for your iced tea? Your computer and phone? Electricity and lights? Cars, books, TVs. Simple pleasures denied to much of the world. Make the mundane marvelous and extraordinary.

- *Savor and reminisce with friends and family.* This is particularly important, and staying connected takes work. Don't think about calling, call. Don't think about visiting, visit. Something good always comes of such gestures.

- *Transport yourself.* This is positive reminiscing. It can also be a daily, 10-minute scheduled meditation; we *all* have 10 minutes in the day. When practiced regularly, you not only realize your blessings, but you relieve stress. Make fond memories continuously to give yourself plenty of material. You may want to even keep notes. Many accomplished people make notes on the day. Some turn them into memoirs passed on to grandchildren.

- *Celebrate good news by sharing it.* Take pride in your accomplishments and that of others. Boast a bit; it's okay. You deserve it.

Find joy in living in the *present*, as this heightens and preserves pleasure in addition to lessening mental and physical illness.

- *Be open to beauty and excellence.* Be forever thankful for the artists past and present who, for example, devote a lifetime to the classical guitar, Asian brush painting, sculptures that adorn our cities, piano concertos, beautiful gardens, innovative buildings, and much, much more. Marvel at all the creativity and craftsmanship of which people are capable and they've given us to enjoy. For example, tucked into the Mountains of North Carolina, a small, rather ramshackle glass-blowing studio sits at the end of a road, left open with an honor jar for purchases. The artist's petite glass chickens are featured in the Smithsonian!

- *Be mindful.* More people are discovering and profiting from becoming highly aware, that is mindful, of their surroundings versus the mindlessness of stray and scattered thoughts that distract and disturb us. Mindful people are ". . . [more] flourishing, happier, [more] optimistic, self-confident, and generally satisfied . . . " than their counterparts, who are likely to be ". . . depressed, angry, anxious, hostile, self-conscious, impulsive or neurotic."[172] Mindfulness meditation is simply being open to what we see as if we're seeing it for the first time. This is practiced by many titans of industry, sports, entertainment, politics, and even the military.

Marvels abound. Look, and you'll find much to savor.

The Strategy of Gratitude

Why highlight gratitude in this discussion? Rightminded leadership persistent in improving the common good can't be accomplished without the right frame of mind, the right balance of positive attitude and insightful perspective. This returns to the leader's role in building a resilient staff and organization. An attitude of gratitude, which all people can generate and contribute, a lack of fear around failure, and collaboration from the bottom up and back are critical to a well-functioning organization. A significant part of this personal balance is realizing, even within a tumultuous day, that many possibilities exist for seeing the good in every moment.

Well-being takes practice, and one of the most important components of well-being is having and expressing gratitude. Think back to a time when someone expressed sincere gratitude to you. How did it make you feel? Chances are it boosted your spirit, gave you a positive feeling, and assisted in enhancing your well-being. We know experientially that when we express gratitude, it not only boosts the spirit of others but our own spirit. It's clear anecdotally that having an *attitude of gratitude* is of benefit.

Sometimes we get lost in the stress of daily life. We forget what's important and abandon it for the current crisis at hand or the next goal we think will make us happy. A technical term known as Hedonic Adaptation, or the Hedonic Treadmill, means that after the initial excitement of accomplishing a treasured goal, we return to a baseline level of happiness. For example, after winning the Super Bowl, Deion Sanders said he felt empty, even after accomplishing this goal he'd longed for his whole life, an accomplishment few will attain.

> **An attitude of gratitude, which all people can generate and contribute, a lack of fear around failure, and collaboration from the bottom up and back are critical to a well-functioning organization.**

What does this tell us? To achieve lasting happiness, a sense of well-being, we need to stay focused throughout our lives on what truly matters most, a life well lived. That kind of life includes being able to feel and express gratitude for *all* our good, daily and beyond. In fact, a solid body of contemporary research demonstrates that gratitude promotes well-being and increases happiness. In a recent research study, researchers determined that with just five minutes a day of expressing gratitude through journaling, research subjects increased happiness by as much as 10 percent.[173] Research demonstrates that gratitude can relieve stress,[174] build social capital,[175] increase health,[176] make memories happier,[177] and provide a host of other benefits.

Additionally, expressing gratitude rewires our brains to be happier according to researchers at UCLA who induced gratitude in research subjects and studied brain activity using MRIs. During these studies, the brain showed increased activity in the areas of the brain that are associated with moral and social cognition, empathy, emotional responses, and value judgments.[178]

Practicing gratitude isn't difficult, but it requires building good habits. These few simple steps will get you started:

- *Identify one thing for which you're appreciative or thankful.* You'll think of many, but begin with one. It might be a person.

- *Express thanks.* When you wake up in the morning, build the habit of expressing gratitude for one item or person you're thankful for at that moment.

- *Develop the habit.* Keep a journal on the nightstand and journal your gratitude, which builds a good habit of expressing gratitude. One sentence of a few words is all it takes. Even a single jotted word helps preserve a fleeting thought worthy of reflection.

The research is clear. Expressing gratitude improves health—both mental and physical. New Wave Leaders understand that being thankful is important for our well-being and the well-being of those we touch. We build our core around being others-focused, values- and virtue-centric, and character-based. Seeking to accelerate ourselves beyond what we thought possible, we energize our mental and physical capacities and enhance our well-being.

> *However beautiful the strategy, you should occasionally look at the results.*
> – Winston Churchill

Five Practices to Support Well-Being

In keeping with our theme of simple, suitable, and sustainable, the following five practices adapted from Lyubomirsky also support well-being. They help us maintain a set point of resilience from which we can build increasing antifragility.[179]

- *Develop positive emotions.*[180] Look for reasons for positivity and you'll find them. Do whatever you're inspired to do to feel ". . . joy, delight, contentment, serenity, curiosity, interest, vitality, enthusiasm, vigor, thrill, and pride. . . ."[181] These emotions are cumulative, compounding, and easily habit forming.

- *Recognize optimal timing and variety.*[182] Getting used to any emotion is a natural human response. Thus, guard against boredom and thwart adaptation. Refresh and vary your positive emotions often and regularly.

- *Develop and give social support.*[183] Find people who validate and sustain your strengths and validate their strengths in return. Give and receive support freely without expectation. You can do this with only one sincere person, but even better, with an accumulated network of true friends, acquaintances, and loving family.

- *Cultivate motivation, effort, and commitment.*[184] Living well isn't a given; discipline and dedication are its foundation. *Resolve* to do the work of expanding and re-creating yourself. *Learn* how it is done, and work at it. Commit! No turning back—for any reason. No, you're *not* too busy.

No, you can't delegate it to the New Year's resolutions list. The magic to a better life lies in saying what you will do then doing it.

- *Make it habitual.*[185] Here it is again. To make a permanent change, you must make your new behavior a habit. This is the definition of sustainability, what we're after. Make your good lifestyle changes habits and soon those healthy changes will be part of your life and well-being. Good and right thoughts are a substantial start; but we are judged by our words, deeds, and actions.

Remember, the task of finding happiness, which is fleeting, is about achieving well-being, which is not fleeting and much within our power. It's all about the pursuit. The journey itself becomes the focus of our day, and by that, we gain continuous betterment—another definition of well-being. As a quick review, living well results from the following:

- *Developing a strong conscience* – Learning right from wrong and living virtuously with values.

- *Enlisting hormonal reinforcement* – Cultivating positive hormonal stimulation through doing good and releasing stress.

- *Revising the unproductive* – Catching unproductive or harmful impulses and reversing them.

- *Aiming for sophrosyne* – Adjusting behavior to the Golden Mean.

- *Balancing body, mind, and disposition* – Conditioning the body and following holistic practices.

- *Strengthening relationships* – Nurturing relationships with friends and family.

- *Collaborating with others* – Combining efforts for the benefit of the whole.

- *Accepting failure* – Considering challenges and failures as growth opportunities.

- *Thinking positively and cultivating joy* – Looking for the good, being thankful, and finding your joys.

When we make these activities and attitudes habitual, we can more easily handle the ups and downs of the day and life in general. The goal is to have an overall satisfaction with our lives and be reasonably accomplished in contributing to the common good.

> **Remember, the task of finding happiness, which is fleeting, is about achieving well-being, which is not fleeting and much within our power.**

Keep in mind that many people never reach retirement, and many who do are enfeebled. Still more are ill equipped to take advantage of what can be the most productive years of their lives. Much is at stake, so we need to practice and persist in the strategies of well-being as early on in life as possible.

As we learn to become a New Wave Leader in whatever role we find ourselves in, we have an obligation to model and teach the wisdom of continuously becoming more.

The Importance of Being a Mentor

One of our greatest legacies can result from mentoring children, ours and others. Churchland reminds us, "Typically, children intently watch and pick up styles of behavior such as kindly interactions, generosity, warmth, and friendliness as well as their opposites."[186] Because attention from being cooperative feels good, they repeat those preferred behaviors in virtuous cycles. The flip side is they're also reinforced with attention when they don't cooperate and thus repeat vicious cycles of unacceptable behavior.

A child is blessed with eons of evolution and learning social practices of ". . . stability, safety and prosperity. . . ."[187] We are born with a ". . . neurological platform that undergirds our caring for family and friends, and the set of customs [that help us] cope with the many demands in the physical and social environment."[188] More learning happens in the first few years of life than in any other period. How much better if the teacher is eager, caring, honest, humble, sharing, loves knowledge, and is a bit witty and humorous.

We model behavior, good and bad. Others, especially children, are absorbing our examples from birth, and some say even in utero, where they inherit their first hormones from their mother. As role models for children, we have a responsibility to practice virtuous/holistic living enough that it becomes second nature.[189] Children are watching us. We are compelled to make moral choices, which then are developed over time, lengthening and strengthening neurological foundations by practice. Our own internal "wonder drug" oxytocin, for example, enhances positive feelings of bonding to group members.[190] Again, we have positive feelings when we contribute to the common good and when we're welcomed and respected in return.

As role models for children, we have a responsibility to practice virtuous/holistic living enough that it becomes second nature. Children are watching us.

Following Personally Speaking about experiences mentoring a child begins Section III, in which you'll discover more specifics about the journey to becoming your best and how to thrive. You'll also find out more about New Wave Leadership in all its facets—as well as what leadership is *not*. Stay the course to see how you can considerably enhance your life and your leadership.

Personally Speaking

Mentoring—and Learning from—a Child

James Klopovic

Our leisure is a time for having good, clean, renewing, productive fun—sometimes with a child, which confers added benefits. I'm aware that one of the greatest contributions I can make is influencing a child's health, motivation, and especially morality. The impact of such association goes both ways. Ah, the *joy* of having a child in tow!

Over the years, I've aimed to spark curiosity in my daughter Nicole by showing her that nature is the gateway to so much more. In fact, understanding the natural way of things is an essential part of becoming fully human, which is the epitome of a natural growth process.

Trips with my daughter into the wild and not-so-wild facilitate the study and development of virtue and character and how to truly thrive, which is quite experiential. There's nothing like hands on. Yes, we can learn from books, but we learn more by doing things—and all the better together. The memories galore are frosting on the cake. Imagine father and daughter in our sleeping bags with nothing between us and the Pacific Northwest skies but the purest of air and the hum and buzz of the night. The profusion of stars is the same that Native Americans marveled at for millennia.

I've seen joy erupt on Nicole's face while landing her first fish, a 35-pound king salmon, after flying into the Alaskan outback on a float plane. And, yes, she was at the stick, too (under the eye of the pilot of course).

Joy again broke out when she boated a 190-pound tarpon off Miami Beach. This after an hour and 45-minute battle in which the fish danced over the ocean on its tail and towed the boat another mile offshore. On that trip, we learned from our experienced guide that the female tarpon can release up to 12 million eggs at once and produce up to 20 million eggs per season. These fish can see 100 million colors, whereas we humans may see one million. The tarpon, the guide informed us, is one of the most evolved creatures on the planet and essential to the balance of our waters. It's a true, still-living "dinosaur." Its lifespan is decades, and it can breathe air! Fishing trips can be most educational.

Nicole and I also rafted the Middle Fork of the Salmon River, Idaho. She accomplished the entire six days of the rafting trip in a one-man (or woman) dinghy, rapids and all. I stuck to the cargo raft, watching the sky drift by and soaring in my mind with the bald eagles that inspected us on their frequent flybys, sharing their river with gracious but majestic acceptance.

We observed the living stories of Native Americans in petroglyphs of hundreds of years ago or more and learned how they collaborated with one another and nature to thrive for millennia. The night sky as we camped was unimpeded by even a speck of dust, which allowed us to contemplate the impossible vastness of the cosmos. So inspired, we touched on what it is to live the Good Life and how to do it. Rare moments for father and daughter.

Another time, we bicycled Holland, studied the five stories of a hand-built old-time wooden windmill and marveled at its engineering and the builders' understanding of wind dynamics. All the blades of the windmill could be turned into the wind.

Then we stood before the Dutch Masters and marveled at how Vermeer captured light, which seemed to beam from the painting. Back then, painters had to mix all their own linseed oil-based paints with hand-ground mineral colors. How can one not be inspired by what man can achieve and, in turn, be stirred to create?

What a great way to spend leisure time and mentor an eager young mind and soul. These are the best of times, spent with my daughter as she made more connections with her inner and outer worlds, her place in life, and her responsibilities to it. It's not only building legacy that she will carry on, but such fun can't be adequately described.

So I ask *you*, also, to remember that one of the greatest contributions you can make in life is to heighten the well-being, motivation, and morality of a child.

Help a young child pack his or her smiley-face backpack with a favorite blanket, a plush toy, a bottle of water, some gummy bears, and a book. Oh yes! You must pack a book. Walk 50 feet from the car to a campfire to roast weenies and tell stories. You will change the child's life—and yours—for the better . . . and for a lifetime. That child teaches *you* so much.

Look *intently;* listen *intensely;* learn *insightfully.*

SECTION III:
THE JOURNEY EXPLAINED – LEARNING TO THRIVE

Section Overview

As we experience life and work, it takes years to educate ourselves on how to live with virtue as a whole person and to develop the skills of introspection and humility. In other words, it takes time to develop into a New Wave Leader. Those talents cannot be immediately assumed; they take years to be realized and become the fabric—some say the soul—of the individual. Therefore, we explain New Wave Leadership as a most personal journey.

Effectiveness as a person, let alone leader, is a rigorous maturational process requiring stern commitment and dogged persistence. Character does not leap from a page but is harvested from reading, studying, practicing, and living life. Also, the journey means we never stop as we can learn and improve throughout the whole journey, which is the way we want it. Such advancement becomes the preferred way to live.

The chapters in Section III flesh out what it takes to become a New Wave Leader so you can better visualize your own personal journey.

Chapter 8: The Natural Pursuit of Virtue and Well-Being defines the basics of becoming this New Wave Leader, living with virtue and character while improving well-being and learning to thrive.

Chapter 9: Becoming a Part of the New Wave – An Equal Opportunity establishes the fact that living life with consequence is realistic for anyone—and the rewards are many and significant. This chapter discusses how to spend your time to MAGNUS effect and explores how the ancient Samurai Way informs New Wave thinking.

Chapter 10: New Wave Leadership – Myths, Principles, Imperatives explains how leadership is changing and what it is not in the new era as well as the principles of successful, legitimate leadership. It presents the imperatives to live by and the way ahead.

Chapter 11: Phoenix Factors – From Inertia to Thriving further illuminates the emergence of the New Wave Leader. It expands on the factors that spark and distinguish the New Wave individual, organization, community, and leadership.

Chapter 8

The Natural Pursuit of Virtue and Well-Being

*The best Armour of Old Age is a well spent life preceding it; a Life employed in the
Pursuit of useful Knowledge, in honourable Actions and the Practice of Virtue;
in which he who labours to improve himself from his Youth, will in Age reap
the happiest Fruits of them; not only because these never leave a Man,
not even in the extremest Old Age; but because a Conscience bearing Witness
that our Life was well-spent, together with the Remembrance of past
good Actions, yields an unspeakable Comfort to the Soul.*
– Marcus Tullius Cicero

Cicero (Roman, b. 106 BCE) followed a line of Greek philosophers who encouraged a life of virtue and well-being: Socrates (b. 471 BCE) began the discussion of how virtue defined character. Plato (b. 428 BCE) made the case that happiness depends on living virtuously. Essentially, Aristotle (b. 384 BCE) argues that to live well, that is live a meaningful life, one must be virtuous. Living virtuously allows us to conduct our days morally. Together, these Ancients make a compelling case that the pursuit of virtue is the way to conduct a life worth living and worthy of the work. Not only that; such a pursuit is the key to success and happiness. Because along the way we learn what it is to succeed and what it is to be happy. It's not about having a fancier car. It's about learning to live the Good Life by pursuing virtues and holistic living, thereby being healthy, accomplished, respected, and happy, with a life of well-being, content and thriving.

Living virtuously may at first appear to be a lofty ideal—but no. Anyone can achieve it with the proper mindset and practice because it's a way of realizing our potential. Plus, it's a process that continues after a career to earn money ends. We can make our later years some of our best years, as Cicero suggests, if we prepare for them by continually bettering and expanding ourselves.

> **This journey is an exceptional way to pursue meaning in life. Timeless rewards include a deep sense of accomplishment, satisfying relationships, health and vitality, and an intergenerational legacy.**

A Most Personal Journey

Once you learn the how of becoming MAGNUS–OVÉA, your path will be as unique as you are, yet quite realistic and ever rewarding. You arrive at what it means for *you* as you read this book and take it to heart. Then more understanding derives from doing.

> *We throw all our attention on the utterly idle question whether A has done as well as B, when the only question is whether A has done as well as he could.*
> – William Graham Sumner

Your commitment to becoming a New Wave MAGNUS–OVÉA individual is an earnest, sacred, devoted promise to yourself, as it should be. How you define your path, how you travel it, how you overcome straying from it is up to you. Your resolve will be tested, especially at first. You must find the doggedness to push through. Your ideals will be tested so you must be certain that living with virtue is worthy. Study the Cardinal Virtues, invest in yourself. Find fellow compatriots for mutual support.

You'll need to have or develop the discipline to live holistically in body, mind, and inner spirit, as the Ancients prescribed. As you begin this journey, your belief in being MAGNUS–OVÉA may cycle up and down. Keep reminding yourself that this journey is an exceptional way to pursue meaning in life. Timeless rewards include a deep sense of accomplishment, satisfying relationships, health and vitality, and an intergenerational legacy. You will affect those you can't imagine and continue to affect people *after* you're gone by building permanency in what you do. Ultimately, the experience will bring a lasting happiness, or well-being. Define what you'll do and how you'll do it in a way that's as uncomplicated, appropriate, and manageable as possible. Eventually, you'll find that the process of becoming MAGNUS–OVÉA is a natural part of your every waking hour—and you'll notice it's working. The journey becomes the goal.

Following the S³ Formula

We return to the how of getting things done; the S³ Formula. Once you know about the what and the why; its all about the how.

Committing to better yourself is potentially a life-changing moment; but it's only the first, albeit remarkable, step. It's remarkable because most people fail at this crucial point of beginning. They don't know how to begin. If they know how to begin, they don't persist. If they persist, they don't know how to pursue continuously becoming better. The answer to these realities is to just begin.

> **Becoming a New Wave MAGNUS–OVÉA Leader means you *age gracefully*.**

Keep the formula *Commitment = S³* in mind. Keep your path simple, suitable, and sustainable. Let's use physical conditioning as an example of how to apply the formula.

- *Simple* – Study what it means to be conditioned, not just active, not just "in shape." Develop a routine you can do for a lifetime and do it at least three times a week, combined with other exercise. The body craves variety. Curiously, this is not only one of the best uses of your time, but it multiplies the time you have to do other things you want to do because it adds long, productive, and content years to your life.

- *Suitable* – Make sure your routine suits *you*—at *your age*. Work into whole-body conditioning based on body weight and light resistance. Body-weight exercises can be maintained. Remember to include a variety of exercises you're capable of doing but that challenge you enough to increase your strength and agility to where you want it.

- *Sustainable* – Consistency and sustainability are key. You may find you can up-level your routine as your body becomes better conditioned. At your annual physical, track your basic body functioning, resting heart rate, blood pressure, and weight. If you're already in good condition, aim to at least maintain, if not improve. Set your sights on what's simple, suitable and sustainable for you personally. Becoming a New Wave MAGNUS–OVÉA Leader means you *age gracefully*.

Once you incorporate this formula into your life, you'll be surprised at its near universal application. Observe how it saves time, increases productivity, and most important, reduces stress. Now let's consider in a little more detail how to put the formula in motion.

Your Inner OVÉA

OVÉA—**O**thers, **V**alues, **E**thics, **A**cceleration—is the nucleus and activator of MAGNUS. True modern leaders of today and especially tomorrow have the spark of OVÉA as their inner activator.

An active OVÉA converges in the three leadership dimensions of Influence, Inspiration, and Aspiration effected by a New Wave Leader, who can:

- Persuade others gently and effectively. *(Influence)*

- Communicate enthusiasm to others' minds and spirits. *(Inspiration)*

- Trigger the ability to *learn* more, *do* more, *dream* more, and *become* more. *(Aspiration)*

The convergence of these dimensions doesn't happen automatically. Few have it naturally. However, we believe many can *learn* the required knowledge, skills, and practical application to become dynamic, accomplished leaders. Many can *activate* their inner OVÉA for daily individual improvement and thus the betterment of family, work, and community. One such way is to follow the suggestions in this book. Over time, you'll find yourself influencing and inspiring others more and more to be their greater selves.

Practicing Character Strengths

Becoming a New Wave Leader isn't about trying to achieve an unfathomable ideal; it's about continuously studying, learning, and expressing what is best *in* you *for* you. The learning addresses the strengths of character, which you see in Figure 4: The Practices of Character – Strengths and Behaviors. Chris Peterson and Martin Seligman identified these 24 character strengths and how they're expressed in their 2004 book *Character Strengths and Virtues.*[191] You can also find them on the VIA Institute on Character website.[192]

With regard to becoming a New Wave Leader, we want to keep our practice simple, suitable, and sustainable. Thus, in this book we emphasize and discuss only two main character traits—*introspection* and *humility*. In addition, we focus on the Cardinal Virtues of *Justice, Wisdom, Courage, and Temperance.* Together, these six traits guide our personal progress. Peterson and Seligman add Humanity and Transcendence to the Cardinals to describe further character traits, which are aspirational.

The chart in Figure 4 lists the virtues, or traits, under which are character strengths, and below that, ways in which we can express each strength. We suggest you focus on the *expressions,* or *behaviors,* which are what we *practice* to develop character. For example, the trait of Temperance is about the strength of Self-Regulation. Related behaviors include being disciplined, exercising self-control, and managing impulses and emotions.

Figure 4: The Practices of Character Traits, Strengths, and Behaviors[193]

The Opposite Sides of Character

We strive to reach deeper and deeper to find our generosity, loyalty, devotion, self-control, determination, and on the list goes. But good character, which mimics life, comes in opposites,[194] such as dishonesty, unkindness, rudeness, greed, cruelty, selfishness, and on that list goes, too. Becoming better recognizes both sides of our human condition, excessive vices and virtues, then considers the acceptable middle ground and acts on that.

Consider patience versus anger. It's natural to be patient. But what happens when patience wears thin? We tend to get angry; its natural, part of the human condition. Having to make a call to customer service for a computer problem for the nth time comes to mind. Anger is also part of good character—yes, *good* character—but wonton anger is destructive. It's silly to deny the steam that rises at an injustice. Anger at the right time, at the right level, and directed appropriately is *not* a bad thing. Thus, the study and growth of what we consider a positive virtue can't fully progress without knowing its opposite; judicial patience and managed anger go together. When understood in pairs, we learn to balance the two extremes and find the mean, or middle path. *Then* we progress.

Perspective and attitude matter. We hear over and over that attitude is paramount, particularly when handling the many downsides to life and minute-to-minute swings we experience daily. This is wisdom about how to survive, even thrive, through crises, betrayals, and heavy loss, especially that of the heart.

> **Becoming better recognizes both sides of our human condition, excessive vices and virtues, then considers the acceptable middle ground and acts on that.**

We needn't hang on to being angry, depressed, or vengeful, as everything changes and passes. We turn to the Ancients—Asians this time—for a memorable parable, simple and elegant, to strike home the point of balancing character traits. The story illustrates seeing difficulties for what they are—temporary with unforeseen ramifications.[195]

The Chinese Rice Farmer

Imagine an ancient Chinese farming village with humble houses handmade from rustic brick and sturdy bamboo. Out back are lush vegetable gardens, which the chickens keep bugless. Acres of rice paddies, artfully irrigated, form rows in mathematical precision and geometric patterns. Families work shoulder to shoulder; only the very youngest at play. . . .

One day in this village, a farmer's horse ran away. Upon hearing the news, his neighbors came to visit saying, "Such bad fortune." They were full of sympathy.

"Maybe," replied the farmer.

The next morning, the horse returned, bringing with it three wild horses. "What great fortune!" the neighbors exclaimed.

"Maybe," the old man replied.

The following day, the farmer's son tried to ride one of the untamed horses, was thrown off, and broke his leg. His son would forever limp.

"What terrible fortune!" the neighbors cried.

"Maybe," answered the farmer.

The next morning, the army came through the farmers' village to conscript young, able-bodied men for the war. Seeing the son's limp, they passed him by.

"What wonderful fortune!" the neighbors exclaimed, congratulating the farmer, who answered . . .

"Maybe."

We can't know which experiences and events will turn out to be fortunate and which will be unfortunate because everything is constantly changing. Today's misfortune is tomorrow's fortune. It's impossible to control the future, though we can prepare for it and stack the deck in our favor. While it's tough to suffer misfortune, especially when it seems senseless, we can learn from it and get up the next day expecting good things and making them happen. As rapper J. Cole says, "The bad news is nothing lasts forever. The good news is nothing lasts forever."

The next time life takes a downturn, see if you can stop worrying. Take the middle path of "Maybe." Good change is always just around the corner, especially if you do something productive and train yourself to realize it when good news happens. Therefore, as a perceived misfortune weaves its way through your life, you can maintain your equilibrium and keep working on challenging, lasting, and positive changes for yourself and communal betterment. And do something fun to lift your spirits, too.

Now let's continue the discussion of how to live well, accomplished, and content by being virtuous and living holistically. Begin at the beginning nearly 2,400 years ago when the Ancients were deeply debating what constitutes the Good Life. Aristotle made an indelible case for pursuing happiness through virtue.

Living Virtuously – Simple, Not Easy, But Worth It

These pages offer realistic tips for beginning the journey gathered from a select few of our greats, ancient and modern, who suggest *how* we can pursue an exemplary life. It doesn't take much to earn respect, be involved in making lives better, and realize that adequate material comfort is enough. Those who take this path inevitably become much the better for the work of it and are well thought of, accomplished, and genuinely happy. What better way to pursue what matters than by committing to serve the greater good while doing it nobly! The words *generous, worthy, kindly, forgiving, dependable, honest,* and *fair* spring to mind.

Realistically, attaining true virtue is difficult—impossible, most say—but what matters is that you try. Say you will do it and do what you say. Thus, becoming MAGNUS–OVÉA is a way of life, a way of learning, thinking, speaking, and behaving. Progress doesn't come in lightning bolts of insight, and you're not likely to reach the pinnacle of virtuous being. Life is full of every twist and turn imaginable—but you'll be in a better position to handle whatever comes your way. In the very least, you will be better, perhaps much better, for the work you put into becoming a New Wave individual who understands what is important and how to culture it.

Everyday Moderation – Sophrosyne

We're constantly bombarded by images in advertising and the media cleverly enticing us to over consume. If we aren't aware and don't challenge these influences and our impulses, we end up overeating, binge watching, or buying things we don't need.[196]

> *"Out of moderation a pure happiness springs."*
> – Johann Wolfgang von Goethe

As we've mentioned, *sophrosyne* is an ancient Greek word that describes a healthy approach to moderation based on a growing sense of self-awareness. This approach to life begins by acknowledging our excesses and then carefully, accurately recognizing the difference between need and want. Once we recognize why and how we over consume, for example, the

> **Becoming MAGNUS–OVÉA is a way of life, a way of learning, thinking, speaking, and behaving.**

concept of sophrosyne suggests that we focus on what we will gain rather than what we will lose by changing our habits. This moderation way of thinking isn't a constraint on our wishes and pleasures; rather it's a source of balance that results in peace of mind and soul, or harmony. Of course, change takes time and effort. It's important to face our excesses with patience and compassion, especially if we slip up.

We can start by asking, *Is this a need or want?* Imagine the peace of mind gained when investing the afternoon in activity that's truly meaningful. Even doing nothing, relaxing properly, is meaningful. Consider the money we could save when prioritizing needs before indulgences in our monthly budget. Then we could put that savings toward eliminating debt and retiring from work early. Think of the extra space gained without clutter of mind, conscience, and household. Attention to moderation helps us create contentment as we reap the benefits of increased health, true wealth, wisdom, and respect. Growth, your upward trajectory in character, tends to be geometric.

This leads to another point: Committing to the morally grounded way of New Wave Leadership is synergistic. Practice and frequent insights from working on one worthy endeavor lead to similar practices and insights in another, whereby all improve and strengthen. Thus, as we learn the lessons of frugality, for example, we also have insights into right over wrong, learning to love learning, and being determined even in adversity. Continuous practice in applying these insights leads to habits of the best kind.

By now, you've realized that this journey to thriving includes every aspect of our being. Let's look a little deeper into what that means.

Holistic Thriving

The Ancient Greats defined the human condition as comprised of body, mind, and spirit, or inner being. Strengthened together, we learn to *thrive* in a contented life not merely exist to watch the clock until quitting time. Thriving is another way of understanding happiness. Good all-round health and happiness affects our intellect, curiosity, and endeavors, which determine our zest for life, our spirit, in a self-perpetuating virtuous cycle. A discontented spirit will bring down our body and mind, but it also works the other way around. The ancients also observe, which experience bears out, that when we work on this trilogy—especially our weakest link—we grow physically, in well-being, and in purpose. Here, too, we must remember sophrosyne and not go overboard in any one area.

Body – Physical Health and Hardiness

What follows is a commonsense way of approaching how to develop yourself physically based on a reasonable diet and the physiology of exercise. It's realistic and encouraging. Getting this part of holistic living right is immeasurably valuable. It will give you the longevity to realize a fantastic state of life. You'll enjoy a long retirement in which you don't have to work for money and have the pep to explore what you've dreamed of doing.

We learn to be unhealthy, given all our creature comforts, and likewise, we can unlearn it. How often do we cruise a parking lot in our air-conditioned car to find a parking space close to the door of an air-conditioned store? And how often do we take an elevator up one story to escape a "cruel" flight of stairs? How many times do we grab a fast-food meal to avoid grocery shopping or cooking?

Health is part of our nature, but often we don't appreciate it until it's gone. Our bodies crave nutritious foods and proper vigorous exercise. The task, then, is to support our natural, healthy vitality—and the sooner the better so we can thrive as we age.

That said, let's consider a few simple suggestions to help maintain and improve the strength and energy of our bodies.

Nutrition – Study and practice the basics of good nutrition. For example, learn the recommended proportions of carbs, proteins, and fats. Saturated fats (solid at room temp) are a modest necessity, but for the most part avoid artificial trans fats created when liquid vegetable oils are hydrogenated to make them semi-solid. Both saturated and unsaturated fats are naturally occurring, and some natural trans fat is found in meat and dairy. However, artificial trans fats can create negative health effects if consumed too heavily. These fats are in many bakery items and, yes, they're tempting. But too many doughnuts, for example, do not a good diet make. One of the healthiest fats is olive oil, a staple of the Mediterranean diet, and especially extra virgin olive oil, or EVOO, which is cold pressed, thus retaining its nutrients. Surprisingly, coconut oil, a medium-chain triglyceride, provides several health benefits.[197]

Learn to shop around the perimeter of the grocery store, where you'll find what grows in the soil rather than what walks on it. To provide your body with the proper range of nutrients, eat a variety of fruits and vegetables in many colors and whole grains. And don't forget your leafy greens! A 2017 Rush University study showed that those adults who ate just one serving of leafy greens a day (e.g., spinach, kale, collard greens, arugula) could think more clearly, remember details and names better, had less brain fog, and were more productive every day than those who didn't.[198] If you eat meat, make it fresh and lean, including chicken, fish, and other seafood. Maple smoked salmon has a remarkable taste and is an even more remarkable food. So what about those center aisles?

When shopping the inside aisles of the store where all the packaged and processed foods are shelved, learn to read labels. If one of the first three ingredients is sugar or fat and a long list of items you can't pronounce, back on the shelf it goes. Keep healthy food in the house, which means banning the likes of sugary drinks and chips. If you don't drink alcohol, don't start. If you do enjoy an "adult" beverage, keep it to one a day. If you don't have that discipline, it's best not to drink at all.

Again, you needn't be perfect! Enjoy a holiday feast; just fill your plate modestly . . . once. And a delicious slice of pic is good for the soul. Aim for steady improvement and keep the benefits of healthy eating in mind. Conserve your willpower for the discipline of nutrition, conditioning, and working on your state of well-being and your body will respond to reward you. That's it; nothing mystical, just simple, suitable, sustainable. Commit! Stick with a healthy eating regimen for six months at least, or long enough for good nutrition to become habitual and to notice how good you feel.

Conditioning – Exercise vigorously, regularly. "But I have no time . . . the gym is too far away . . . I need a coach . . ." No excuses! Do this as if your life depends on it—because it does. Study the difference between being active, exercising, and conditioning. People mistake gardening or even walking a pet for exercise. These are worthy activities, but they do little for overall, life-sustaining health. Focus on conditioning, which enhances, strengthens, and perpetuates your cardiovascular systems and functions. Tax your muscles and joints along with your heart and lungs. Eliminate excuses not to get into condition, which means pushing your whole body to a reasonable limit. That's the point at which all your bodily systems work at peak efficiency with your musculoskeletal systems. Again, make sure you have a regular physical so you can monitor your basic readings.

Since longevity is the goal, you'll want to touch five key qualities several ways every week through your conditioning program: speed, coordination, flexibility, strength, and endurance. This is a hierarchy for sustained conditioning that recognizes the needs of aging. As you age, you'll notice a decline in speed, coordination, and flexibility, which is addressed with age-appropriate body-weight routines, full-body stretching, and yoga. All of these attributes are crucial for preserving your quality of life with age, and the hardest to maintain is speed. You don't need to train like a track and field athlete, but recognize that slow movement is *not* a characteristic of youth and vigor. With that, you'll want to keep your training simple, suitable, and—you guessed it—sustainable.

Also keep your program rich with variety. Maintain enough consistency in your conditioning to see progress, while including enough variety to keep it engaging and enhance your ability to overcome novel physical challenges. As you age, the issue becomes more and more about being able to do life's tasks and enjoy life's pleasures. You may need or want to carry a heavy bag of groceries or dog food up a flight of stairs, easily bend over to pick up something, or play ball with your grandchild without getting tired. It's essential to vary exercises nearly daily to keep the body stimulated. Your body acclimates to conditioning routines within a few days. Variety introduces healthy shock to that which makes you strong. More important, variety is the bulwark against boredom and lack of discipline. Approach conditioning with religious dedication. Even if injured, you can still go to the gym for the whirlpool and steam bath. Keep the habit alive and you'll accrue the health and wellness that's essential to well-being.

> *"We have more ability than willpower, and it is often an excuse to ourselves*
> *that we imagine that things are impossible."*
> – François de la Rochefoucauld

Mind – Psychological Toughness and Mental Enrichment

The care and development of your mind are just as important as the nurturing of your body. Included in this category are the emotions, as they stem from the thoughts you have and affect the whole body. As we've discussed, negative emotions and mental habits can trigger hormones that depress or excite your physiology. The habits suggested in this book will help train your neuroplastic brain toward the positive and build mental toughness and well-being you need for the vicissitudes of the day. Simply, you need to be mentally capable for what's going right as much as what's objectionable or difficult. You'll gain psychological hardiness through commitment, control, courage, perseverance, and passion, which will help you deal with crises as well as your everyday life.

Beyond just being mentally resilient, developing and enriching your mind can expand your experience of life and help you lead. So first, take Ben Franklin's advice and *read*—extensively! Libraries and the internet and audio books allow you to read and absorb knowledge without warehousing all those books, magazines, and journals in your home. That said, you may find it gratifying to see your library grow as a record of your path through life. In addition, you can now take advantage of endless videos online and on TV. Still, nothing replaces or is as assuring as a good, hardbound book. If you own them, you can write notes in them to help you remember what's worth remembering. Or, better yet, note the many insights you have. Noted books are another bit of your legacy. Who knows who will find that book?

Travel is also a way to feed your mind and soak up novel and fascinating experiences. Get out in the world as best you can—and travel this marvelous country of ours, even if it's just the next state over. Explore! Plan tours of our national parks and historical places. Enjoy a variety of natural settings such as beaches, mountains, and forests, or take a trip on a river boat. All are educational when you seek learning. You can imagine the Native American who carved a petrograph on a rocky overhang along the Middle Fork of the Salmon River hundreds of years ago. If you can find a way to visit different countries, it will widen your horizons and open your mind to other cultures and ways of thinking. Be adventurous! Possibilities abound.

By learning, thinking, and doing interesting things, you become a more interesting person and thus attract other interesting people to you. This great virtuous cycle affirms the aphorism that you're judged by the company you keep, not to mention greatly enriched by it. In addition, the more you learn, the better you're able to communicate, lead, and *live*.

Challenge yourself! If you stumble and fall, get up, and do it again. Though you may fall, you're still further along for being willing to take a challenge.

These practices promote a deeper understanding of life and a sense of well-being, which includes what we all seek—happiness.

Spirit - Love and Zest for Life

Beyond thoughts, emotions, and behaviors is meta-motivation, an energy that comes from a place of love and caring for life and people. We can learn to love anything and anyone. Read about the Greats, our Founding Fathers, and Abraham Lincoln. These people had remarkable platonic love for close friends. How they wrote of it is endearing and life affirming. Lincoln's close ties gave him strength to preserve the union, abolish slavery, and change the course of history, making a better world far into the future. Every century needs a Lincoln to teach us what's possible with grit and the awareness of humanity's greatness. It's the spirit behind OVÉA, a respecter of all things and the inspiration that gives life meaning.

Spirit is the lifeforce or zest that sparks and sustains action when you *do something bigger than you are.* Yes, challenge yourself! If you stumble and fall, get up, and do it again. Though you may fall, you're still further along for being willing to take a challenge. Zestful experiences build on one another. Cicero asserted that zest in life is the antidote to being ". . . slack, sluggish, and somnambulant."[199] Certainly, you don't want to waste your life in such a state when so many enlivening experiences beckon that will add to your own life as well as that of others.

To be clear, zestful action doesn't mean excessive action. Remember the Golden Mean. We're still talking simple, suitable, and sustainable as well as meaningful, virtuous, and healthy. Sensibility goes a long way to sustain what may be a simple and routine yet satisfying path that has anything but simple and routine results. Especially when traveled with zest and a love of life and fellow man.

Why Should I Commit?

You may be asking, *Why should I commit to the New Wave MAGNUS–OVÉA Journey? Where will I find the time? What can I expect? How will it affect me and mine?*

In answer, you will achieve more personally and get more—much more—from life by committing to this better way of living. You will grow in self-awareness and become more cognizant of what matters. Taking the steps to become better, advancing toward your best, will quickly become routine. You will be much more resilient as you go through the ups and downs of a career. As you become a better and better person, you will become a better parent, spouse, friend, and professional and be more successful at home, on the job, and in the community. Most important, you will continuously develop your strength of character as your depth of understanding right and wrong, good and bad grows. You are going to grow one way or another, so why not grow to become better?

> *. . . [B]y the endeavor [of seeking a virtuous life, I became] a better*
> *and happier man than I otherwise should have been.*
> – Benjamin Franklin

Personally Speaking

Worth It—a Thousand Times Over!
James Klopovic

I often say to the younger folks I meet, and most are now younger, that they're not working out for being 30, 40, or even 50 something. They're working out for being 80, 90, and 100 something.

Face it. If we're not conditioned and at a good "fighting" weight when we hit our senior years, hope is lost for all but a few of us. It becomes more and more difficult as time goes by to recover healthy vitality and strength once they've dissipated. The pity is we're our most powerful when we reach our 60s because that's when we've developed a degree of wisdom and have much of life figured out. We want to have enough vim and vigor to use that wisdom in our retirement doing whatever it is we enjoy.

Personally, I'm committed to the concept of MAGNUS–OVÉA, which requires dedication to be sure, but it's well worth it. Take diet, for example. I don't expect this to be everyone's "cup of tea," but here are a few of my personal favorites. Breakfast includes whole grain cereals, hemp seeds, and fruit. A good barista coffee with a dash of half and half and just enough of my beloved honey tops it off. My lunch is likely to consist of chicken with veggies and rice, and for dinner, I often have fish or chicken with more veggies and perhaps a baked sweet potato. I like to drink a popular flavored "live" water or filtered water.

I make my routine sustainable by allowing myself a few extras such as one alcoholic beverage in the early evening. If a birthday or some such occasion comes along, I'll have a special dinner; I just don't eat half the cake!

When it comes to exercise, I can't seem to do it at home. Therefore, I've found a gym staffed by conditioning coaches who tailor exercise regimens to the individual train*ees* not train*ers*. They watch over this aging body, which sometimes remembers being 20 something and tends to attempt "stupid guy" stuff. Another good thing about having a qualified conditioning coach and guided workouts is I have exercise mates who bring companionship, comradery, and a little competition to a common cause.

I've found that a good regimen for me combines regular High Intensity Interval Training (HIIT), mostly with bodyweight, perhaps a short jog, some swimming and biking, plus stretching, yoga, and a daily 10-minute guided meditation. I don't slight meditation because it teaches true relaxation, which permeates my day.

I suggest you work up to something similar—but you need to approach it with near religious dedication. I can tell you, it's worth it. At one point, I had my shoulder repaired and at this writing, the other shoulder has also been mended. It was elective, preventive surgery. I was doing fine but could notice deterioration in major rotator and bicep connective tissue. I confidently signed the release, and the doc proceeded to disconnect and reconnect that tissue.

Well, you know the tiny print at the bottom of the release that says, "Hey, we might kill you, but it's not our fault"? You'd best take that seriously. A day or so after surgery, I experienced torturous pain caused by *three* pulmonary embolisms, which took hours of being on the rack to locate. I later learned that one such embolism is more dangerous, kills faster, and is more insidious than a heart attack or stroke.

Fast forward to my first post-op visit with the surgeon, who said to me, "Jim, you're most probably alive because you're well-conditioned." He didn't say "healthy" or "active" or "in shape"—he said, "well-conditioned." All those hours at the gym were worth it—a thousand times over—yes! I'm still alive, and I can continue my path of becoming, hopefully making a difference, making memories, leaving a legacy, and having *fun*.

The grim reaper came to me with his hand outstretched that day, and I told him, "Not today, Mr. Grim Reaper, not today!"

Chapter 9

Becoming Part of the New Wave – An Equal Opportunity

First say to yourself what you would be; then do what you have to do.
– Epictetus

Let's be clear. Becoming a New Wave MAGNUS–OVÉA Leader and living the good life applies to anyone, in any career, in any circumstance in life. As Epictetus says so clearly, it's about deciding what you want for your life and then doing what it takes to be it and have it. So besides decision, it takes commitment and determination. Is living a happy, healthy life—a long, vital, and vigorous life—worth making a few changes? Is doing well and doing good, being respected and leaving a commendable legacy worth committing to the journey? The choice is up to you.

We all have the capacity to be just, wise, brave, and frugal. But those capacities need to be awakened and charged, or switched on, as if bringing light to a darkened room. OVÉA is the light switch to your MAGNUS persona. It's the motivational force for what you can become. Your potential, your MAGNUS, needs the spark of OVÉA to be realized. Once your natural propensity to be good and do well is ignited, you're ready to gain necessary and relevant knowledge, skills, experience, character, and attitude for the journey of becoming your best self. It's been our experience that this journey is not only indescribably rewarding, it's infinitely *enjoyable*.

No impediments prevent you from beginning your journey; no obstacles block your progress. Think of the many people who have what most would consider impediments to life and happiness, yet they're accomplished in their own way and *happy*. A blind piano player, a blind opera singer, a world class surfer with one arm lost to a shark come to mind. In fact, difficulties can uncover hidden talents, resources, and strengths. To someone on a virtuous path, troubles are opportunities.

How many times have all of us experienced what seemed at the time like the end of the world—not getting a long-sought promotion, losing a job or a relationship—only to see things work out for the better in the long run? The difference in how we travel the path is attitude. *Anyone* can be magnanimous. We turn again to the wisdom of an Ancient:

> *What matters most is what sort of person you are becoming,*
> *what sort of life you are living.*
> – Epictetus

Spending Time for Optimal Effect

Time, time, time. We all have it, but what do we do with it? One person with 24 hours a day supports self, family, and community and builds a lasting reputation with earned respect by being humble and of good character. Another with the same amount of time has little to show for it and complains about life.

Every way you spend your time is important. The trick is to know what you're achieving from each category of activity and how you're doing it. Accomplishing each one in its own way is vital to sustaining yourself physically and especially mentally, while taking on endeavors that are fun and productive.

We can have leisure moments any time throughout our lives, but here we explore that leisure can be a pleasant and productive reward for a lifetime of work. How we take advantage of this time depends on living a meaningful, productive life up until then based on the journey of virtuous and holistic living.

Leisure takes preparation and perspiration. Plainly put, you can't just hang up your spurs then decide to do a triathlon, plow through your bucket list, master the guitar, and do something "big." Whenever you retire, those years can be the most productive, happy years of life if you are vital and vigorous and ready for them.

> **Those who choose the journey must strive to maximize the use, efficiency, and effectiveness of their time for the greatest effect.**

Those who choose the journey must strive to maximize the use, efficiency, and effectiveness of their time for the greatest effect. Let's first look at the various ways we spend our time, including personal maintenance, working, resting, relaxing, and leisure.[201] We need every category properly invested.

Personal Maintenance – Satisfying Physical Needs

This category addresses satisfying our bodily requirements for sleep, food, sex, exercise, and personal hygiene. Although these pursuits may fall under "maintenance," foregoing them can have serious consequences, and for most of these needs, can even be life threatening. Due diligence is necessary, so we need to build time into our day for the necessities (including grocery shopping and preparation of food for good health).

Although necessary, these pursuits are extrinsic as opposed to the intrinsic nature of leisure, which is the "higher" pursuit, beyond the basics. How we use our leisure time is even critical to character-building.

Work – Careers and Working for Pay

We work to sustain ourselves and our families as well as offer our gifts to the world. There's much satisfaction in doing a job well and contributing to society. Many are fortunate to have paid work they enjoy that also improves the lives of others. That said, labor for financial compensation differs from work we freely choose in a pursuit to better ourselves, for pure enjoyment, personal development, or because our "Inner OVÉA" motivates us to help others without compensation. Such are the endeavors we might choose during retirement from work for pay[202] but also on the way there.

Rest – Pure Inactivity

Productive, sustained work is complemented by rest and relaxation. How many of us have learned to periodically "shut off" our brain for the complete rest it needs? Very few. Complete rest is doing nothing. We differentiate this way of spending time from recreation, which is purposeful amusement.

Consider this science of true rest. Our brain has two main modes of processing. The first is action oriented, which lets us concentrate on tasks, solve problems, and process information. The second is called *default state/mode network,* or a task-negative state, which gives our mind a chance to sort things out subconsciously. This time is when our brain makes cortical connections. We need true rest to consolidate input and make sense of it all. Our brain can then solidify lessons from memories and work out problems when we're stuck.

Leonardo DaVinci would finish the day by reviewing it mentally just before sleep. This queued up his unconscious brain for growth and creative problem solving. This is a great reason to keep a pad and pen on the nightstand. The default mode network naturally kicks in right before we fall asleep. We can further support this brain "recovery" by deliberately resting our brain through the conscious release stage of real rest. We rest to replenish the brain's finite stores of attention and encourage productivity, clarity, and creativity.

So, remember how important it is to intentionally allow your brain to disengage. The purposeful relaxing and non-doing may not seem actively productive, but when we carve out time for pure inactivity, we release tension and allow this complex organ to rest.[203] Even 10 minutes of daily meditation is beneficial and why people have practiced meditation for millennia. By doing "nothing" for even a few minutes, we actually save time by returning to the task at hand more at ease, calm, and renewed. Let's look at how that differs from simply relaxing.

Relaxation - Recuperation with Restorative Activity

Relaxation is a pursuit that allows us to be at peace, to calm down. You may find great relaxation reading books, visiting with friends, playing a video game, being in nature, sitting on your porch with a cup of tea, or watching a baseball game on TV with a (single) bottle of ale. This is amusement, a respite, a "remedy" from the toil of work. True relaxation is not rest but renewal, which helps establish balance, the Golden Mean of living. One of its scientifically proven benefits is it fights aging by reducing vascular inflammation and improving metabolism.[204]

Leisure - Purposeful, Productive

Leisure is the capstone to a life well lived. It's the reward for our working—sometimes at various jobs for decades. The Greats wrote that work for pay is much less important than leisure time, as this is when we reach our full potential! But most people waste it because they fail to develop creative pursuits and healthy lifestyles.

> **The best leisure according to the Ancients is when we strengthen ourselves to, in turn, strengthen our families, our neighborhoods, our communities.**

Leisure time is productive time, so it must be used purposefully. To have a balanced life, we need to give time to actualizing our potential, which might mean taking up a musical instrument or writing—and giving back, whether that means volunteering or starting and running a foundation.

A noble way to spend time when we are free to choose is to cultivate the arts, pursue a public service or hobby, perhaps even take up another profession, or spend quality time with grandchildren.

We need to begin fostering leisure during our working years. It comes with an attitude of personal and communal betterment. The opposite of tediousness, which destroys motivation and direction according to Aristotle, neither is it idleness. Rather, it's a key to productivity and contentment.

Leisure gives us time to do something bigger than ourselves, whether we do it in a few moments during the day or as a devoted life pursuit. The best leisure according to the Ancients is when we strengthen ourselves to, in turn, strengthen our families, our neighborhoods, our communities. Opportunities abound.

Essentially, a state of true leisure is achieved by working on living well *preceding* the cessation of working for a living. Productive, meaningful leisure takes preparation. Learn what is worthy of pursuit—that which will help you give back and continue growing. Learn how to go about using your leisure time, and develop determination to do that worthy thing born of the time in which to do it.

The journey of becoming better and better supports a long and healthy life. This implies that early on we become quite serious about living well by practicing the good habits we've been discussing. Remember that Boomers will live an average of 35 years longer than their grandparents—still alert, able, and active—and those who are younger could live even longer. Many of us will live to a dynamic and spirited 100! We could potentially spend an entire "career" in noble leisure, a process that's constantly evolving, engaging, exciting, fruitful.

Sadly, many people retire completely ill prepared, and, in a few months, they go reluctantly back to work for "something to do." If one plans well for the day when there's no clock to punch, retirement to leisure is by far the best time of life.

So, remember to plan for leisure. It's the best time to grow after a lifetime of accumulating wisdom, capability, and knowledge of desires, wants, and needs that matter. All the wisdom, experience, and good work you've accomplished are mechanisms for practicing virtue and expressing gratitude for your many blessings.

We maintain that a life is better spent when we plan to repay our good fortune during retirement rather than merely resting, relaxing, and recreating because we "earned it." Oh yes, plan to take vacations, visit the grandchildren, take up that hobby in earnest, make memories! Just don't squander your retirement. Aristotle tells us that productive leisure is uniquely human as it sustains our souls and minds and strengthens our personal relationships. It can also enhance the human species by allowing grandparents an active role in educating grandchildren practically and by example. Anticipating a retirement well spent makes our working years more endurable, even enjoyable, with the bright promise of making a lasting mark.

> **Plan for leisure. It's the best time to grow after a lifetime of accumulating wisdom, capability, and knowledge of desires, wants, and needs that matter.**

True Equal Opportunity

The Greats throughout history practiced what they preached. Cicero became one of our greatest orators by life-long study and practice. Miyamoto Musashi was one of Japan's greatest samurai because he lived The Way. Benjamin Franklin became one of our most accomplished and revered Founding Fathers by acting on his 13 virtues as a young man and to his dying day. All had the pursuit of virtue in common. They acted on a sense of responsibility to improve what needed improving for the benefit of the community. All started humbly and lived lives worth living, making the world a much better place. Their enduring message is that everyone, yes everyone, has the capacity to be better tomorrow than they are today and consequently enhance their world. Are we all as great as these remarkable men? No. Can we practice how they lived within our capabilities? Yes. It simply takes intention and purposefulness.

Never Too Early, Never Too Late

Better late than never is relevant to beginning this journey—even though it's best to begin early. Of the many theories of how the mind works, one of the most fascinating is the dual capacity for fluid and crystalized intelligence.[205]

- *Fluid intelligence* – ability to reason and think flexibly.[206]

- *Crystallized intelligence* – knowledge, facts, and skills acquired throughout life.[207]

Both types of intelligence have to do with reasoning. The problem is we're best at reasoning when we're younger, and our ability to reason declines somewhat with middle age. However, as we reach middle age, we have data and experience—or crystallized intelligence—to guide our fluid intelligence. Thus, as we accumulate information, experiences, and insights, we augment reasoning. As mentioned earlier, we continue to shape the neural synapses in our neuroplastic brain. Both obviously work together and, more important, enhance one another. Thus, we increasingly perform better into middle age and well into our senior years. Churchill, for example, became prime minister of Great Britain for the second time in his 70s. Then he continued to write, winning the Nobel Prize for Literature, and travel, paint, lay bricks, and enthrall audiences into his 90s.

The fallacy of celebrating only our agile youthful reasoning is that it's further developed by information that comes with age. It's called aging gracefully by recognizing that a wrinkle is testimony to earned elegance. Accumulation of knowledge is the *work* of years, of a lifetime. So as the fluidity of early reason fades, we become better at reasoning based on the wealth of what we intellectually accumulate. We become more capable and wiser as we age.

So go ahead and take that job based on your crystallized wealth of intelligence.[208] Dazzle the youth with reasoning derived from a reservoir of knowing how people and things work seasoned with the dash and flare of having "been there, done that."

While personal success is a worthwhile pursuit, significance is the more noble aim. Significance is others-centric, the New Wave way. When we pursue significance, we realize our purpose and meaning and how we can positively impact the world around us.

> *To laugh often and much; to win the respect of intelligent people and the*
> *affection of children; to earn the appreciation of honest critics and endure*
> *the betrayal of false friends; to appreciate beauty; to find the beauty in others;*
> *to leave the world a bit better whether by a healthy child, a garden patch,*
> *or a redeemed social condition; to know that one life has breathed easier*
> *because you lived here. This is to have succeeded.*
> – Ralph Waldo Emerson

The Samurai Way – Practical Then, Practical Now, Practical Tomorrow

The elements of virtuous living have been advocated in major cultures over the centuries, and following them is something anyone can do who has the intention and determination to do so. You might want to think of yourself as a samurai warrior as you practice becoming virtuous.

Miyamoto Musashi, Japan's most famous samurai warrior-philosopher defined the samurai "Way," which comes gradually by study, training, and experience. He asserts, "If you practice day and night . . . your spirit will naturally broaden."[209] The Way captures specific, doable advice on how to live, which incidentally aligns with the Cardinal Virtues. Miyamoto Musashi's nine strategies of the Way constitute remarkable life advice, yet they are simple, suitable, sustainable, *and* profound. These strategies are presented in Musashi's *A Book of Five Rings*.[210] Here's an overview.

1. *Do not think dishonestly.* The Master understood that thoughts lead to words, then actions, then behavior, then character. He also recognized that it takes *more* effort to develop bad character than it does good character. This strategy of truth equates with the Cardinal Virtue of Justice.

   Musashi understood the primacy of knowing right from wrong and acting justly such that it becomes automatic. It's not coincidental that the Asian belief about the preeminence of Justice parallels that of Greek and Roman philosophers. They all understood that the dishonest thought leads to the dishonest word, to the dishonest deed, to the dishonest character, to the dishonest reputation, from which there's no turning back. At that point, all is lost; what else matters? Our reputation is part of our legacy, which lives after us and reflects on our children. Ask yourself again, how do *you* wish to be remembered?

2. *The Way is in training.* It's not enough to read, study, and think. We must practice virtuous holistic living—the trilogy of body, mind, and disposition in concert. Every proficient person practices what they intend to do well. It's said that a great guitarist must first put in 10,000 hours at the six strings and practice almost daily for 10 years just to find out *if* he or she has the justification, motivation, and ability to continue. If so, then the dedication and *real* work begin. Stories aplenty tell of legendary musicians who sleep with their instrument nearby to capture those few magical, mystical words and notes that come from the unconscious only at night. Yes, they even dream music.

3. *Become acquainted with every art.* This strategy is about becoming a well-rounded person. Obviously, you can't become proficient at everything, but you can learn to appreciate the beauty of art and music, the discipline of sports, and how a well-crafted book communicates images, emotion, and a message. When you diligently improve your writing skills, you become a much better orator and communicator. You can appreciate the color and

form created by a master gardener and the calming balance of an Asian four-panel screen. Learning to create remarkable art takes years of dedication, and deeply appreciating art also takes years. An art lover once asked Picasso to create a painting for her. He slashed a few squiggles on a sheet of paper, stating a heart-stopping fee. When the art lover resisted such a fee for something so simple that he dashed off in no time, Picasso countered that it had taken him years.

4. *Know the ways of all professions.* Every way of earning a living offers lessons for how you conduct your own career. A carpenter, for example, builds a home with a good foundation, meticulously measures more than once, then makes his cut before the walls go up and the roof goes on. A master carpenter teaches careful planning and attention to details for an enduring structure. This lesson applies to nearly every endeavor.

5. *Distinguish between gain and loss in worldly matters.* Simply put, money isn't everything. Would you rather have a good reputation or another home for an occasional vacation at the cost of endless overtime and few friends? Never mind the endless to-do lists that command any visit. Learn what enough is, and when you have it, surprise yourself at how little it takes to keep hearth, health, and a bit of humor satisfied.

The next three parts of the Way have to do with the ancient wisdom of knowing the difference between Sight and Perception. Sight, or what appears to our senses, is weak, shallow, and a poor basis for a decision. Perception is strong because it's about the *meaning* behind what our senses tell us. Perception accrues through years of living, reading, studying, observing, and understanding. Socrates spent his time on the streets with the people, asking questions, learning, then teaching. Thank goodness a few students understood his profound insights and did the writing for him. Perception preserves our integrity and reputation. It considers the *effects* of words and actions, which can be harmful, even devastating, for the remainder of a lifetime.

> **Sight, or what appears to our senses, is weak, shallow, and a poor basis for a decision. Perception is strong because it's about the *meaning* behind what our senses tell us.**

So consider that word hurled in anger, the imprudent decision to cut a corner, the little lie. . . . Pause a moment and think about this for yourself, then read on.

6. *Develop intuitive judgment and understanding for everything.* Be able to look at a few situational facts then deduce the correct and often hidden meaning and subsequent prudent action. Consider especially the result of it, including hidden, long-term, and unintended consequences. Also consider the effects of your actions on others—especially the yet unborn! This suggests that every Cardinal Virtue comes into play when making decisions. Such judicious decision-making comes from lots of experience and saves backtracking and explaining. Even if that's possible, it's best not to have to do so in the first place. Be clear, knowing that a right course of action, especially on the fly, is tough. Don't be afraid of making decisions and taking action, but know when and how to make them.

7. *Perceive those things that cannot be seen.* Hidden meaning, usually the most important, lies below the surface of just about any circumstance. Seeing what can't be seen with the naked eye or meant from spoken words is also a matter of experience and a large part of being wise.

   For example, a group of entrepreneurs "saw" a quick, easy, secure way to pay for things, and now we have the ubiquitous PayPal. Elon Musk saw the day when electric cars would dominate the roads and manifested the Tesla. Now every major carmaker is racing to manufacture the next generation of electric vehicle; whole new industries are springing up; roads and cities are being redesigned, and much, much more.

   We also have Jennifer Doudna, who knew she wanted to be a biologist, against current advice, because she wanted to know how things work. The world would no longer be the same when she saw that RNA, not DNA, was the key to gene therapies. Oh—and the Nobel Prize came with that insight and the grit, determination, and vision to make gene editing possible.

   Are we as great as these people? Certainly not in the way they are. Do we have what it takes to improve our households, our neighborhoods, our wider communities? Yes! Let such people inspire you to "see" what is yours to see and do.

8. *Pay attention even to trifles.* This doesn't mean to fiddle with endless, mindless details to the point of stopping a worthy project or harming the

common good. Continually analyze whether a trifle is meaningful, contributes to progress, is not too expensive in time and effort to pursue, and contributes to worthy goals. Furthermore, you don't need to consider every facet to be 100 percent sure of an action; reasonable surety is okay. Dithering is the enemy of progress. So, take aim at your target, pull the trigger, and let the results tell you how to adjust your scope.

9. *Do nothing that's of no use.* Finally, consider how you use your time. Accomplished people are rarely idle. Even their rest, relaxation, and leisure are meaningful. It's exciting to be around people who are energized by a good and useful life trajectory. Would you like to be one of them?

One of the greatest rewards you will get from pursuing this ageless wisdom is that many people follow the Way, and you will find them or they will find you—and your life will be enriched. Clearly, moral attitude is a primary, if not *the* primary, good character trait of MAGNUS–OVÉA. One of the most important and repetitive lessons of the Way is having the right attitude, including and especially the practice of determining pertinent and valuable hidden meaning and impact.

The Twofold Gaze

A student asked his teacher, "Master, what is happiness?"

The master replied graciously, knowingly, "Grandfather die, son die, grandson die."

The stunned student cried, "Master! How can such unspeakable tragedy be happiness?"

The master answered, "Because that is the natural order of things."

This is the epitome of perspective, of "seeing" the real meaning in everything, and especially in human interaction, whether it's a thought, word, or deed. Perception largely determines how well we function in the world.

Musashi tells us to learn the "twofold gaze of sight and perception" to view self and the wider world.[211] Always "see" with perception. Take, for example a problem, obstacle, or unfortunate circumstance. Repeatedly, we're conditioned to see difficulties as obstacles "in the way" of life instead of to be expected and accepted as ways we can learn and better ourselves. But learning from adversity is not haphazard. Develop the habit of pausing and asking, "What does this really mean?"

A simple everyday example is saving money. We might go out to lunch nearly daily at remarkable annual expense and with an inefficient use of time. Packing a lunch is more nutritious, it saves a veritable moun-

> **Perceiving meaning is a skill that develops only with long and consistent study, experience, and growth.**

tain of gold, and that time can be used for a noon workout. This money plus money from similar spending could be put toward paying off a house and long-term wealth building, in which it compounds many times over. Soon, saving becomes an extremely rewarding habit. Thinking your actions through will save you from many rash and wrong judgments and their significant consequences. This doesn't mean to overanalyze everything. In the end, *reality* shows us the paths to goals and accomplishments. Understand this twofold gaze in your self-reflection.

Perceiving meaning is a skill that develops only with long and consistent study, experience, and growth. The ancients call it practice. Practice needs to begin early and continue throughout life. One insight leads to the clearer view of two more and so on. Thus, we grow. Perception is also perspective; it is learning about self.

Musashi's *A Book of Five Rings* was one of a few volumes in Napoleon's mobile command post when he was captured at Waterloo—and it's still available. (See the Bibliography.) Although it's written in martial terms, it can and must be read and reread for its hidden meaning and application to daily life. New insights occur with each reading. Be *methodical* about acting on those insights!

The question is not what you look at, but what you see.
– Henry David Thoreau

Your Journey, Your Way

You will never be a Musashi, an Aristotle, a Franklin, a Wright brother, a Mother Teresa, a Steve Jobs . . . nor need you be. But they *inspire*; and you can learn from them to be the best *you*. You can do some of the things they did in your own way to learn what life has to teach you on your own journey. You can aspire to become better and better because anyone can develop the habits of virtuous living with character and a zest for life. Proven philosophy, step-by-step strategies and tactics, research, theory, and science make the journey *practical*. The best part is you have people all around you to show you how to take the journey, to give you continuous encouragement and purpose. If you look, you will find the inspired New Wave Leaders among us.

The blessing of approaching life as a journey is that you never arrive, and that is the way you want it. Because, as a process, a continuous journey allows and reveals continuous improvement. A goal ends by its nature, whereas a process never does; thus, it has in it a bit of magic. You can always gain another insight, arrive at a better understanding, see further, and have revealed to you the true meaning of something.

This journey is *not* a prescription, a "ten best" list of things to do. How can a way of life be reduced to a presentation, opinion, or checklist? It cannot. Becoming your best is just that, yours. It is very personal. You design the process, and how well and faithfully you pursue what you design is entirely your decision. If you accept the journey as worthy and make it happen by providing commitment, discipline, and dedication, you will inevitably benefit and, yes, prosper. Each accomplishment, each insight, only affords a better view of what is next and who you can become.

A flourishing life depends on our responding, as best we can,
to those things uniquely incumbent on us.[212]
– Epictetus

Personally Speaking

Interest Begets Interesting

James Klopovic

One of my ongoing purposes in life is to become the kind of person with whom I myself would wish to keep company. I think of my skeet-shooting buddy. Not only does he improve my game by being much better than I am, but the whole experience is enhanced by his interesting conversation.

My life is enriched by his company, and I wish to likewise enrich others.

I've found that to become an interesting person who attracts other interesting people, first and foremost, it's important to read. Some say travel first to experience other countries and peoples, but you can read almost anywhere any time, and you don't need a passport. I've built a small library of books on topics such as travel, ancient philosophy, health, managing wealth, cooking, biographies, hobbies, and good old fiction and nonfiction adventure tales. I often read in stolen moments during the day, and I enjoy learning. Besides, reading is a key to good communication and thus communicating your point in conversations, teaching, and yes, leading. In my opinion, unless you're scuba diving, there's no excuse to be without a book. Of course, if you'd rather watch than read, you can view the best lecturers in the world and other educational programs online from just about anywhere.

When reading or watching isn't enough, I like to travel to interesting places and experience all that's on offer—especially the history. I've seen Lenin in his glass sarcophagus, and I've looked down on eagles soaring above the clouds *below* me on the Appalachian Trail at 3,600 feet. Likewise, I've watched a rare pair of condors floating, circling, and "guarding" the rock formations at Zion National Park. The sheer drop-offs of hundreds of feet still make my heart flutter when I think of them.

With all that's available to see and do on this third rock from the sun, there's a reason much of the world comes to this country for their vacations. Let's take advantage of the wonders out our "back door."

While I've done my fair share of backpacking, lately I've gravitated to car camping. I no longer relish hauling a 35-pound pack to a campsite at 4,500 feet, then having to set up camp in the rain. Still, I have fond memories of my backpacking adventures and even wrote *The Honest Backpacker: A Practical Guide for the Rookie Adventurer over 50*.[213] Backpacking led to day-packing on England's Coast to Coast trail, hiking from one picturesque, homey BnB to the next. I've gathered memories galore—from chocolate-covered orange rinds to visiting the present owners of a former Viking farm.

Anyone can become more interesting by taking up a good hobby or two and undertaking challenging activities. As I mentioned, I like to shoot a little skeet. (Sometimes it makes me say indiscrete things, but I always come back. Can't get enough of it.) Meeting fellow shooters has led me to rafting world renowned rivers, bird and duck hunting, and fishing for world-class fish (mostly catch and release). More adventure!

It's often interesting to make the acquaintance of strangers. I find they wish me to make the first move. These connections mutually build upon one another more than might have occurred without my first overture. I struck up a conversation with a fellow who asked to shoot a round of skeet with me. This was on a Friday. By Tuesday morning, I was in Miami, Florida, with the "Tarponator"—the uncontested best tarpon guide in the world, not an exaggeration. Given my long life so far, I've found that if I'm engaged and involved and inquisitive enough, I'll have something in common with just about anyone.

Shifting venues to the home front, I also like to cook a bit. Learning the culinary arts began when I won an apple pie baking contest at age 53. The silver bowl and blue ribbon rest on my bookshelf of life mementos as proof. That led to cooking dinners for close friends, which included about seven hours of too many stories to count and laughter aplenty. There's much to learn and do to enrich life!

Therefore, my advice to you is to learn, think, and do as many interesting things as you can. In becoming an interesting person, you'll attract interesting people around you in a virtuous, energizing cycle. These practices promote well-being, which brings true happiness.

*Twenty years from now you will be more disappointed by the things that you
didn't do than by the ones you did do. So, throw off the bowlines,
sail away from safe harbor, catch the trade winds in your sails.
Explore, Dream, Discover.*
– Author unverified

Chapter 10

New Wave Leadership – Myths, Principles, Imperatives

Where there is discord, may we bring harmony. Where there is error,
may we bring truth. Where there is doubt, may we bring faith.
And where there is despair, may we bring hope.
– St. Francis of Assisi

Leadership again? What more can be said? We are living the reality of the new enlightenment activated by science, technology, creativity, and innovation. This dramatic new era demands a timely reinterpretation of the wisdom of the ages. Riding the cusp of a wave of innovation in which machines do more and more of our work, we'll have more time to reach our potentials. So yes, leadership again. These historically exciting times demand a response. What will we do with such opportunity?

Principles of Successful Leadership in a New Era

Great leadership is not simply "yesterday's news" to be ignored. It's imperative that we rediscover old truths and principles of leadership and combine them with today's realities, insights, opportunities, and discoveries to create our tomorrow. The world has endured many seismic shifts, from the COVID-19 pandemic to the advance of communism to the exploration of space and our own genes. We, the people, need leaders that bring us meaning, identity, and hope[214] and guide us to compel progress for the highest good of all.

Of course various levels of leadership exist, from the president of the country to CEOs of companies to the heads of agencies, various organizations, and yes, families.

Leadership going forward is not formulaic, and anyone can lead in his or her own sphere of influence.

When we understand New Wave Leadership, we see good examples all around us—and *within* us. It's not the kind of leadership that comes from a particular combination of skills, knowledge, and abilities. No longer are only certain people responsible to lead, nor does achieving certain results or numbers define leadership.

> **The essence of successful New Wave Leadership is expressed in dedication, devotion, and love for serving others, and in being values driven and ethical in all you do.**

Understand that *you* are an ethical being with a guiding vision of the organization you lead, no matter its size. Leadership for this New Wave is not a secret or reserved for the chosen few; it's a matter of knowing you can make a difference.

The essence of successful New Wave Leadership is expressed in dedication, devotion, and love for serving others, and in being values driven and ethical in all you do. For example, all of us have the capacity to be quietly generous. This hierarchy ends in love, romantic and platonic, because it's the most positive of emotions, and it sparks acts great and small that make a difference. Because love encompasses the *joy* of play, *interest* in exploring, *contentment*, which is savoring life's beauty, gifts, and pleasures, and the *integration* of all three.[215] With love, you link directly to the concept of OVÉA because positive emotions are activators. Genuine love creates within you a positive hormonal reaction that significantly enhances your well-being and helps you create a productive, worthy life—and thus to lead well.

Again, we get our inspiration and example for how to take command from the wisest of us, from ancient to modern leaders, who admonished that we must live virtuously before we can lead well at all. This applies no matter who we are, no matter where we are, no matter the circumstances in which we find ourselves. In fact, exemplary leaders may be standing right next to us. So, the question is not about a specific definition of leadership, but about how we rise to the moment by demonstrating New Wave principles.

An attractive personality can be a great asset in life. Other people will like you,
which is important. But if your character is fundamentally flawed,
you'll never know the true meaning of success.
– Steven R. Covey

More Timeless Advice from Past Millenia

Cyrus the Great was a "New Wave" Leader over 2,500 years ago! What did he teach us about ourselves as leaders? The answers validate major themes of this book:[216]

- *Serve as a moral compass to others.* Ethical principles are the only way to prepare for responsibility and ensure we progress with it.

- *Take constant care to secure the well-being of all around you.* Build a followership of collaborators who know how to thrive individually and, especially, collectively.

- *Absorb as much knowledge as possible.* Cyrus began from childhood to imagine empires in his mind before he fulfilled that destiny.

- *Seize the unexpected opportunity.* This implies the principle of perceiving the meaning of what you see: perception beyond sight. Opportunities abound, but few see them or know how to take advantage of them.

- *Inspire your collaborators/followers with a vision.* Be the symbol of a vision by your character, word, deed, and connection to those you serve. Earn the right to be admired.

- *Know when to keep your own counsel.* Seek the advice of others, yes. But be truly introspective so you know your strengths and weaknesses. Have a wealth of knowledge to know when and how to decide, act, and make that action work.

- *Make people all they ought to be.* Learn to be ethical and brave in taking worthy challenges. In any position, even the most obscure, work hard at being outstanding. Encourage and inspire others to do the same.

A key to leadership, then, is to learn to live early on with virtue, character, and morals so you can be a beacon for others. As you immerse yourself in this process, you will realize you're content and secure and have no need to chase the fleeting nature of happiness. Rather, you will embody it.

Many of our greatest leaders rose from obscurity, first doing whatever jobs they landed, but doing those jobs *very well*. Eisenhower, a major at the time, was an assistant to General MacArthur. McArthur commented that Major Eisenhower was the best aide he'd ever had when good people were needed for key positions in

World War II (WWII). Hence, Ike became General Eisenhower—and later our 34th president. Had he not done his absolute best from the beginning, history would have been written by others. We all can write a bit of history in our own spheres, and that is enough.

Three Essentials of New Wave Leadership

Who you are today is not who you will be a day from now, a year from now, decades from now. Imagine yourself epitomizing the following essentials of leading, adapted from General Stanley McChrystal's seminal work on leadership, *Leaders: Myth and Reality.*[217] (Read it, again and again.) New Wave Leadership displays these elements:

- *Vision* – A New Wave Leader can *conceive a different future* and reminds us that something better *is* possible, especially in rough times.

- *Character* – A New Wave Leader symbolizes how to *be an exemplary human* and inspires such character in all.

- *Competencies* – New Wave Leaders captivate audiences and *communicate the best of human values* in word, deed, and manner. They are ethical, brave, wise, and moderate *every* day.

These are the essentials we aim to achieve, personally and professionally, little by little, day by day. As McChrystal asserts, "Get the leader right and all else falls into place."[218]

Leadership Fallacies

Many often misconstrue how leaders come into being. One of the most striking realizations arising from this research is that most of our more effective and illustrious leaders had no formal training in leadership. They achieved their status by developing massive knowledge from study and experience and emulating mentors. These leaders learned from ancient philosophy, the exploits of modern leaders, and the legends and biographies of successful people. They represent New Wave Leaders in that they formed their own path by educated instinct, moral practices, understanding the human condition, and hard work. Many of these forward-thinking leaders knew they could shape their own destinies—and they did!

As we introduced in Chapter 2, McChrystal observes three myths concerning leadership: the Formulaic Myth, the Attribution Myth, and the Results Myth. Let's take a deeper look at these misconceptions and learn from them.

Formulaic Myth

Leadership offers no formula. It's largely contextual,[219] meaning that fate and luck play a huge hand in leadership effectiveness. In the days of the sail, the lash, the cannon, and the broad sword, naval battles were sometimes determined by an ill or favorable wind! Admiral Nelson at Trafalgar simply was up wind. All he had to do was turn at a right angle to slice right through the French and Spanish fleets. First, however, he had to perceive, not just see, the advantage of a crosswind that presented itself. Then and only then could brilliant technical seamanship prevail. Nelson went against naval convention, which held that tall ships would glide past each other broadside and blast away, the winner being the last boat afloat. Furthermore, in this famous, world-changing battle, Nelson was in the lead ship; he had to prevail. Result: The British captured 19 ships and lost none. Consequence: Lord Nelson put a halt to Napoleon's plans to invade and subjugate England—the beginning of Napoleon's end. All because the wind blew in the right direction in front of a man who perceived what it meant and knew what to do.

Most of our more effective and illustrious leaders had no formal training in leadership. They achieved their status by developing massive knowledge from study and experience and emulating mentors.

How did the Admiral prepare himself for this day? He had great enthusiasm for his job, a deep sense of duty to his country, courage, an aptitude for sailing, and love for the men he led.[220] Other than that, he couldn't have prepared for that particular situation. It was up to the wind. The battle of Trafalgar demonstrated a complex, chaotic reality. The Brits were outgunned and outmanned. But Horatio Nelson, a brilliant, brave man standing five feet four inches tall with only one eye and one arm perceived at the time what he needed to do to be successful—and became a giant of history. The world tilted on its axis the few hours of that battle, favorably for Britain because one man prepared himself to inspire and lead and was able to seize the moment!

Winston Churchill grasped the opportunity of WWII to express the totality of his legendary gifts only after spending a lifetime of becoming prepared for this "darkest hour." He suffered years of sting, even humiliation, hammering alone on the threat of Hitler. Leadership is not formed from a cookie cutter. Making good decisions without fear depends on personal preparation and momentary realities many times missed by the herd.

Great military leaders won battles, yes; then they did the most important work of managing what they had won. They did it with genius hands-on participatory guidance, which is why their work and legacy endure. Take the example of winning WWII. This could have resulted in something like the Treaty of Versailles after WWI, which punished Germany. Thus, it made the Germans more fierce enemies, who began scheming the next world war nearly before the ink of the treaty was dry. The United States brilliantly closed WWII by implementing the Marshall Plan conceived by George C. Marshall to collaboratively rebuild Europe into democracies and trading partners, stronger than ever before. *That* is leadership.

In execution, therefore, leadership is highly contextual, wedding circumstance, inspiration, and good judgment for success. Plans must bend to reality; the New Wave Leader adjusts and takes action from preparation, constitution, and intuitive decision that defies the regimentation of equations. The prepared, able individual recognizes how to put people and resources to work depending on the situation and its practicalities. The New Wave Leader ". . . (encourages) a whole organization to become great together"[221] via earned mutual trust and respect.

Therefore, don't look for a magic potion or a list of proven skills, whether you're leading your family or a corporation. There is no recipe. Be ready for leadership, and you will know it when you get it right. It feels good because you earn respect, and your organization can see and feel advancement.

The Attribution Myth

Neither is good, intuitive leadership about *attribution*. It's not automatically bestowed on those who attended the right schools[222] or those born into the right family. While those people may be conferred responsibility or position, winning the day goes to the one who understands that calling the shots is an immediate, dynamic, fluid situation. The best leaders plan while expecting reality to alter circumstances. A plan is only a beginning to anticipate and answer commotion. What was done one time merely informs the next instance but doesn't determine it. Timing is ultimate.

Thus, the New Wave Leader must be responsive, which gets back to moral grounding: Is the action right? Do you have the knowledge base to make good decisions? Do you have the courage to take that action? Are you frugal with the effort, especially with your human capital? Greatness arises not from one who inspires superior individuals, but from creating conditions where everyone is great together.

Attribution ignores the reality that the leader is bound to followers who innately defy the restrictions of regimentation. People can be unpredictable, moody, demanding, disappointing—yet dynamic, deep, and driven not merely to succeed but to do the good, the great, and at times, as in Churchill's England, the glorious. Our institutions depend on people, and all the

> **The New Wave Leader's job is to cultivate collaborators, not followers nor individuals who compete against one another.**

better when those people are inspired to do the gritty work necessary to accomplish good things well, all rowing rhythmically, forcefully in the same direction to the meter of "our leader." The organization knows when it is being led by a leader who "gets it."

The Results Myth

The third myth is that getting *results* is more important than what the person in charge stands for. Again, not so. Results—usually "the numbers"—are a byproduct of a well-oiled, well led organization. How do we get good results with these new realities? New Wave Leadership. Effective leaders symbolize character, values, and a dream—a vision of something grander than any one person, something just out of reach that can only be achieved by energized collective effort.

New Wave Leadership, then, is bound in a *system* of people who are taught to collaborate on a goal over the horizon. This is another dimension entirely than just cooperating on projects to get them to the end of the day. Thus, the New Wave Leader's job is to cultivate collaborators, not followers nor individuals who compete against one another.

Leaders for today and especially tomorrow share successes and defeat and press on. They find their place as part of the system, not at the traditional top looking down. Thus, they provide firsthand meaning and guidance, eye-to-eye in a network that engenders human potential. They realize the wonderful burdens of a position that's not about glamour can be painful and confusing, but it's worth every minute it affords. Succeeding at something bigger than we are provides a near ethereal feeling.

Yes, these are the realities of necessary leadership for tomorrow that we need to establish today. We drive home the point that all this matters little if the responsible people are timid in acting. Perhaps they are worried about looking bad, concerned about protecting their position, or fear failure. Successful people make decisions on 40-60 percent of the possible information and analysis, but with input from collective wisdom, they know when that decision is good and right. They fear the risk of not trying much more than the risk of taking a chance.

Napoleon lost more battles than he won! Steve Jobs got fired from his beloved Apple. They didn't let that stop them. Napoleon became emperor in his 20s, left us the Concordat, which officially ended the French Revolution, and much more. Mr. Jobs ended up revolutionizing six, yes six, major industries[223] and fulfilled his vision of putting "a ding in the universe." So, *act* as a New Wave Leader. Leave a legacy.

Effective leaders know what style of leadership applies to their role and particular situation.[224] How do they know it when opportunity falls at their feet? They can "see" it, even feel it, from experience, study, practice, and innate perception. Attention to reasonable detail matters, reasonable analysis matters, and being reasonably prepared for the unexpected matters. But being 100 percent prepared is impossible, and trying to be is the enemy of progress. Forward movement happens with just enough analysis, thought, and preparation that allow the "feeling" that it's time to act. Action is born of collective thought and consultation and knowing that leadership is about making decisions.

Myths, Realities, and New Wave Leadership – A Brief Comparison

We need to understand the basics, the nuances, the *how* of becoming a New Wave Leader so we can bring it to the student, the internet, the classroom, and the factory floor. A direct, simple comparison will help. Figure 5 summarizes leadership myths, realities, and the New Wave path.

Myth	**Reality**	*New Wave*
There's a *formula* for leadership.	*Context* matters, which often is complicated, dynamic, fluid, and unpredictable.	Leaders perceive the *meaning* of the moment and act accordingly.
Leadership is an *attribution*, or appointment.	*System* matters. The organization is a system of people collaborating toward a common good. The whole is greater than the sum of its parts. Inspired followership matters.	The *path* (journey, process) is primary because it leads to meaningful ends.
Numbers mean successful *results*.	*Symbolism* matters. Meaning, purpose, and symbolism of virtues and values energize the action.	Goals are achieved by *collaboration* between matrices of partners and coworkers focused on a motivating vision led by an inspiring person.

Figure 5: Leadership Myths and New Wave Realities

Leadership Going Forward

Realities demand a new wave of leadership that's not solely about rules and regulations imposed from the top but about *meaning*. It doesn't matter how good the rules and policies are if the character and conduct of the leader don't drive the work. Thus, a primary, if not the primary job of the leader is to inspire, yes, but to create good followers who know they have an essential part of the whole and can make their part work. Effective leadership is founded on the legitimacy of those in charge, which in turn is based on the leaders' moral fiber, character, and vision. Leaders must be congruent in thought, word, and deed, and even in appearance. They must understand they are fulfilling the collective need, the basic human instinct and drive, for accomplishment.

The corrosive statement by Machiavelli that "The end justifies the means" is, well, Machiavellian. Oppressive management can appear to get results but, in the end, the "whip" begets only a shell of what *could* have been achieved. The path, the *journey*, the "how" matters. The old rules, epitomized by "The end justifies the means," rarely have value, especially in a moral context, and rarely succeed to actualize individual and organizational potential in the long term.

We need to study and master how to mentor, motivate, and move the organization as a collaborative unit. Individuals matter, of course, but their collective will and momentum matter more. It's not about motivating the "servants" on the bottom of the pile; it's about motivating the whole shebang—line staff, management, and leadership—as nodes of a people-centric network interacting and acting as one. Top down, hierarchical command-and-control bureaucracies may survive, but they will *not* flourish in the new normal of this new century.

It's always been about multiplying strengths. We've stressed throughout this book that the whole is always greater than the sum when individuals are taught how to work in matrices of problem-solving collectives. There's a reason luminaries of New Wave industries such as Facebook, Apple, NetFlix, and Google have flowing offices that allow staff to mingle. Creative ideas and combined energies become reality compelled by a well-spoken narrative of inspiring ideals. The public, and especially other private sector companies, can learn from these successful examples.

Thus, leaders are not about collecting a given list of skills, knowledge, and abilities. Per General McChrystal, "They should be *equipped* with an understanding of leadership as a system, see themselves as the *enablers* of that system [that builds collaborators], and learn how to *adjust* their approach based on the *needs* of that system."[225] (Italics by author)

Leadership going forward, starting now, is about more than how we learn to lead; it's about how we prepare new generations of New Wave Leaders. That mentorship is a major part of our legacy. In other words, our responsibility as the next wave of leaders is to teach those who follow how to be collaborators who build healthy systems, who encourage feedback and participation. New Wave Leaders are called to be good stewards of all with whom they're entrusted. Good stewardship provides:

- *Meaning* – With this, we teach the simplicity of moral living because this guides our words, deeds, and actions. When we grasp meaning, we are more inclined to promote the good for all. Said another way, what we do we do for others thus we do for ourselves. It behooves us to do a good job—no, the *best* job we can—and thus we all win.

- *Purpose* – We have a place in this world and an obligation to improve it— but as New Wave Leaders, we go beyond obligation and duty to caring.

- *Identity* – We realize our common identity as human beings. With this, we affirm the worth of those we lead, treating all with dignity and respect.

- *Hope* – We emphasize what is promising, especially in troubled times. Essentially, we envision tomorrow as truly a brighter day.

The progress of society begins with individual commitment to consistent, persistent dedication, if not devotion, to acting with values. Thus, we become that person we ourselves admire, good stewards of those in our charge, and role models to others around us. This is how we pay it forward. When we do it all with meaning, purpose, identity, and hope, it is good.

Imperatives to Live By

Imperatives move us way beyond our current understanding of how we manage organizations and lead people today. Getting New Wave Leadership right is vital going forward in the new reality, the new normal of artificial intelligence, gene editing, interplanetary colonization, and hydrogen fuels with all their serious cautions and fabulous possibilities. Anyone in *any* circumstance of importance must be dynamic, insightful, and flexible. They'll need to be: *dynamic* in their ability to adjust to the ground realities of the moment; *insightful* in recognizing what it all means; and *flexible* enough to adapt given the best decisions of the moment.

Thus, we come to the imperatives of New Wave Leadership—how to begin then accelerate our ability to lead well. Although you'll recognize that this whole book is steeped in these imperatives, it helps to repeat them in a slightly different way, just as a teabag provides more flavor each time it's dipped in hot water.

Accountability, or personal and communal responsibility to behave ethically, is paramount for any individual and especially for a group collaborating on a vision.

Imperative of Building Character

As noted in previous chapters, character is built by ongoing habitual action to build personal physical, intellectual, and social strengths and resources. As we make good decisions daily, it becomes easier to make the next good decision. Likewise, as we make bad decisions, it becomes easier to make bad decisions. We build our character one decision, one action at a time.

Consider those you've noticed are struggling though life. Does a criminal start with the most egregious crimes? Not usually. They commit small crimes and graduate to more serious crimes, one decision at a time. Conversely, think about the impact of good decisions. When you resist temptation, it becomes easier to resist temptation the next time. Whether you're seeking to exercise more, become well, learn to thrive, be more patient, or improve yourself in some other way, start with building the resources of character.

It is impossible to improve our individual lives or our society without genuinely caring about and striving to improve personal character.
– Russell W. Gough, author of *Character is Destiny*

Imperative of Living with Virtue

Virtue is moral excellence. As we strive for moral excellence, we need to be self-aware, willing to evaluate where we are in our life trajectory compared to where we desire to be. When we evaluate ourselves, we can seek to strengthen those virtues we desire or need to strengthen through daily, even minute-to-minute, practice.

Evidence and stories of how to live with virtue fill libraries. The topic goes back eons. As humans emerged, we had to decide how to live well. Make this a lifetime pursuit and study. It will put you hand in hand with some of our greats and how they became great. Choose someone you would like to emulate—and be inspired.

Imperative of Being Accountable

Accountability, or personal and communal responsibility to behave ethically, is paramount for any individual and especially for a group collaborating on a vision. Many of the struggles we see around us come from an unwillingness to properly prioritize accountability. Consider the significant loss for any employer who must spend precious dollars, time, and energy to investigate employee misconduct. Such costs of bad behavior are galactic and chip away at our fabric as a country.

What if every employee took accountability seriously? How much better if they self-corrected in a timely manner. Even better if the error or misbehavior was prevented to begin with—for example, with character training, which fosters self-accountability. The savings would be considerable, and the resulting improvement in character would benefit not only the organization but the municipality and country as a whole.

Imperative of Having a Positive Attitude

Attitude matters, which is another major theme of becoming a New Wave Leader. A positive attitude is infectious. Try passing on a cheerful thought or offering someone, anyone, a simple sincere greeting and a smile. Watch what happens to that person and notice how it makes you feel. Conversely, a bad attitude can also be infectious. The good news is, no matter what we encounter, we can control our attitude toward the circumstance. We can use our attitude as another tool to become better and better, more and more resilient.

In reference to Barbara Fredrickson's Broaden-and-Build Theory of Positive Emotions, she writes:

> *People should cultivate positive emotions in their own lives and in the lives of those around them, not just because doing so makes them feel good in the moment, but also because doing so transforms people for the better and sets them on paths toward flourishing and healthy longevity.*[226]

The significance of Fredrickson's study is that a good attitude is critical to our well-being, which, we maintain, is the basis of thriving. Our ability to thrive happens *over time*, and a positive attitude is a factor in achieving robust longevity. The ability to keep our attitudes in perspective through both victories and adversity is necessary to our success in life—on the job and especially at home. As Fredrickson notes, we can radically better all aspects of who we are simply by adopting a positive attitude.

Leaders now and of the future develop positive attitudes that step up their ability to maintain top performance.

Imperative of Being Responsible

In discussing responsibility, we consider what lies beyond duty and obligation. Duty is based on moral law, which we accept and adhere to as we perform, such as when we take an oath of office in the military or an oath of fidelity in marriage. We do this willingly and are expected to follow our oaths. Obligation, on the other hand, is born of societal standards we hold to facilitate communal living. We formally commit to do something, which might be to accept a job and its responsibilities. The provider wants to legally obligate the consumer to be accountable for the transaction. While both are important and play a roll, we do well to recognize the differences. Personal responsibility, automatically doing what is right and proper, matters. This could range from taking care of your children to not littering the streets to picking up after your dog to being responsible for the safety of your employees. It means acting out of respect for everyone involved and doing your part for the highest good of everyone involved. It takes thought and consideration, whatever the situation.

> **The ability to keep our attitudes in perspective through both victories and adversity is necessary to our success in life—on the job and especially at home.**

The New Wave Leader in Action

Let's look at some of the qualities portrayed by leaders who have done remarkable things—not by formula or through appointment due to rank or pedigree or by achieving certain numbers at the end of a quarter:[227]

- *Kinship* – Creating an environment where the group acts with a *common spirit.* People are invigorated to come to the job and work to build something good. Kinship is about building excellent relationships. The New Wave Leader understands the intricacies of the human condition and behaviors.

- *Connection* – Encouraging others in times of trouble, inspiring others in times of crisis, and being gracious with success. The New Wave Leader mutually *bonds* with people, individually and collectively.

- *Tenacity* – Displaying *determination*—sometimes nearly beyond endurance—such as pursuing a career for decades and rarely diminishing the effort of it. Committing to a cause and seeing it through. The New Wave Leader understands a job continuously done well is a virtue compared to the vices of perfectionism and carelessness on either side of professionalism.

- *Action* – Taking action, a leadership theme from antiquity through today. For example, Bill Gates predicted the COVID-19 pandemic five years before Wuhan. Plus, he had the contacts, resources, funds, and especially plans to put the best drug development innovation, effective strategies, and complex logistics to immediate effect. He was ready for this moment because he reads voraciously and made himself action ready. You can't know without perception. The New Wave Leader perceives the meaning of real-time facts, which enables him or her to make the best decisions and *act* in that snapshot of time.

- *Example* – Symbolizing the best. Understanding the work of the organization, what motivates people, and that little things matter. New Wave Leaders live, even radiate, *the best* of the organization. They know their followers watch, learn, imitate, and in turn, lead. It is by example that the leader creates a *team* of leaders.

How does our present conception of leadership relate to New Wave Leadership? This is crucial to understand for three elemental reasons: First, so we can prepare ourselves for increasing, novel responsibilities, both personal and corporate. Second, so we can become and model the best of New Wave Leadership. Most important, so we can educate and develop the next generation of leaders who can thrive in our rapidly evolving systems of governance and industry.

This new blueprint of leadership has implications for how we teach leadership by combining the realities of the present with the demands of the future to craft what McChrystal calls the ". . . visceral sense of the possible."[228]

Action Items from New Wave Forerunners

Again, let's go right to the top for specific examples of how to lead in the new normal, the new reality. In Chapter 2, we mentioned the seminal work of Doris K. Goodwin in her book *Leadership in Turbulent Times*. She profiles four of our presidents who were significant for the crises they endured: Abraham Lincoln, Theodore Roosevelt,

---

This new blueprint of leadership has implications for how we teach leadership by combining the realities of the present with the demands of the future.

Franklin D. Roosevelt, and Lyndon B. Johnson. These leaders changed our republic for the better and set the bar for the future New Wave Leader. They embodied transformational leadership, crisis management, and vision with historical struggle and consequence. They *foretold* New Wave Leaders. They are most instructive, particularly Lincoln, because they offer proven, practical New Wave action items you can employ now. Following, in no particular hierarchy, are some of the most pertinent:[229]

- *Understand the emotional needs of others.* Never forget you work in complex, human systems. Getting your organizational human capacity right is paramount to successes small and big.

   I don't like that man. I must get to know him better.
   – Abraham Lincoln

- *Be accessible and approachable.* This doesn't mean being one of the staff but rather sharing the burdens of the job with them. Know their situations, even of their families; empathize, learn their difficulties, sincerely connect. This consists of more art and heart than technique and a play book. People *recognize* sincerity.

- *Learn from failure and try again.* Those who succeeded surmounted a litany of continuous woes and failure and continued anyway.

- *Gather real-time and front-line information. Ask questions—a lot of them.* Being informed includes much more than years of study and experience. It's difficult to overstate the importance of experience, accurate information, and data interpreted by your front line.

- *Find time and space in which to rest your mind.* It's important to isolate yourself properly. Use this time judiciously. Don't allow isolation to invite unproductive (senseless) rumination, repetition, and even irrational fear. Many successful people devote a regular time and place to just sit, away from any stimulation. They've learned to meditate to calm the mind and be present in the moment—a good, productive practice that allows healing of the nervous system and insights that may not have surfaced otherwise.

Truly resting the mind is also a time to concentrate on breathing properly. Science now proves good breathing habits are linked to physical and mental health and *longevity*.[230] Deep, correct breathing, as the data show, is a greater predicter of longevity than diet, exercise, and heredity! The lesson: Learn the ancient arts of meditation (10 minutes a day) and yoga (only two sessions per week) as if your life depends on it . . . because it well might.

- *Find ways to cope with pressure, maintain balance, and replenish energy.* This is much different from finding time and space to think. Everyone needs time to maintain themselves, relax, recreate, and do leisure activities for personal betterment. We discussed this before in the ways to use your time. Learn what each involves; there's a significant difference. Making the time to do so actually *saves* time in that you're ready and able to address the stresses and challenges of the day.

- *Compromise when possible; decide when necessary.* Compromise can be unending quibbling about this detail and that, searching to satisfy all. So are foolhardy, uninformed choices. Know when to act; that is the only way to see what works. Never compromise on universal moral principles.

- *Anticipate opposing viewpoints.* Differentiate between contrary, antagonizing views meant to tear down from constructive comments meant to build up. Prepare for the first, encourage the latter. Full advocacy, pro and con, aids decisions and the vital timing of them. Free-flowing exchange from a diversity of viewpoints ensures you see things more clearly, understand strengths and especially weaknesses, and tap the best ideas and solutions.

- *When you decide, assume full responsibility.* This points to another quality of a New Wave thinker—self-analysis. When a thing is done well or especially not so well, it's a particularly good habit to ask, *What did I do (well or) wrong?* Then adjust. You are ultimately the cause of the result. Things won't improve unless you do. When you engage in automatic accountability and take extreme ownership, you build trust and self-respect.

- *Shield your collaborators from blame.* This fits with assuming responsibility. Misplaced blame, or finger pointing, ruins morale. It's to be expected in good collaboration that someone will err, but as the leader, you are ultimately complicit in whatever happens.

- *Transcend personal vendettas.* Life will tempt you with recrimination. People malign each other; that's the plain truth. Your reaction to this unhealthy human condition matters. Realize when it's happening and resist confrontation when possible. If it's unjust, bring the matter, well considered, to the offending party. Don't let the situation deter you from recognizing the offender's overall contribution, especially if both parties make amends. It takes huge restraint to be compassionate and patient. Ask yourself how you or your system might adjust to avoid such situations.

- *Set a standard of mutual respect and dignity, and control anger.* Biographies of the greats are fascinating for many reasons. One of the most compelling reasons is seeing how uncontrollably angry they could get yet still restrain themselves with enormous effort. Our George Washington was famously volcanic, which few witnessed. Those who did made legends of the event, blistering language and all. Washington knew the damage of it, thus held himself in check, let a little time pass, and regained his equally legendary composure, dignity, and moderation. Usually, a piercing glance of his blue-grey eyes was all that was needed to command respect and commitment, if not a little fear.

- *Maintain perspective and composure with praise and especially with abuse.* The human response is to preen or return barb for barb, respectively. Each, though prevalent, is imprudent. Basking in praise or returning abuses distracts from the truths of the matter; a battle may be won but the war lost. Use your energy to understand what the accolade or rebuke really means.

- *Keep your word. Say what you will do and do it.* Consider carefully what you will do as your word means you will see the thing to its natural end. Understand the implications of commitment, make sure what you intend to do is a worthy and doable thing, then do it. Have the courage to accept when further effort is futile and abandon the work. That, too, is keeping your word. Make your word your bond. It's the basis of mutual trust.

- *Know the difference between prudent restraint and prudent action.* In the vernacular, know when to hold 'em, when to fold 'em, and when to play 'em. This is the essence of decision making: intensely considering all the variables involved then acting appropriately. Something must happen beyond deliberation unless the decision is not to act.

- *Combine transactional and transformational guidance.* Be the master of the transaction; that is, be adept at gaining support and swaying conduct. At the same time, transform the organization by symbolizing, or exemplifying, good temperament and values with the message that the organization is doing something necessary, big, worthy. Develop shared purpose and direction.

Such are the lessons we can learn from four of our most eminent presidents. What we're describing here is Aristotle's Magnanimous Man. As the greats argue, life is a struggle; make it worthy. They rightly observe that nothing less than happiness results from the earnest struggle of the life's work of becoming a person with a noble, selfless soul.

A nation that forgets its past has no future.
– Winston Churchill

The Way Ahead – Beginning as a Great Follower

Great leaders begin as great followers. What does this mean? First, we need to clear up a common and outdated misconception. Ira Chaleff, author of *The Courageous Follower: Standing Up to & for Our Leaders*, observes that the kind of followership we're used to is people gathering to accomplish a goal.[231] He explains the outdated view is that roles are fairly well defined; the leader essentially leads and others are expected to follow, top down, in a hierarchical

> New Wave Leaders realize that true effectiveness derives from the front line collaborating with supervision, management, and leadership. This creates a culture of safety for ideas.

manner. How many of us have heard variations of "It's my way or the highway"? Here, followers either see themselves or are seen as docile, conforming, just taking direction. In the extreme, this implies that a follower is weak and possibly a failure when it comes to contributing to the potential of the group. Leaders discourage discussion, even professional argument—and thus stifle creativity. Such a viewpoint is the diametric opposite of successful New Wave Leadership and followership, *both* of which are multi-disciplinary and participatory. The sooner we move beyond this belief and get comfortable with the idea of influential *collaborator*-followers supporting powerful leaders, the sooner we can fully develop and test models for dynamic, self-responsible, synergistic relationships in our organizations.

Followers in the New Wave naturally have new responsibilities to reflect this next wave, the revolution of industry, and our development as a country. They need to learn how to be accountable to the community of the organization, and with that, learn how to hold present leadership accountable—respectfully, dutifully. Yes, they still take directives from leadership, but here is the New Wave twist: They also ensure information travels back up the organizational hierarchy as well as down. This assumes that present leadership establishes a no-fault environment in which mistakes will be seen as part of the process, ways to learn, opportunities to get better. Also, New Wave Leaders realize that true effectiveness derives from the front line collaborating with supervision, management, and leadership. This creates a culture of safety for ideas in which people can fail forward within reason. Mistakes are part of the productive process of progress. In this environment, followers can become stronger, more creative, and more disciplined by becoming more and more capable. They help build an organizational culture in which members benefit from the disorder of figuring things out and delivering on promises. This describes the organization that nurtures increasingly vibrant followers.

The great insight of this way forward is that just about anyone can learn to lead if they put their back, mind, and soul into the work of it. This brings up another point. Yes, we dwell on describing the practicalities of New Wave Leadership, but those of us writing code, bending wrenches, driving the forklift must be responsible also. The wisdom of being as strong as the weakest link comes to mind.

You don't want to be that weak link. You are integral to the foundation of the organization being built. You are working for a man or a woman, not a god. Understand and help that person when he or she stumbles. Be a symbol of ethics and character. Understand the significant difference between cooperation and collaboration and be that collaborator-follower. Realize you are part of the next wave of New Wave Leaders and take responsibility to learn, to be ready. This takes more than your sweat; it takes your creative ideas, your problem solutions, collaboration. So, give it. Recognize the best job you have is the one you have right now. Remember you are the heartbeat of your organization. Everyone leads, even the least of us.

> *. . . [L]eadership is now about improving the overall progress of humanity.*
> – General Stanley McChrystal

Personally Speaking

Making My Way

James Klopovic

I must confess that as a young Air Force Airman First Class, A1C, on my first assignment to the Far East for 18 months, it was all about the countdown. Even six months away from "rotating" back stateside, we ticked off the days to the final day, which we counted down in hours, then minutes—yes, minutes!

For that year and a half, we put our heads down and worked. We had assigned duties, we did them, then we moved on to the next one, 10 hours a day, sometimes six days a week. We marked the passing months by the looks of our ballcaps as they became a bit tattered, stained from aircraft lube, and comfy, worn at just the right angle.

In those early days in the Air Force, we would say with some truth, "We do the difficult every day; the impossible takes a little longer." We progressed by saying yes to the difficult but worthwhile and making it work. Looking back on that troop of boys, many of us still teenagers, we didn't know that what we were doing couldn't be done, so we did it.

Some of us grew up and some grew more acrimonious. It's all about perspective—the difference between surviving moment to moment to seeing and living the big picture and thriving in the process. Succeeding through adversity is self-motivating, self-affirming, self-fulling; it's learning to thrive.

I can still smell the tropics, see the torrential monsoon skies, and taste Friday fried shrimp at the chow hall. When I returned to my town, the streets I grew up on, everything looked small, even my old home. Lilliputian really. I had been in the wider world—on the other *side* of the world, to be more specific. It had been scary, confusing, even dangerous—yet fantastically promising and exciting. And I had made my way in it.

Long after that career, I realized what an honor it was—and still is—to have served, especially in a war theater. It's part of my legacy.

I am still learning.
– Leonardo DaVinci

Chapter 11

Phoenix Factors – From Inertia to Thriving

Life can either be accepted or changed. If it is not accepted, it must be changed.
If it cannot be changed, then it must be accepted.
– Winston Churchill

New Wave Leadership is evolutionary and thus is symbolized by the mythical phoenix, which continuously rises from the ashes—renewed, better. Phoenix Factors describe possibilities and how organizations can evolve—must evolve—from inertia to thriving in this era of bits, bytes, thinking machines, and the possibilities of gene editing.[232]

Chapter 11 describes the potential of becoming MAGNUS–OVÉA, from the individual to our wider society. In the new wave of improvement in self and governance, private, private nonprofit, and public, we can learn to achieve more and more well-being and thus learn to thrive and flourish. This has to be a precursor to the kind of enlightened leadership these times demand and suggest for the future. We may not

> **Phoenix Factors describe possibilities and how organizations can evolve—must evolve—from inertia to thriving in this era of bits, bytes, thinking machines, and the possibilities of gene editing.**

realize it as it's happening, but on reflection, we'll see we have indeed improved and will continue to improve by taking the New Wave MAGNUS–OVÉA Journey. One success is the success of two and so on, geometrically.

As Klaus Schwab of the World Economic Forum observes:

We stand on the brink of a technological revolution that will fundamentally alter the way we live, work, and relate to one another. In its scale, scope, and complexity, the transformation will be unlike anything humankind has experienced before. We do not yet know just how it will unfold, but one thing is clear: the response to it must be integrated and comprehensive, involving all stakeholders of the global polity, from the public and private sectors to academia and civil society.[233]

Character-based staff, energized organizations, thriving communities are the vision and work of the budding current and promising next generation of New Wave Leaders. These leaders build from the bottom up to contribute to the well-being of communities where people live, work, play, raise their children, and seek happiness. This is the definition of thriving.

The focus must be on well-being in response to this rapid advancement of the community spurred by AI, near instant communication, and increasing expectations from organizations and agencies, public and private. The Phoenix Factors represent not only an advancement of the individual and organization; they comprise the next evolutionary step in the progress of how we conduct and deliver services. The Factors begin with reimagining the character-based professional from the perspective of family and personal development. They then expand to how that advancement manifests in bettering the organization and the wider community. So much is at stake as countries jostle for dominance. We have to get this one right.

New Wave MAGNUS–OVÉA Themes

Phoenix Factors are synergistic in that one blends into another, sometimes using the same concepts and terms for definition. They arise from the journey of becoming a New Wave MAGNUS–OVÉA individual and then leading as such. The blending is a result of having the mutual objective of building well-being, which cuts across the collective effort of individuals and organizations. Thus, you will see the following themes running through all the Factors:

- *Well-being* – We start with the ultimate goal of well-being. This state is considerably beyond being medically healthy; it's about thriving and being generally happy or at least content, accepting of many areas of life.

- *The Golden Mean* – Growth derives from seeing what is possible and achieving it not through extreme measures but by how we spend our time and make decisions daily, even minute to minute. Because it isn't drastic, moderate change provides time to work out the kinks of the day and of our evolution over time, which means lasting improvement.

- *Continuous character-based education and development* – A virtue-driven life is just that. When practiced daily, it drives us toward excellence. Each accomplishment encourages another, and life, living becomes self-fulfilling.

- *Growth mindset* – Each Phoenix Factor describes the attitude for how we improve personally, professionally, and as part of our family and the larger community. This is true collaboration, not merely cooperation.

- *Matrix solutions* – The private and especially the public sectors simply can't satisfy all service demands as single agencies, whether they're corporate or municipal. Some services will have to be delivered in collaboration with sister agencies, indeed entire supply chains of materials, supplies, components, and people—or not at all. For example, Crisis Intervention Teams to decriminalize mental illness[234] represent just one significant service that a number of agencies must deliver to support the program's recipients.

- *Reversing top-down mentality to bottom up* – Top-down, command-and-control leadership has evolved, even in the military. What the foot soldier, so to speak, has to say matters. Leaders of the New Wave are urged to construct collaboration with all levels, especially the line level. Communication needs to flow not only top down but back up again in a continuous cycle of idea sharing in the relentless pursuit of improvement by learning, doing, analyzing, and doing again.

- *Project capacity building* – New Wave Leadership will improve the general good with targeted, self-sustaining services. Any service project idea, private or public, has the best chance of sustaining itself if it's planned, implemented, and sustained by building in the permanent capacity to deliver that service.[235]

- *Legacy* – The work of becoming MAGNUS–OVÉA leads to good that's lasting, thus improving the lives of those who follow. Once begun, it will hopefully become an intergenerational aspiration.

These themes suggest the synergy that's vital to cultivating New Wave Leaders and force multipliers and organizations. We welcome challenge and, yes, failure, because it's fertilizer for growth. Every failure is a chance to mend things, improve things, cement the way forward. When individuals become a single-minded body—one being nourished by the progress of the other, it multiplies the force of their effects. This can only happen by fostering the well-being of the individual.

> **While progress may seem glacially slow as we live it daily, reaching for a Phoenix Factor is truly rapid and will reshape organizations by strengthening individuals.**

A Practical Call to Action

Our present state of routine—how we work, individually and in groups—has taken generations to develop. That era has passed, even long passed. While the status quo works to an extent, we're overdue for the next step of private and municipal governance. From the *what* to the *how* of being increasingly efficient and especially effective, we need an overhaul in light of the new realities. It's always been about the how.

To contemplate these transitions from inertia to thriving *in their entirety* is daunting, discouraging, even hopeless. Taken individually, however, each factor is highly achievable. This approach is a dream, but a highly realistic one when taken in digestible bites. While progress may seem glacially slow as we live it daily, reaching for a Phoenix Factor is truly rapid and will reshape organizations by strengthening individuals. Change for the better we will—and start we must. Inertia, no matter how comfortable, will not do. As the evolution of nation-states go, this New Wave will be dramatic. The ride can be exhilarating.

For an overview, Figure 6 lists the Phoenix Factors in a single table. Collectively, these factors describe pathways and possibilities that redefine organizations and the people who drive them.

<table>
<tr><td colspan="2" align="center">PHOENIX FACTORS: NEW BEGINNINGS
From Inertia to Thriving by Becoming a New Wave Leader</td></tr>
<tr><td align="center">How It Is</td><td align="center">How It Can Be</td></tr>
<tr><td colspan="2" align="center">MAGNUS–OVÉA – New Wave Individual</td></tr>
<tr><td>Stagnation</td><td>Productive activation</td></tr>
<tr><td>Lack of healthy vitality</td><td>Productive longevity</td></tr>
<tr><td>Trainer</td><td>Mentor</td></tr>
<tr><td>PTSD</td><td>Post-traumatic growth</td></tr>
<tr><td>De-escalation</td><td>Pre-escalation</td></tr>
<tr><td>Retirement clock watcher</td><td>Lifetime legacy mentality</td></tr>
<tr><td>Hypervigilance</td><td>Service mentality</td></tr>
<tr><td colspan="2" align="center">OVÉA: Others—Values—Ethics—Acceleration</td></tr>
<tr><td>VUCA</td><td>Counter VUCA</td></tr>
<tr><td>Volatility</td><td>Vision</td></tr>
<tr><td>Uncertainty</td><td>Understanding</td></tr>
<tr><td>Complexity</td><td>Clarity</td></tr>
<tr><td>Ambiguity</td><td>Agility</td></tr>
<tr><td>Fixed mindset</td><td>Growth mindset</td></tr>
<tr><td>Burnout</td><td>Vigor</td></tr>
<tr><td>Avoidance</td><td>Engagement</td></tr>
<tr><td>Routine procedures</td><td>Practical practice</td></tr>
<tr><td colspan="2" align="center">MAGNUS–OVÉA – New Wave Organization</td></tr>
<tr><td>Budgetary cycle uncertainty</td><td>Life cycle cost effectiveness stability</td></tr>
<tr><td>Best practices</td><td>Effective practices</td></tr>
<tr><td>Technical skills training</td><td>Character development</td></tr>
<tr><td>Cooperation</td><td>Collaboration</td></tr>
<tr><td>Administration of projects</td><td>Capacity building for program permanency</td></tr>
</table>

PHOENIX FACTORS: NEW BEGINNINGS From Inertia to Thriving by Becoming a New Wave Leader	
How It *Is*	**How It *Can* Be**
MAGNUS–OVÉA – New Wave *Organization* (continued)	
Risk tolerance	Risk and liability reduction
Human resources administration	Multiplied social capital
Hiring for skills – Firing for character	Hiring for character – Rarely firing for skills
MAGNUS–OVÉA – New Wave *Community*	
Cooperation	Collaboration
Silo services management	Matrix governance
Vicious cycles	Virtuous cycles
Guessing	Proof
MAGNUS–OVÉA Legacy – New Wave *Leadership*	
Medical wellness	Holistic well-being
Obstacles	Opportunities
Stagnant inertia	Forward thinking evolution
IQ and skills	Emotional Quotient (EQ) for personal development
Opinion	Science-based and proven practice
Top-down governance	Cycle between top-down, bottom-up
Extremes	Golden Mean

Figure 6: Phoenix Factors

The Emergence of the New Wave Leader

As you can see in this table of the Phoenix Factors, five distinct yet synergistic areas or domains flow from MAGNUS–OVÉA and New Wave thinking and doing: the Individual, OVÉA, the Organization, the Community, and New Wave Leadership. Each area is described as how it is now in juxtaposition with how it can be, rather *must* be, to rise to the demands of this New Wave evolution.

Let's look at each area in depth, beginning with the refocusing of the individual, and through individuals, imagining a more efficient, effective, and harmonious way of governing our enterprises.

MAGNUS–OVÉA – New Wave *Individual*	
How It *Is*	**How It *Can* Be**
Stagnation	Productive activation
Lack of healthy vitality	Productive longevity
Trainer	Mentor
PTSD	Post-traumatic growth
De-escalation	Pre-escalation
Retirement clock watcher	Lifetime legacy mentality
Hypervigilance	Service mentality

Figure 7: New Wave Individual

Phoenix Factors in the New Wave Individual

Basically, in New Wave evolution the individual, organization, and community change focus from top-down organization-assigned duties and responsibilities to directives considering character-driven, collaborative actions and input from all levels, which is how all our sectors need to evolve going forward.

It all begins with the individual from the bottom up—the surest way for our institutions to evolve. If new people aren't hired for basic moral substance, there's no guarantee they will decide to change. It they don't make that commitment, no amount of mentoring, training, education, discipline, or termination will materially rewire their basic character flaws. According to leaders, character flaws cause most of organizational difficulties—for example, in alarming risk and liability expenses, claims, and payouts. Misconduct is one of the most expensive costs of doing business. Organizational improvement happens with individual improvement. It begins by hiring for character, not merely education, skills, and a good interview.

Once good character has been established, the most sustainable improvements in an organization are likely to happen from the line employee up. This evolution from the bottom up and back down again allows the flow of ideas, creativity, and positive change throughout the organization. In addition, collaboration is a force multiplier that substantially increases the return on investment in manpower.

This view is materially different from the stereotypical command-and-control, top-down hierarchical system. The New Wave way of doing things recognizes the contribution of all employees—bottom up, top down, and back again, or wherever an idea starts. Each loop makes things a bit better, one idea at a time. This approach was exemplified by Hubert Joly, who became the CEO of Best Buy in 2012, when the company was flagging. In his book *The Heart of Business: Leadership Principles for the Next Era of Capitalism*, Joly explained that the first thing he did when hired was spend three days in one of the stores, asking questions and listening to the staff and management team.[236] The information he learned and what he did with it saved the company.

> **According to leaders, character flaws cause most of organizational difficulties—for example, in alarming risk and liability expenses, claims, and payouts.**

A character-driven, bottom-up approach also creates enthusiasm for getting good work done. It breeds an atmosphere of "we," not "they." Employees become active, valued, and cherished team members, involved followers who know their new participatory role. They learn what is beyond cooperation on a project that finishes at the end of the day to true collaboration on what is meaningful, fulfilling, and enduring. People know they are heard and can make a difference. They increasingly see themselves as a part of a mission and know they have a vital purpose in it. Said another way, "work," a "four-letter word," becomes a career for the New Wave individual. Let's consider the aspects presented in Figure 7.

Stagnation to productive activation: Many times, a job is notably stagnant, and people take little joy in going to work. Clock watching is a significant event. Employees may begin with the enthusiasm inspired by a chance to do some good, but the initial spark often fades to "going along to get along." Productive activation to achieve communal goals takes the continuous renewal of enthusiasm by leaders who inspire action by example. These leaders understand the human context of their organization and know success is more than numbers or merely putting in the hours. In turn, staff know they are doing something bigger than they are and thereby have a broader, inspired purpose. The clock matters little.

Lack of healthy vitality to productive longevity. We understand from science that healthy practices contribute to longevity and enhance well-being. Conversely, negative symptoms stem from feeling insignificant like a cog in a wheel. This is exemplified by employees who describe their role as "just a___________." You fill in the blank. This notion downplays the importance of people in the mission, degrades their purpose, and is simply not true. Without meaning and purpose, jobs are stressful and "hypervigilant" unhealthy jobs.

Public jobs, especially in public safety, for example, are legendary for premature burnout and, shockingly, death, sometimes shortly after retirement. Twenty to 30 years of emotionally charged workdays, riding the roller coaster of the stress cycle, take their toll. The modern knowledge worker who sits at a computer for hours and hours may experience the same fate for different reasons. Conversely, imagine a work environment that inspires. An environment that promotes personal well-being by continuously developing character in each person; by supporting holistic health in body, mind, and a zest for life. Imagine every person pursuing a career, not "work," that will allow them another lengthy period of activity in retirement being good, doing good, and having *fun.* Becoming more accelerates when you have a skilled, character-based, likeminded mentor to start and guide you through a fulfilling working life.

Trainer to mentor. Though necessary, trainers concentrate on what the job requires, compliance with policy, rules, and regulations—what has *always* been done, to the exclusion of character-based education. Much training is a result of trying to codify an answer to everything that can get the organization or agency in trouble, which is impossible because it assumes employees are just and make good moral decisions. Yes, risk

> **What if your trainer were also your mentor, your role model, with solid ethical character, a wholesome attitude to life, and eagerness for the opportunities of the job? It's magical when it happens.**

prevention and mitigation are quite necessary, but it's a rigid picture of inflexibility; follow this policy and procedure . . . or else. How many of us have heard a variation of

"It's my way or the highway" from trainers? Training need not be this way. What if your trainer were also your mentor, your role model, with solid ethical character, a wholesome attitude to life, and eagerness for the opportunities of the job? It's magical when it happens. It occurs increasingly as New Wave Leaders prosper, produce, and proliferate, thus multiplying themselves through their workmates. The transition begins by helping to prevent personal stressors, which come with any job.

PTSD to post-traumatic growth – PTSD is widely perceived to be primarily caused by a single traumatic experience. We don't recognize that PTSD more frequently results from being continuously exposed to stressors every day for extended periods of our career, no matter what that career is. This describes many jobs but is notably prevalent in the public sector, often steeped in hyperactivity, hypertension, and hypervigilance. Trust devolves with such a mentality. Consider we have nearly a million people, sworn and nonsworn, to uphold the peace and keep community well-being. This doesn't count the many more in peripheral careers involved in community well-being. The notoriety of PTSD masks the significance of these conditions in many other occupations driven by target goals, competition, and rules in inflexible organizations. There is an answer.

Individuals trained in New Wave Leadership learn to counter chaos, which has implications for all sectors. With the tools and resources presented in this book, they confront and overcome substance abuse, depression, ebbing job performance, and family difficulties. They even become better spouses and parents! People in high-tension jobs learn how to de-stress by continually improving their lifestyles. They discover there's much more to a well-balanced life when they pursue post-traumatic *growth* via the New Wave MAGNUS–OVÉA Journey. This includes methods of healthy preparation for handling stressful or traumatic situations *without* being hypertensive, hyperactive, or hypervigilant. They approach a crisis as normal, yes normal, and see it as the growth experience it is. They realize they can and will work through it because they do it repeatedly.

De-escalation to pre-escalation. De-escalating a potentially difficult or dangerous situation is a skill we *all* need to develop. We need to manage our daily interactions no matter who we are. The same skills are relevant in our daily personal and professional lives, wherever we may work. However, a flaw exists in current de-escalation logic and training, which is that something must be going wrong for the skills of de-escalation to be utilized. Again, using police as an example of facing crises, preparing for "a war out there" is counterproductive, given that much is going well "out there." An acquaintance only drew his gun once in 25 years—and that's the norm. It's not enough to de-escalate a situation; we must prepare for the possibility of confrontations by learning to prevent them in the first place. We also need to learn to cope with any aftermath by learning proper human interactions. Recognize that good can come from our experiences

> **With pre-escalation skills to manage your human interactions, the lion's share of confrontations can be avoided.**

if we learn from them. Situational learning is another mark of the New Wave Leader.

Prepare better responses and, importantly, consider post-traumatic strengthening. This preparation can include self-examination, a primary character trait of a New Wave MAGNUS–OVÉA professional, which strengthens how one is predisposed to handle conflict. Note here we mean the conflict we experience in everyday interactions with anyone. Learn not to escalate, or have a teammate more adept at handling volatile situations step into the breech. Think of the emotional and physical energies, which can then be redirected to personal growth and success with family and work. With pre-escalation skills to manage your human interactions, the lion's share of confrontations can be avoided. If not, they can be handled better, thus diminishing the harmful effects on involved parties. This is taking a long step to living with legacy in mind.

Retirement clock watcher to lifetime legacy mentality. A major point of the New Wave philosophy is that focusing on legacy matters. Leaving a career with the respect of respectable people matters. Fulfilling purpose matters. Fulfilling mission matters. The New Wave professional works hard at the job, and he or she looks for the challenge that will contribute to the general good even if it's a bit frightening to contemplate.

Learn to say yes to challenges. Even if you fail, it most likely will be failing forward to progress. With struggle, the rewards are more meaningful. This is the way legacy is built—one challenge at a time, modeling the best of behavior and making a positive difference one day, one achievement at a time. Your perspective then becomes one of looking beyond the work at hand, over the horizon of many years after a career, so you, the New Wave professional, can give back and enjoy the Good Life.

Hypervigilance to service mentality. We touched on hypervigilance and its corollaries, hyperactivity and hypertension, and their result, mental instability. These are states that feed on compounding apprehension, which eventually weakens us. So many jobs are marked by pressure from peers, bosses, deadlines, and the ultimate pressure—that which we demand from ourselves. A better, healthier way to avoid this continual tension is to focus on contributing to the general good, something loftier. We can see a good day's work as a building block to an accomplished career that provides great rewards as we learn to accept and even conquer the stressful times. This does *not* mean one is to stick with a dead-end, dull, or inappropriate job. This behavioral model encourages the strategic job move. Note that the sum of the parts of a career matters, even though it comprises several jobs. Realize all these states of being hyper are harmful and misplaced.

New Wave professionals realize it's futile to stress over things that may never happen. They channel their energies into being more irrepressible and hardy, positive, socially collaborative, self-aware, and focused.[238] Thus, they generally think better, act better, and are much more productive than the average worker. Keep in mind that channeling good stress to doing what is right and good rewires, strengthens, and grows the brain to do more of the same.[239] Imagine, again, if the energy of hypervigilance can be redirected to service to the greater good, which epitomizes New Wave thinking. Becoming a New Wave individual is self-generating, self-fulfilling, and self-rewarding.

Now let's consider OVÉA, the spark, the activator that inspires the realization that doing good is rewarding and energizing.

OVÉA: *Others—Values—Ethics—Acceleration*	
How It *Is*	**How It *Can* Be**
VUCA – Volatility	Vision
VUCA – Uncertainty	Understanding
VUCA – Complexity	Clarity
VUCA – Ambiguity	Agility
Fixed mindset	Growth mindset
Burnout	Vigor
Avoidance	Engagement
Routine procedures	Practical practice

Figure 8: OVÉA

Phoenix Factors in OVÉA, the Spark

OVÉA describes the activators that compel our progress to character-based thriving and becoming part of the New Wave. With *others* as a focus, we find the sense of accomplishment that comes with improving ourselves and the lives around us and beyond. When we study and embody character, *values* guide us, and *ethics* provide our moral standards. Together, they deliver the spark, the energy, the *acceleration* to persist. Making the right decision at the right time for the right reasons—even when no one else is around—becomes routine, even automatic, innate, part of our strengthening character.

VUCA to Counter VUCA. Volatility, Uncertainty, Complexity, and Ambiguity, daily crises, big, small and seemingly never ending. VUCA is varying degrees of chaos due to moment-to-moment unpredictability and a rapidly changing world. Everyone, every agency, every business, and every sector are affected by accelerating technology, turmoil in global politics, and social issues boiling in our lives—all exacerbated by the media. This is not to mention the distresses that plague our personal lives. Likewise, in our work lives, we never know when something unexpected will demand our immediate attention. This runs the spectrum from urgent calls, texts, and emails to something foundationally disruptive. What more if it's a destabilizing calamity out of the blue, which many times changes the way business is defined and done—often not in a good way.

Generalized crisis mode operation when no real crisis exists isn't productive. Soon, we have no time to build a business or service because staff is being whipsawed by seeming crises. While each condition can be countered separately, the best strategy is twofold. First, we need to personally become antifragile and resilient. Next, we need to build an organizational environment to counter crises *before* they critically affect us personally and organizationally. We can suffer under VUCA, or we can be ready for it then respond to it rationally and productively.

The usual responses to a calamity are to fight it head on or to ignore it, which aren't the best approaches. We can become more stressed, perhaps lose sleep, or internalize it all, thus inexorably diminishing our health and quality of life. How, then, to do it?

We can more effectively counter setbacks by working day to day on our character and our physical, mental, and emotional well-being. In his seminal book *Principles*, Ray Dalio begins his insightful look into living well by saying, "Embrace reality and deal with it."[240] Dalio would recommend becoming a "hyperrealist." Being a hyper-realist means to see things for what they truly are, analyze them thoroughly, decide an action, assign corporate responsibility, and respond.

Don't be obsessed with imagined impending doom. Stay centered and grounded and focus on what's important to family, job, and the wider world. Chaos, when embraced as a reality, is a genuine opportunity to calm things down, sharpen our wits, and focus our purposes. Imagine taking a vacation and enjoying it because you're confident you have the strength to withstand an ill wind or find answers to the stressors of the day and life.

When a leadership environment grows its social capital, invests in collective character development, and exemplifies job collaboration, it can work to counter reversals. Such an environment can lessen chaos.

> **Being a hyperrealist means to see things for what they truly are, analyze them thoroughly, decide an action, assign corporate responsibility, and respond.**

The following exposition on VUCA is adapted from leader, writer, and speaker Wayne Pollard.[241]

- **VUCA –** *Volatility to Vision.* Volatility at its worst is the tendency of things to change quickly and erratically and descend into worsening situations. This epitomizes the nature, speed, and magnitude of undesirable change.[242] You can counter volatility with a long-term vision to help you clearly see your purpose and how to realize it. Volumes have been written on how to define a vision for your intentions, with uncountable suggestions for how to get there. As a New Wave Leader, you take two overarching actions with that inspiring statement of what the organization can be. First, you ensure *input* from all levels of the organization and from the people served. Second, you constantly *test* the validity of the vision to make sure it's a true beacon of where you desire to go. Volatility isn't compatible with a strong vision.

> *If you are working on something exciting that you really care about,*
> *you don't have to be pushed. The vision pulls you.*
> – Steve Jobs

- VUCA – *Uncertainty to Understanding.* Uncertainty is the lack of predictability and the prospects of surprise.[243] The antidote here is a hallmark of the New Wave organization—the learning environment. Knowledge diminishes uncertainty.

A lover of knowledge is naturally inquisitive and analytical, qualities that are antidotes to uncertainty. New Wave organizational leadership encourages self-study, formal education, and professional development at *all* levels, with an emphasis on entry-level staff. Beyond skills training for carrying out daily duties, this means developing job knowledge, interpersonal perception, depth, and character in all employees. With knowledge comes understanding and progress. Uncertainty is incompatible with the well-read person.

- VUCA – *Complexity to Communication.* When things are complex, they can be confusingly intricate. Complexity is the epitome of chaos.[244] To answer complexity, we return to a major theme of New Wave Leadership—hew to what is simple, suitable, and sustainable. Complexity is often necessary, as in assembling a new Tesla automobile. However, assemblage happens one bolt at a time, one component at a time, one system at a time. It all comes together in an extraordinarily complex, yet efficient, safe, and aesthetically pleasing ride, rolling off the assembly line. Everyone has a job, an essential contribution to a revolutionary car. Complexity is incompatible with the rationally simple, suitable, and sustainable solution.

> **Knowledge diminishes uncertainty. A lover of knowledge is naturally inquisitive and analytical, qualities that are antidotes to uncertainty.**

- VUCA – *Ambiguity to Agility.* Multiple states or ways of interpreting information can be ambiguous and lead to potentially misreading the reality confronting us.[245] Again, the New Wave organization has the answer. Collaboration is the heartbeat of agility, flexibility, and responsiveness, all of which answer ambiguity. Agility is exemplified by another New Wave tenet: matrix solutions to basic problems.

  Consider the Tesla again, the first successful auto manufacturing startup in 90 years and at the time of this writing, the most valuable car manufacturer ever! Imagine how many disparate companies, supply chains, sub-manufacturers, etc. it takes to build a Tesla automobile. Your Model S starts down the assembly line as a huge aluminum coil that weighs up to 20,000 pounds. Out the other end rolls a space age car in about *three days*—1,000 cars a day, 7,000 cars per week! All year long! All with the aid of 160 multi-functional robots envisioned by a mix of our brightest scientists, engineers, and inventors from our major universities and industry. Now *that* is matrix thinking and doing; *agile* New Wave thinking and doing. Ambiguity is incompatible with collaboration.

Much can be said about how the private sector innovates and accomplishes objectives. We all need to learn from it and go beyond the fixed mindset of "Don't rock the boat. We've always done it this way" to a growth mindset of creative possibilities.

Enlightenment begins when you change your mindset — from a blaming mindset to blessing mindset, from a negative mindset to a positive mindset, from a fixed mindset to a growth mindset, from a linear mindset to an exponential mindset.
– Amit Ray

Fixed mindset to Growth mindset. We learn to be set in our ways of thinking and doing; it's comfortable. Routine sets in quickly, dampening creativity and locking in bad habits that end up wasting time. Streaming the evenings away, for example, can be a major hindrance to personal growth and progress. One "must see" season leads to two, leads to bingeing. We generally like the predictability of routine action and, especially, thinking. It takes work, if not a little "fear and loathing," to upset our mind-numbing sameness and take on a challenge. Thus, we tend to limit the extent of our abilities, and our confidence can wane to near timidity. We close ourselves off from creative ways of doing things, pursuing new ideas, imagining possibilities.

> **When we reach a goal after a struggle, we feel more capable, sometimes for years.**

A growth mindset is conversely quite expansive; we *believe* we have the brains and drive to take on something a "little beyond us" and succeed, and thus we do. When we reach a goal after a struggle, we feel more capable, sometimes for years. The feeling is intoxicating, so we reach for more expansion with gusto. Everyone wins. This path to growth of reaching to overcome obstacles and take on challenges is central to New Wave Leadership.

Burnout to Vigor. Feeling overall vigor is a direct outcome of New Wave philosophy and practice to develop a healthy mindset. Retirement was established because we tire of working for money. (We are most fortunate; few in the march of civilizations had or have the privilege of *not* having to work for pay.) Burnout is an all-too-common state in our working lives, often occurring early in our career.

What more can we accomplish when work energizes us? In a New Wave organization, an overall contentment, if not excitement, from work is a highly realistic state. People enjoy the challenge of doing more because it has significance. A vigorous agency is led by talented, character-based, inspired people who, in turn, inspire those with whom they work. Thank goodness those of us who have done the work of character-based holistic living will live well into our 90s, age appropriately vital, vigorous, and valued. What more can we reap from a career, from life, when we feel *invigorated?* Being energized by personal growth and accomplishment at home and on the job leads to legacy at the end. This is the heart of OVÉA. *Achievement* comes to those who do great things for themselves. *Success* comes when they empower followers to do great things with them. *Significance* comes when they develop leaders to do great things for and with them. But *legacy* is created only when leaders develop their organization such that it can do great things *without* them.

> **It's far more fulfilling to be engaged and capable by understanding how to productively follow *or* lead. The New Wave individual knows when and how to do either.**

Avoidance to Engagement. How many of us actually work at becoming *invisible* at home, on the job, and in the community? We might avoid engagement because of fear, apathy, risk avoidance, or unmanaged stress. But those are *not* MAGNUS–OVÉA traits. When was the last time you volunteered to take the lead, to take responsibility, to risk failing? It's risky to be at the head of the line and even riskier to appear eager to join in a collaboration with a challenging goal. MAGNUS–OVÉA Leaders show up ready, willing, creative, energized, and able to work; ready to be part of a purposeful mission not just a cog in it. It's far more fulfilling to be engaged and capable by understanding how to productively follow or lead. The New Wave individual knows when and how to do either.

People are more relaxed with the right amount and the right kind of motivating stress, so yes, professionally managed stress is a good thing. In fact, stress is necessary, even productive, until it moves to distress.[246] Days go by more quickly when we confront and answer our challenges, make progress, and achieve goals because we're engaged and enjoy what we do. Engagement eventually leads to legacy.

Good things happen when we're in pursuit of meaningful goals that make life worthwhile. We can balance work and private life while looking forward to productive longevity—a third act, as it's termed. Although a clever meme notes it's doubtful we'll want our tombstone to read, "I wish I'd spent more time at the office," we *can* truly enjoy our work. We just need to know how to get out of the avoidance mindset and confidently into the proactive engagement mode. Routine work then becomes something else entirely: meaningful, practical, and productive practice.

Routine procedures to Practical practice. Much of our workday is about the routine, the compliance issues of the job—this rule and that regulation. It seems that little of it results in action that rewards the sweat of our diligence or leaves us eager for the next morning. In the New Wave organization staffed with MAGNUS–OVÉA practitioners and propelled by New Wave Leadership, it's all about what works, accomplished in a collegial atmosphere of collaboration. In such an environment, the results are much greater than the individual efforts. We notice a multiplier effect when motivated, inspired people do practical, productive work. Many in a New Wave organization realize unexpected, uncommon rewards in life-affirming ways. Imagine, for example, a program to address mental illness that keeps mental health sufferers out of the criminal justice system, in the community, and being *productive*.[247] This is a practical, money-saving result with a rewarding moral imperative to boot!

Next let's imagine the possibilities for the organization that lives by the give and take of organization-wide, bottom-up New Wave Leadership to promote well-being.

MAGNUS–OVÉA – New Wave *Organization*	
How It *Is*	**How It *Can* Be**
Budgetary cycle uncertainty	Life cycle cost effectiveness stability
Best practices	Effective practices
Technical skills training	Character development
Cooperation	Collaboration
Administration of projects	Capacity building for program permanency
Risk tolerance	Risk and liability reduction
Human resources administration	Multiplied social capital
Hiring for skills – Firing for character	Hiring for character – Rarely firing for skills

Figure 9: New Wave Organization

Phoenix Factors in the New Wave Organization

When Phoenix Factors manifest in continuously better employees, all levels of staff are invigorated by the collective creativity and energy of delivering what the individual and organization are meant to do. The organization can't help but benefit *if* New Wave management is concurrently concentrated on the greater good based on continuous, career-long, organization-wide character development. Such is manifested in a career development workplan mutually agreed upon between a staff member and management. The concurrent goal of well-being continually raises capability with more effective allocation of resources and a big-picture focus, which enables the organization to achieve much more than isolated project objectives. Done right, it's infectious. New Wave Leadership produces a win–win–win between team members, leadership, and the recipients of the goods produced or services delivered.

Budgetary cycle uncertainty to Life cycle cost effectiveness stability. Let's use the public sector as an example for the private and private nonprofit sectors, as budgeting drives all three. Local municipal service programs depend on a flow of funding that's anything but steady as

> **A New Wave program is conceived considering its entire life cycle. Thus, it's planned, operated, and sustained by building in the capacity to support the idea *permanently*.**

their funds are usually "soft" money, most likely funded by one-time allocations such as a grant, needing to be reauthorized annually. The question then becomes how to ensure cost-effective stability.

A New Wave program is conceived considering its entire life cycle. Thus, it's planned, operated, and sustained by building in the capacity to support the idea *permanently*. The usual model of program implementation begins by delivering the service without building the support infrastructure to continue it. Many good ideas die before they begin to reap their potential. Therefore, one of the first critical milestones of capacity building consists of planning for reliable operational resources, including multi-sourced monetary streams. Diversity of funding sources becomes reliable over time as the program establishes a history of predictability, which means budgets become more realistic so people can plan more accurately. Then, a program idea can last as long as the service need or problem it addresses. When New Wave professionals involved in developing local service programs learn the skills of program life cycle planning and implementation, their success rates soar.

This has implications for the private and private nonprofit sectors as well. Both focus on budget and profit matters as well as delivering a service. Thus, both are better served by considering how to sustain operations so the bottom line remains healthy and the service remains viable. In other words, building capacity for infrastructure of production and services helps to ensure organizational permanency. (For an example of capacity building for public service programs, see *Decriminalizing Mental Illness: A Practical Model for Building Sustainable Crisis Intervention Teams.*)[248]

This approach to service programming is a highly effective practice but *not* considered a "best practice." Let's look at why not.

Best practices to Effective practices. The terms we use have a significant effect on what and how we accomplish things. No common term is more illustrative of this point than the ubiquitous "Best Practices," a term that purports to indicate prescriptions to follow. When determining how to develop service programs, there's *no such thing* as a "best practice." What works in one town doesn't guarantee it will work in another. In fact, it usually doesn't—especially if the practice is applied as an immutable template with the expectation of repeating results experienced elsewhere. Every attempt at implementing a new idea must be flexible, because every locale is different. Context matters! Cookie cutter templates of governance policies, corporate prescriptions, agency lessons learned, or service ideas and programming don't apply universally. At best, they are a starting point. Consider how many businesses fail copying other, even similar businesses.

We need a proper shift in terms to understand what an idea means and its general application to programming—no matter the locale. To wit: What works in Lizard Lick, North Carolina is little indication of what works in Bee Lick, Kentucky (yes, real places). Each place is defined quite differently by its politics, personalities, processes, procedures, demographics, view of the immediate world, and even the weather! A best practice in one place is simply *not* a best practice in another. Therefore, best practices will likely struggle and, at worst, fail outright—

> An *effective* practice based on lessons learned is general, practical, and proven advice for getting things done in the proper sequence by the suitably responsible person or agency.

after a great amount of effort, misdirected resources, and costs. Plus, such failure snuffs out enthusiasm for new ideas. It's difficult to impossible to start another program on the heels of such a disappointment. We can never know how many good, practical, needed ideas silently die out of fear of failure. An effective practice proven in another locale but *outlined to be flexible with capacity building when taken elsewhere* makes all the difference.

An effective practice based on lessons learned is general, practical, and proven advice for getting things done in the proper sequence by the suitably responsible person or agency. Each organization is free to adapt the checklist of effective practices from another site to fit its own. The kernel of a good idea is thus preserved, proliferated, and proven further with each application. This is the epitome of the New Wave evolution of creativity and getting good things done with permanent impact.

Technical skills training to Character development. Being technically competent is a must for any leader but must be rooted in good character—an important distinction made throughout these pages. Skills training alone assumes a new hire already has good ethics and morals. A good moral compass takes many years to develop.[249] It begins early in life with our families but needs to continue.

> **Continuous character-based ethical education for all staff is the "gold-standard" of staff development.**

This is why the New Wave organization needs to prioritize continuous character-based education and development *along with* skill-based and professional training. Continuous character development must come first, as technical competence is no measure of good judgment. Otherwise, the organization misses the opportunity to optimize the potential of the individual and support and promote the best of what the collective can deliver. Reflect again that one of the largest expenses for an organization, private or public, are people not exercising good judgment or acting badly.

Training budgets are often limited and spent on mandatory technical and professional skills training. After all, the company must avoid grievances, legal expenses, and liability claims. Yet professional and character-based training is even less well funded and usually reserved for employees in senior positions. Continuous character-based ethical education for all staff is the "gold-standard" of staff development.

New Wave organizations have a strategy for and philosophy of *human-capacity* development, beginning from the hiring process to the most senior positions, as it should be. Agencies and organizations that adopt this way of doing business see it as a strategic imperative to building a true team of employees. Many tangible results transpire from this practice. Public organizations, for example, greatly enhance community collaboration, lower crime rates, and reduce huge liability expenses and payouts. This hints at the multiplier effect of character-based development, which is remarkable. Ethical behavior is not achieved by one-time training. Everyone needs time, study, contemplation, and practical application about how one must be and act ethically and morally to come into their own as they mature as an employee, teammate, and senior leader. This type of character development and education also recognizes that staff begin to lead from the *first* day on the job.

> *Nearly all men can stand adversity, but if you want to*
> *test a man's character, give him power.*
> – Abraham Lincoln

Administration of projects to Capacity building for program permanency. The theme of capacity building as explained under the topic of *Budgetary cycle uncertainty to Life cycle cost effectiveness stability* continues. Here, however, the focus is on building stable programs as opposed to managing budgetary issues.

Administrative efficiency within bureaucracies usually serves the purpose of compliance only, but governance must take a wider view. When an agency wishes or is asked to participate in inter-agency programs to work on an overarching idea to improve the community, more administration will not build that idea to self-sustaining permanency. There's a world of difference between *cooperating* on an *intra*-agency terminal project and selecting people to *collaborate* on a multi-agency program focused on the well-being of the wider community. Both are necessary; both can work in concert for the greater good. The latter has the potential to deliver wider and wider benefits to issues and people who need it most. New Wave organizations work toward true collaboration. The vehicle to do this is capacity building for the individual, agency or organization, and those served.

Capacity building exemplifies New Wave thinking and *doing*—and it's also a way to manage risk and liability.

Risk tolerance to Risk and liability reduction. Risk and liability claims and subsequent settlements in the public sector are "just a cost of doing business—besides, we have insurance." This attitude has genuinely tragic impact. *The Wall Street Journal* reports that misconduct is the largest percentage of claims payouts for most (police) agencies.[250] This bodes implications for municipalities in general. For example, in 2010, the cities of New York and Chicago recorded that 72 percent and 89 percent, respectively, of all claims were paid for people making moral, lack-of-judgment, lack-of-character mistakes. Payouts for misconduct don't include the many other reasons claims are paid, and they certainly don't include all the direct, indirect, insidious hidden costs and, worst of all, unintended consequences of administering and litigating those situations. Many large agencies have law firms on retainer or in-house attorneys and staff "manning the barricades." Then, they have the costs of litigating accused staff, not to mention shadow costs in loss of careers and agency credibility and reputation. These negative effects last for years and sometimes decades as

> **Character education and development pays; it does not cost.**

a scandal becomes legend. "Taxpayers foot the bill for settlements one way or another." The true tragedy is that grievances, litigation, and settlements take time, resources, and billions of dollars away from people and programming that keep a community safe, sound, and productive. The first law of economics, economists say, is "There's no such thing as a free lunch."

There *is* a better way. New Wave agencies that focus on a progression of character-based education and development report reductions in grievances, claims, and payouts for misconduct. Concurrently, they report indicators of more efficient and effective service delivery. Simply put, character education and development pays; it does not cost. Character development must be a life-long, overarching strategy for staff, beginning with the hiring process and extending to retirement. It thus lays the groundwork for an individual's productive longevity. A healthy, happy, involved retiree is valuable to us all.

Human resources administration to Multiplying social capital. This factor elaborates on collaboration and working in matrices. Both multiply individual contributions such that the whole becomes greater than the sum of the parts. Individual human *resources* become human *capital.* While human resources administration is becoming more staff centric than compliance oriented, it can evolve further. Although this simplifies reality, based on experience, the HR department may treat staff as an asset, not unlike a capital asset, to be recruited, hired, trained for a skill, put in a position, and finally managed with compliance rules and regulations. The department may even deem staff an "asset" in terms of a return on investment, considering an employee a profit-and-loss entity. After all, the numbers matter. Such an approach lacks humanity. Yes, this is an oversimplification of how it is across the board and unfair to all the extremely good HR professionals. Still, we aim for a leadership philosophy that considers staff to be people with remarkable collaborative social capital and real potential.

Social capital means the compounding of talent that occurs when people are self-motivated to work with and help one another. This combined talent generates capabilities and possibilities unrealized when people are counted as "assets" largely to be managed for compliance. Such collaboration is the essence of the success of inter-agency matrix solutions previously discussed. In the context of MAGNUS-OVÉA with the guiding goal of well-being, people can tackle more difficult and complex programs when working in a matrix and all prosper with the undertaking.

The whole of social capital is largely self-motivated, self-sustaining, and self-renewing because it's built on healthy personal relationships, give and take, up and down the chain of command. "One for all, and all for one," if you will. People so organized, motivated, and led are largely trusting, respectful, and generous. Yet they're realistic about what it takes to work for a living based on personal growth and contributing to the whole. In other words, *all* are New Wave Leaders, not just the people at or near the top. Content and accomplished employees mean continuing success organizationally and especially where needed services reach intended target groups. All have a stake in leading. Performance happens. Growth happens. Legacy happens.

Hire for skills—fire for character to Hire for character—rarely fire for skills. Organizations are known for hiring criteria based on experience, education, and job-specific skills. This process begins with the interview. HR staff normally don't make the effort to determine good character, as it's so intangible. Conversely, hiring for character assumes a natural moral compass that's still forming and will take guidance, instruction, and example to strengthen. A young person needs years to develop morally, even if she or he has had a good grounding growing up. Organizations must continue that education and encourage the development that largely comes with maturation.

> In the ideal hiring process, candidates learn that character matters and how they fit into the vision, creed, and goals of the organization.

In the ideal hiring process, candidates learn that character matters and how they fit into the vision, creed, and goals of the organization. They're put on a career development plan, the core of which builds character and goes way beyond skills training and professional development. The plan continues the process of developing a morally grounded, collaborative team member. Bringing new staff on board requires that New Wave Leaders welcome and get to know and appreciate a new employee they may spend decades interacting with, shoulder to shoulder.

The current hiring template unfortunately glosses over or ignores assessment of the emotional maturity and good character needed to function well in the New Wave organization. Assessing and developing character must be first and foremost. Thank goodness continuous, simple, suitable, and sustainable assessment can be accomplished with one assessment. The Bar-On Emotional Quotient Inventory (EQ-i™) assesses emotional maturity as character maturity progresses with five scales and their competencies.[252]

- *Intrapersonal* – Self-awareness and self-expression. For example, self-regard is the ability to accurately perceive, understand, and accept oneself.

- *Interpersonal* – Social awareness and interpersonal relationship. Empathy, for example, is to be aware of and understand how others feel.

- *Stress management* – Emotional management and regulation. For example, stress tolerance is to effectively and constructively manage emotions.

- *Adaptability* – Change management. Reality-testing, for example, is to objectively validate one's feelings and thinking with external reality.

- *General Mood* – Self-motivation. Optimism, for example, is to be positive and look at the brighter side of life.

The EQ-i offers many advantages and applications. It's understandable, observable, measurable, and applicable to anyone in any organization and can be given by the individual, HR, or a supervisor. It can be used to maintain progress, and conversely, if an area needs improvement, it provides specific suggestions. Most important, the individual can easily self-monitor progress.

Regular testing, counseling, and mentoring will improve individuals intrinsically and thus their performance on the job.

Regular assessment, mentoring, and practice help to monitor individual progress. The idea is that regular testing, counseling, and mentoring will improve individuals intrinsically and thus their performance on the job. Building character takes time. Why not monitor it and give people specific suggestions for how to improve?

Aristotle observed that an individual isn't mature enough for these life lessons in living well in service to the greater good until advanced middle age! We believe New Wave Leaders with the right education, mentoring, counseling, and practice can accelerate the building of their character and make the right decisions when frequent moral dilemmas arise.

Character doesn't sprout from a workshop or even a course on ethics. Unless a prospective hire presents with a questionable background, it may be tough to gauge a person's integrity. Not so, however, with the New Wave philosophy of hiring for character with assessments and a philosophy of pre-hire to retirement human capital development. Yes, an agency needs to have skilled, experienced people *and* it's possible to assess character before, during, and especially after the onboarding process. While this doesn't guarantee a good moral scope, it's a significant start. Potential new team members know that character matters and they have the main responsibility for their moral journey, which is important and supported by their employer. They know the company will support them with a career development plan of skills and professional training with a large dose of moral guidance.[253] In addition, the organization's leaders act as role models and symbols of moral character.

The whole person is the emphasis. Periodic retesting can monitor progress on employees' character development. The best part of these periodic checkups is that it gives the employee the significant task of self-monitoring and personal responsibility for growth. It's only common sense and right to adopt a policy to select people of good morals then guide them in ethics and character from day one to retirement, when they can flourish in their chosen activities.

Let's continue now as we see how this forward-thinking way of doing business manifests in the communities or sectors New Wave organizations serve. Here again are the major themes of continuous character building, collaboration on matrix solutions to vexing problems, and the focus on well-being, which manifests as communal thriving.

MAGNUS–OVÉA – New Wave *Community*	
How It *Is*	**How It *Can* Be**
Cooperation	Collaboration
Silo services management	Matrix governance
Vicious cycles	Virtuous cycles
Guessing	Proof

Figure 10: New Wave Community

Phoenix Factors in the New Wave Community

Remember, Phoenix Factors are not singularly defined, isolated entities. Each has aspects of other factors, reflecting the synergistic nature of the New Wave organization. Such organizations are refocusing from the inertia of today to more vibrant, responsive entities, as demanded by growing exigencies and galloping progress.

In communities, we see a change from isolated organizations providing silo services, necessary though they are, to working collaboratively from the bottom-up with those served in the community. The nature of a republic and its foundational strength is its townships, even neighborhood to neighborhood. Our cities and towns must focus on well-being for strength to continue to build infrastructure and solve long-term difficulties. We are undergoing a significant restructuring of the community and the services it requires. The people who grow well-being from inertia to thriving are a community's greatest assets.

Cooperation to Collaboration. We continue the discussion of the difference between cooperation and collaboration but from the perspective of the agency or organization within a community, an important distinction. Recall that we *cooperate* on a *project*, which is usually terminal, and *collaborate* on a *program*, which usually has an unfolding lifespan characterized by unending progress. Programs address long-standing needs and are usually best served by *inter*-agency, not single *intra*-agency, work. Thus, silo operations have a terminal nature and matrices of services have an expansive nature.

Cooperation is usually rules and compliance bound. Agencies are good at cooperating within the agency to complete a project, which is relatively routine. People are assigned to a job; they get it done; the numbers are agreeable; they move on. When a project is completed, the "team" may break down to be reassembled for the next project. Direction comes down the chain of command. This repetitive, terminal work usually holds little excitement, little creativity, and less intrinsic motivation. Some sense of accomplishment may be in evidence, but not what it can be when tackling something bigger than the individual or even the team or agency. Such satisfaction occurs when people collaborate on a program to accomplish ongoing good in the community.

> **Our cities and towns must focus on well-being for strength to continue to build infrastructure and solve long-term difficulties.**

Collaboration on a program is a flowing process that can become continually more functional, efficient, effective, and rewarding—even fun. It creates a big change in perspective and motivation. Imagine you are asked to help with an idea to conduct aftercare for at-risk youth that keeps youngsters in school through to graduation. You become part of something bigger than you are, a vital part of an alliance, a mission, a vision. You learn that keeping children in school through graduation is the greatest predictor of them staying out of the criminal justice system and assists them to become a contributing member of society. The whole community wins.

Working on a program such as this has the potential to be quite rewarding, if not life-affirming. You aren't just on a payroll; you're doing something to make a difference. Yes, you can be a New Wave professional achieving necessary daily project tasks, perhaps innovating and always doing your best. However, you can also seek ways to help with programs aimed at wider needs, either for your career energies and inspiration or as a volunteer. This is social capital at work at its best. Add to this collaboration between services and you have greater power to effect change.

Collaboration divides the task and multiplies the success.
– Unknown

Silo services management to Matrix governance. We have interspersed this factor throughout our explanation of the potential of the New Wave individual and organization; and now for a little more detail. Collaboration to tackle a permanent problem-solving idea takes forming inter-agency even inter-sector matrices. Your mobile phone was made possible by near numberless entities. Likewise, a matrix focused on a single vision or solving a single problem combined with program-specific talent, groups, and resources has the best chance of solving communal issues that cut across different services and possibly sectors. These problems could not otherwise be addressed adequately or at all by narrower agency services.

This isn't to say single agency services aren't needed or wanted because they certainly are. Companies big and small, schools, the library, street maintenance, sanitation, and the fire department, for example, represent skilled and assigned people who specialize in those areas for a reason. That said, every community needs inter-agency programming that addresses a difficulty or need for overall communal well-being. A great example is the collaboration between safety and mental health providers to keep people suffering from mental health issues from being incarcerated and get them help. Thus, we have collaborative, intra-agency matrices for character-based Crisis Intervention Teams.

We must overcome the reluctance to combine efforts in a matrix to do something lasting and positive about local priorities of things to "fix." New Wave thinking and leading is a way to approach log-jammed efforts and resources.

Oftentimes, no *one* solution will universally apply. New Wave professionals and agencies must think in terms of a multi-faceted, inter-departmental solution of selected agencies, talent, and resources for their unique contribution to resolving the problem at hand. Separate agencies many times duplicate services or assume other agencies provide a certain service. The New Wave professional thinks in terms of matrices for solutions that are as simple as possible, suitable (to what the target recipients say they need), and sustainable (with self-perpetuating funding streams and support). The goal is to build the comprehensive wholesomeness of the community at large where people can thrive.

Between the extremes of vicious and virtuous cycles exists a realistic mean.

Vicious cycles to Virtuous cycles. A typical job, especially in the public sector, can be marked by, even perhaps mired in, vicious cycles. This occurs when solving one problem or finishing one project leads to or even creates another one in a continual, inevitable negative spiral. Pause a moment and visualize yourself spinning downward—an Alice down the rabbit hole. Perhaps you don't need to imagine. It's not a good feeling—not a good way to conduct work for pay.

As with most circumstances, a vicious cycle stands in stark contrast to its opposite, a virtuous cycle. But the Golden Mean comes to the rescue. Between the extremes of vicious and virtuous cycles exists a realistic mean. Another main theme of the New Wave approach is pursuit of a mean that's exactly right and thus realistic, even virtuous. Doing what's intrinsically productive rewards us extrinsically. For example, helping improve a life or many lives simply feels good—and yes, even virtuous.

As this book makes clear, acting for the individual and communal good is also how we encourage our brains and psyche to grow in that direction. Doing good for ourselves, our family, colleagues, organization, and community becomes a continuous virtuous cycle. Thus, it becomes a natural, hormonally activated response. In evolutionary terms, if long ago we didn't learn to work for the benefit of the tribe, we would have ended up conveniently easy-to-catch, tasty food for other species. A dead end of natural selection. But we survived—together; we learned how to sharpen a stick and hunt in packs—collaboratively. Our brains grew in response to overcoming challenges and feeding ourselves well, and now we're on top of the food chain. Instead of a sharpened stick, we're armed with a mobile phone! Quite the advancement, don't you think? And we have just begun our epochal progress.

But *caution:* We can also train ourselves neurologically and physiologically to be immoral and bereft of energy for and interest in life. We get to choose—vicious or virtuous cycles. Committing to the journey of becoming MAGNUS-OVÉA is habit forming, no matter our stage or condition of life. This isn't mere speculation. The benefits, rationale, and proof of pursuing moral development and action are based in science and can be observed, assessed, and tested in real time.

Guessing to Proof. Many "promising" ideas have no basis in proof and hence they don't deliver. The internet is clogged with people and companies touting *the* way to think, plan, do, and achieve "amazing" things. The claims range from the impractical to the preposterous. We may buy in and sputter along to disappointment. There's no end to the latest and greatest of this and that because people want a simple way to "have it all."

What is a truly helpful way to live well, meaning to be relatively content? The New Wave Leadership MAGNUS-OVÉA theory of behavior takes ancient wisdom that's held true for millennia, supports it with science, and verifies it by practice and experience. The result is reasonable proof that living virtuously, with character, and holistically is a great way to conduct life and thrive. You *can* touch happiness. What have you got to lose? Nothing. And so very much to gain.

We see evidence of the effectiveness of this way of life in the New Wave organization as well. When the organization supports character building and ethical operations, at the very least, liability claims and payouts will trend downward while morale and capability increase. Plus working for and with people you know are upstanding and trustworthy is *fun.*

We'll now look at some of the main Phoenix Factors in New Wave Leadership compared to the usual approach to living and leading. As these individuals evolve themselves, they help to evolve their families, workplace, community, and world.

MAGNUS–OVÉA – New Wave *Leadership*	
How It *Is*	**How It *Can* Be**
Medical wellness	Holistic well-being
Obstacles	Opportunities
Stagnant inertia	Forward thinking evolution
IQ and skills	Emotional Quotient (EQ) for personal development
Opinion	Science-based and proven practice
Top down	Bottom up and back
Extremes	Golden Mean

Figure 11: New Wave Leadership

Phoenix Factors in New Wave Leadership

New Wave Leadership reflects our historical evolution in organizational governance. In a relatively short span in the march of civilizations, we have come from buggy whips to spaceships. Steven Pinker, author of *Enlightenment Now: The Case for Reason, Science, Humanism, and Progress*, observes our economic revolution helped us become one hundred times wealthier today than about two hundred years ago.[254] Astounding progress!

> **There's a better way of conducting personal growth and governance by prioritizing character—becoming aware of it, growing it, teaching it, mentoring it, modeling it.**

Plus, that prosperity is more evenly distributed worldwide than ever before. This is just a hint of what lies ahead, which is quite promising. We are *in* the era of the New Wave Leader.

Leadership simply cannot develop, evolve, or be effective unless individuals have a way to personally pursue it. The practical *how* of getting to where we are going matters. New Wave Leadership is at an important moment in the evolution of our municipalities and especially our businesses. Do we continue with the top-down, hierarchical, command-and-control approach we largely have? No. Too much depends on getting leadership right, now and for what the new organization is becoming. There's a better way of conducting personal growth and governance by prioritizing character—becoming aware of it, growing it, teaching it, mentoring it, modeling it. This requires a new look at the old way of doing leadership development and leading. We can learn what works from ancient and modern leaders, understand the science of character-based leadership, then do it. That hints at the thesis of this book: elaborating the process, the journey of character-based professional development for the current and next generations of leaders who recognize *everyone* has a leadership role. Again, Phoenix Factors illustrate how New Wave Leadership functions and what it can be. Never before in history have we made the significant improvements in life we're making now at an accelerating pace. And we live in the country that defined how to do it.

In *The Wall Street Journal* article of 2018, Pinker stated, "People are putting their longer, healthier, safer, freer, richer, and wiser lives to good use."[255] Take great heart. Pinker further elucidates that 85 percent of the world can now read, up from 12 percent in the last two hundred years; life expectancy, which has been 30 brutal years for much of recorded history, is now 71 years and climbing; and more than half of us live in democracies, up from 1 percent of only the most fortunate.[256]

Every significant measure of progress is moving in a good direction. You can listen to endlessly breaking news about a particular story or easily obtain facts to help you make informed decisions and actions.

What will you do with *your* natural propensity to be more and do more?

Medical wellness to Holistic well-being. Wellness, staying physically healthy, is just a start; it's not enough. Wellness focuses on medical wellness via recommendations to eat better, exercise, and avoid stress, adding the dire consequences of not doing so and perhaps a good dose of medicine. Many of us have heard the admonishment, "Lose 20 pounds and exercise." Of course, it's good advice, but it has only a token following—and even those who follow the prescription probably won't arrive at true well-being. Why? Because wellness is only one small segment of well-being, which encompasses much more than physical health. Well-being encompasses simple, suitable, and sustainable solutions to keep *body, mind, and disposition* tuned and prepared to do whatever is asked of it, even for decades after retirement from paid work. It's about learning to thrive with the goals of achievement, legacy, longevity, and contentedness, while continuously improving in virtue, values, and integrity.

If you commit to being physically well, take the next logical steps to wholesome, comprehensive well-being—simple yet profoundly different—and well worth the effort. It's attitude.

By swallowing evil words unsaid, no one has ever harmed his stomach.
– Winston Churchill

Obstacles to Opportunities. Obstacles are opportunities in disguise.[257] This is not a cute saying but a dramatic statement of the correct approach to the possibly tragic realities of life. Viewing obstacles and difficulties this way is a matter of perspective and perception. Rare is the person who goes through a day without facing obstacles of some sort, whether they're catastrophic or running out of mayo for a sandwich.

Instead of avoiding roadblocks, we need to focus on finding a solution. The problem can then become a way to improve, to grow.

We've been trained or have learned to try to avoid obstacles. They're problematic. They display our weaknesses. We fear looking bad and envision failure. Obstacles stop our progress. But negativity is self-fulfilling and spirals us downward. So instead of avoiding roadblocks, we need to focus on finding a solution. The problem can then become a way to improve, to grow. Putting your answer to work is rewarding in many ways. All the doom and foreboding were for naught—making the obstacle worse. Conversely, if we perceive a problem as a real and true opportunity to learn, progress, and grow, we're energized by the challenge and the prospect of overcoming it. This is lifting weights for the psyche. When we do succeed, this too is self-fulfilling. We become stronger, wiser, and a bit braver. The more obstacles we overcome, the more habitual our positivity becomes.

Solving real-world circumstances is how we learn we have capabilities we never knew we had. We have a totally new and optimistic, energized perspective. Our sense of accomplishment is in proportion to the challenge—and we begin to look forward to more *opportunities.* This is forward thinking and acting with the New Wave frame of mind at its best.

Stagnant inertia to Forward thinking revolution. Inertia is where motivation and good ideas go to die. "We've always done it that way" is its motto. *What more can be done* if new hires are carefully fashioned into real team members with collaborative outlooks? What if they're hired for character and proven talent *and* assigned mentors who are personally committed to the New Wave MAGNUS–OVÉA Journey of character development? What if they each have a personal career development plan and are fully supported by leadership, including direct supervisors? What if they know they'll be encouraged and afforded continuous professional and character development throughout their career? What if they know they will be better prepared for more responsibility or a promotion? What if they feel the leader knows how to lead and genuinely cares? What if they sincerely want to be part of a dynamic New Wave team?

IQ and Skills to Emotional Quotient (EQ) for personal development. IQ doesn't measure all the traits of the employee-leader of the future. It's also valuable to know our Emotional Quotient (EQ), which is a peek into how we're equipped to be successful all around. IQ is usually a number established in secondary school, and we're stuck with it. EQ is dynamic in that we can assess it, modify it, and increase it as we develop as moral people.

Currently, many organizations and leaders take only certain skills, experience, and education into consideration when hiring. Promotions often depend on the ability to comply with directives or hit a target number, or worse yet, whom you know. New Wave leaders use EQ to understand themselves and staff for personal betterment and well-being beyond wellness to thriving.

Opinion to Science-based and proven practice. Many times, much of what we're urged to do at work grows out of an opinion promoted by consultants or academics. While these people may have qualifications, they can't identify with our jobs as they haven't been in our trenches. We're left with questions about relevancy and especially how to apply those opinions . . . or not.

The MAGNUS–OVÉA theory of leadership behavior arose from what works in established behavioral theory, neuroscience, social science, and practical experience. Social science is a branch of science that considers how we function as individuals and as a society, and how the mind works individually and collectively. Our study and practice of becoming MAGNUS–OVÉA contributes to this body of knowledge. As this book explains, it's been proven effective by a growing body of disciplines, concepts, and especially science:

> **New Wave leaders use EQ to understand themselves and staff for personal betterment and well-being beyond wellness to thriving.**

- Reversal theory explains mindsets and how we can employ the give and take of social situations to balance our human interactions for better outcomes.

- Neuroscience has and continues to establish the neurological connection to moral behavior. It's exciting to see the proof from brain imaging to track how our brains physically evolve toward being good and doing good. When we act in the spirit of goodness and service to others, we shape our brains with neuroplasticity and synaptic pruning to do more of the same. We witness how the students and practitioners of this new theory improve.

- Neurophilosophy verifies the ancient philosophy of the benefits to brain function of ethical behavior, mainly with positive hormonal responses linked to contributing to the common good.

- The ancient concept of sophrosyne, the mean between extremes of vice and virtue, is basic to the practical application of this behavioral theory, helping to determine appropriate conduct.

All of this is embodied in the *how* of becoming a New Wave MAGNUS–OVÉA Leader and individual.

Top down to Bottom up and back. Principled New Wave Leadership encompasses *all* staff; its projection forward, principles, and practices are inclusive. Principled leaders see that information and ideas from all levels of staff is vital for the systematic betterment of individuals and the organization. It's legendary that great ideas come from people doing the work. But even including all levels of staff in the leadership process is not enough. The gleaning of intellectual product needs to travel to the top, emerge in decision making, and travel back down in endless cycles of inclusive practice. Leadership going forward must be a virtuous cycle of learning, knowing, planning, implementing, reflecting, and learning again. This makes for truly effective, dynamic leadership because followers of a New Wave Leader know they're recognized for who they are and what they contribute. They feel valued, heard, and respected. Inspired leaders foster inspired followers.

Followers of a New Wave Leader feel valued, heard, and respected. Inspired leaders foster inspired followers.

Extremes to Golden Mean. We continue the discussion of this theme but from the perspective of the New Wave Leader. We live among and sometimes put ourselves in either extremely good or extremely bad circumstances, and neither is a good place to be. The task of life is to find balance, a major theme and pursuit of becoming MAGNUS–OVÉA. There *is* enough time in the day for the Golden Mean of appropriate behavior and living. We *can* prioritize what we do.

We have opportunities to manage our day between maintenance (sleeping, eating), work for pay, family, relaxation, recreation, and leisure. How we spend our time matters; our work matters, but what matters more is if it fits into a life well lived. In fact, when we have balance, work proceeds better. We give time to other things that are important, such as health, family, understanding ourselves, pursuing hobbies, building friendships, and learning how to navigate the day and make good decisions morally and ethically. Balance is a major key to being accomplished and content. It reduces stress and increases productivity. Achieving balance includes learning to appreciate simple, meaningful things.

A variant of what happiness is bears reflection: Happiness is the absence of persistent big pain and continuous big troubles. That's it. Pause and think about this. With that in mind, living contentedly and accomplished is a state most of us can achieve. Balance, or harmony, in life matters. It's a significant factor in accomplishment *and* it contributes to longevity.

> *Balance, peace, and joy are the fruit of a successful life. It starts with*
> *recognizing your talents and finding ways to serve others.*
> – Thomas Kinkade

How to Use the Phoenix Factors

Survey the Phoenix Factors as a collective to understand what's possible and use them to devise a vision for yourself or your organization. Then begin with *one* Phoenix Factor that's realistic for you and commit to it with a will to make it work. This keeps endeavors simple, suitable, and sustainable, which can't be repeated enough. It's the practical practice of how to pursue the journey.

Reduce efforts to their essentials, but don't make them so simple or play it so safe that your actions are insignificant or ineffective. Make sure what you implement is appropriate to the people and circumstance, especially you. Don't fear the daunting and let yourself be challenged but not so much you're stunned into inactivity. Make sure your actions can be continuously worked. Most effective change is incremental and thus takes time.

Think of essentials and zero in on what's practical and doable for you in your moment. Even if one person understands and commits to the journey—from one come the many. Over time, many can demonstrate how proper conduct elevates the individual, a team, the business, then the wider community. Others see the benefits for one and commit, if only because they wonder why this person is so accomplished, healthy, and respected, if not *happy*.

Personally Speaking

Perspectives from the Greatest Generation
James Klopovic

I'm grateful to have had the good fortune to visit with a few members of the Greatest Generation, the parents of Boomers, who have seen economic depression, world war, death, destruction, and personal tragedies for two lifetimes. They were generally women, their men long gone; each walking history books and examples of a good—no, great—perspective on life.

When asked her view of life in her last days, Ma Kren, a family friend for over 60 years, observed, "Have fun." Here's a woman who plowed through a tough childhood, defied the depression, "fought" World War II, suffered unspeakably by the early accidental death of a beloved son, and faced down about every major disease there is to have. Ma Kren had come to terms with uncommon tragedy and, in the end, pronounced life good. Sharp as a tarpon hook, witty, and always sharing a smile, her attitude is exemplary. And she always won at Scrabble—because she cheated, with a knowing, wry, grand-motherly smile of defiance that said, "I dare you to check that word."

Then there's my dear friend Betsy, all 94 years of her. Betsy's husband Danny was my senior noncommissioned officer back in the early 1970s. I'm honored that Betsy and The Chief, as she called her chief master sergeant husband, fondly remembered me for a half century. He in his Danish accent would call me *Leftenant*. Luckily, he took me under his ample and knowing wing.

Betsy still has childhood memories of living near London during the Blitz of WWII. Danny was part of the Danish underground as a teenager, a twice-angry bee tormenting the Nazis, risking his life, never mentioning it once. A true, true hero. Now Betsy is his living history. Can you imagine!? And she could not be more cheerful—even to interrupting our conversations with "Just a minute lovey; I need to check if I'm still breathing," then laughing to tears at her own joke.

I mustn't forget Aunt Wanda, within a hop, skip, and a jump of hitting 100! Yes, she has tremors, but twinkly eyes and a whip-crack wit. Doesn't miss a beat, this great grandmother. She's just fun to be with. And oh, the stories . . . She remembers what she wore and the details of when she was a toddler, about two years old, being whisked away in the middle of the night, rescued from oppressive surroundings by her grandmother and mother. She remembers the war years and the 60s happenings just down the street in downtown San Francisco. She's brimming with the wisdom of the years and so glad to have the life she's having.

How many of us have known people who have suffered horrible disfigurements, dismemberments, and disabilities yet are still cheerful and full of hope, bringing light to all they touch, man and beast? To the contrary, we probably know curmudgeons who wallow in endless woe, poisoning the air around them in a blue fog of complaints.

Let's determine to be like these greatest of women, by *living* with virtue—*striving* with character—*thriving* for a lifetime, come what may. Know that our lot is truly fortunate. It's all the more fortunate for those of us born to a republic in which we're free to express our creativity, invest our sweat, and exercise our will to be what we can be.

You are now living and making the good ol' days of tomorrow!
Live well.

Concluding Thoughts

We face another test of the strength of our republic. Extremism can and might take over parts of the world, most times subtly, sometimes violently. The question on the minds of many is whether the atom will be used in another nuclear device in the hands of madmen or in a new power generator to be considered in the mix of sustainable energy provisions. We can edit genes to cure disease or create super warriors; what will we choose? We have at hand all the tools to advance and enhance our lives. This test comes down to how ethical we are and how the intentions and efforts of our local private and public sectors evolve. Will they be directed toward community-building so citizens can thrive? We hope.

> **By living and acting wisely, we improve personally and we inspire those who observe us, then those they touch, and so on.**

As envisioned, our experiment in governance begins with a single right-minded citizen and the realization that life is a great gift but fragile if we neglect its rights, privileges, and great gifts, which must be earned. It continues with how we live to earn respect and be fulfilled while enhancing what, and especially who, we touch. Sustaining character traits such as humility, introspection, and honesty has effects we can't even imagine. By living and acting wisely, we improve personally and we inspire those who observe us, then those they touch, and so on.

> *. . . An individual voice, a single deed, a lone life cultivated to seek health and beauty and brightness can be a blessing to mankind.*[258]
> – Danny Heitman

The blessing of approaching life as a journey is that you never arrive, and that is the way you want it. Why? Because, as a process, a continuous journey allows and reveals continuous improvement and wonderment at all the good and beauty that surrounds us. A goal, by its nature, ends; a process, by its nature, never does. You can always gain another insight, arrive at a better understanding, and have revealed to you the true meaning of things. You will become better at the whole process as you progress to the end, generally satisfied, sufficiently accomplished, and more than a bit happy.

The journey of becoming a New Wave MAGNUS–OVÉA Leader recognizes the individual nature of how to conduct a life. It's *deeply personal.* The design of the process belongs to *you.* How well and faithfully you pursue what you design is entirely your decision. If you accept that the journey is worthy and make it happen with commitment, discipline, and dedication, you will inevitably benefit—and, yes, prosper.

Appendix

PHOENIX FACTORS: NEW BEGINNINGS	
From Inertia to Thriving by Becoming a New Wave Leader	
How It *Is*	**How It *Can* Be**
MAGNUS–OVÉA – New Wave *Individual*	
Stagnation	Productive activation
Lack of healthy vitality	Productive longevity
Trainer	Mentor
PTSD	Post-traumatic growth
De-escalation	Pre-escalation
Retirement clock watcher	Lifetime legacy mentality
Hypervigilance	Service mentality
OVÉA: *Others—Values—Ethics—Acceleration*	
VUCA	*Counter VUCA*
Volatility	Vision
Uncertainty	Understanding
Complexity	Clarity
Ambiguity	Agility
Fixed mindset	Growth mindset
Burnout	Vigor
Avoidance	Engagement
Routine procedures	Practical practice
MAGNUS–OVÉA – New Wave *Organization*	
Budgetary cycle uncertainty	Life cycle cost effectiveness stability
Best practices	Effective practices
Technical skills training	Character development
Cooperation	Collaboration

PHOENIX FACTORS: NEW BEGINNINGS
From Inertia to Thriving by Becoming a New Wave Leader

How It *Is*	How It *Can* Be
MAGNUS–OVÉA – New Wave *Organization* (continued)	
Administration of projects	Capacity building for program permanency
Risk tolerance	Risk and liability reduction
Human resources administration	Multiplied social capital
Hiring for skills – Firing for character	Hiring for character – Rarely firing for skills
MAGNUS–OVÉA – New Wave *Community*	
Cooperation	Collaboration
Silo services management	Matrix governance
Vicious cycles	Virtuous cycles
Guessing	Proof
MAGNUS–OVÉA Legacy – New Wave *Leadership*	
Medical wellness	Holistic well-being
Obstacles	Opportunities
Stagnant inertia	Forward thinking evolution
IQ and skills	Emotional Quotient (EQ) for personal development
Opinion	Science-based and proven practice
Top-down governance	Cycle between top-down, bottom-up
Extremes	Golden Mean

Assessing Cost Effectiveness of the New Wave Organization

While the case for New Wave Leadership and followership throughout an organization is soundly based on proven philosophies and practices, it must make sense economically. We suggest that examining the cost-effectiveness of this new theory will be one of the best ways to determine its efficacy and justify its expansion and continued use. It will be simple, suitable, and sustainable to do so, and your organization will benefit in the process.

To fulfill its potential, the program needs to have a positive effect on the bottom line of your organization, agency, or even department or section. You want to see monetary benefits, for example, in recruiting, retention, turnover rates, and workers' compensation and liability claims. In addition, you want your work on goals to drive collaboration to an exciting vision and increased productivity. Yes, this is all quite possible.

Incorporating a program of New Wave Leadership will reasonably assure you of at least the following:

- You're hiring the most qualified, motivated, and character-driven people.

- Career development plans provide incentive, goals, and a personalized vision of how staff can become more efficient, effective, and satisfied.

- The organization's character-based philosophy, training, and development is made clear from day one.

- Attendant individual and organizational improvements and goal accomplishments are tracked.

- Work and career progression matches each individual's propensities so it's appropriately engaging and fulfilling.

- Efficiency and effectiveness continuously improve, one team member at a time.

Overall, you'll want to assess what your adoption of New Wave Leadership means to the continuing improvement of your team members and thus your organization. Essentially, the agency of tomorrow develops staff from pre-hire to retirement. A great place to start measuring performance is with your new hires to allow for gradual implementation of New Wave Leadership ideas. Go slow. Take incremental steps rather than implement an entire program agency wide. You'll need time to work out processes and how you will measure progress.

- *Pre-hire* – Conduct assessments such as the Bar-On EQ-i™ for emotional-social intelligence. This assessment helps determine if an employment candidate can do the job beyond basic skills, education, and experience and indicates areas in which to improve. (See Chapter 11, Phoenix Factors in the New Wave Organization for more information.) Assessment results become part of an individual's Career Development Work Plan.

- *Career Development Work Plan* – Onboard the new hire with a mentor, and with the aid of the assessment, outline a plan of character development studies, skills training, and professional development. A plan will outline what the individual needs and would like to do. Buy-in matters. Ensure collaboration between organizational needs and individual desires. After the initial assessment, conduct periodic performance and progress reviews on career and character development. Such a process determines readiness for more responsibilities and possibly higher-level jobs in supervision, management, and eventually, leadership. This way, character development has a prominent place in staff improvement, with all its attendant benefits.

- *Periodic assessment* – Readminister the Bar-On EQ-i periodically, say yearly and prior to considering promotion, to monitor individual progress and determine potential areas of improvement as the team member evolves. Besides a picture of progress, regular assessment gives both staff and supervisors a definite course to take going forward for whole-person development.

- *Career progression* – The periodic assessments and Career Development Work Plan help track progress and justify when raises and promotions are in order.

- *Organizational performance assessment* – Choose measures of organizational performance to track, and periodically report these figures to leaders, managers, supervisors, and line staff. Begin with a few simple, meaningful measures that can be monetized, that is, converted to dollars saved that can then be "reinvested." One measure for each factor of performance is plenty. Look for "low hanging fruit" that's readily available and easy to gather and analyze, then create your cost-effectiveness statement. For example:

Turnover and Retention – Determine what it costs to hire, onboard, and train a new hire. Track turnovers. When turnover rates trend down, you can compute savings periodically, say, year over year.

Absenteeism – Employees who miss work cost money. Determine a baseline of absentee days then determine the loss of output in a day. These numbers should also trend down.

Grievances and Legal Settlements – These can be from people within the organization or those served. Grievances can result in costly litigation, out-of-court and court settlements. Any settlement avoided is an obvious monetary savings, and some are most dramatic in terms of millions of dollars. Most often, individual or organizational reputations are also saved, which is of incalculable return.

Workers' compensation claims – Similar to grievances, reductions in workers' comp can result in significant savings.

Overall organizational performance – Track and report goal accomplishments relative to your vision. This adds to the narrative of your cost-effectiveness statement and is one demonstration that your vision is working.

The above measures collectively represent remarkable potential savings and thus additions to your bottom line. They are only suggestions. Choose your own, just a few; these numbers describe *your* performance and *your* vision. Such analysis dramatically demonstrates management and leadership are vitally interested in staff. It also creates competent, collaborative New Wave followers.

Money matters, whether your organization is a nonprofit or for-profit venture. It's critical that you be able to monetize your measures—for example, turnover costs. If that measure can be reduced, the company will realize significant savings. Initially, only a few measures will do to perfect the process of developing metrics that convert to positive bottom-line growth. Remember to regularly return summative data to every level of the organization—from the bottom up. That way everyone can see the individual and organizational improvements and, most important, how each person contributes to building a collaborative team. In the process, you will see, by the numbers and with a few charts, how well your organization performs.

Ultimately, financial solvency and preferably profitability or successful delivery of services is essential to the survival of a company or agency. From the standpoint of a public agency, it can impact the effectiveness of a municipality.

Start with only one data point to work out the process of illuminating your cost-effectiveness. Then expand your data points to paint a bigger, more persuasive picture to justify your programming or the launch of new ideas.

Supporting the Program's Efficiency and Effectiveness

We mentioned that efficiency and especially effectiveness would improve with the New Wave Leadership program. In addition to having happier, more fulfilled employees (a tremendous bonus in itself!), these two measures are excellent reasons to adopt this character-based approach.

Efficiency in this case means that processes result in good, productive, goal-oriented work. They take time to work out and stabilize. Effectiveness determines if something makes economic sense, especially in the public sector. That is: Does the dollar investment in this program have a measurable return, either in sound profit or in improving a needed service? These measures work together; but if an expenditure is not economically sound, it probably won't be funded in the first place or re-funded. Having an idea and all its personal investment summarily axed is devastating to the entire organization. Therefore, the time and effort it takes to track this measure of performance is, in itself, cost effective.

Let's be clear; we aren't referring to the detailed and often cumbersome cost benefit analysis requiring the use of detailed, accepted accounting standards and practices, which has its place in larger organizations. Most small businesses and municipalities need to economize on analysis. You'll be better served if these metrics are relatively easy to monitor, compile, and report—and easy to understand for team members at the line level where the work gets done. Cost effectiveness then becomes highly persuasive when presented well. It's basically saying, "Pay me now (invest in this program upfront) or pay me later (with costly problems that could have been prevented)." In other words, the investment is worth the return.

With continually improving automation, tracking measures is relatively easy, and line team members can do it as a matter of daily work. Line-level data is some of the best and easiest to track. You may find data points are already being gathered so you just need to monetize them. As people see the results of cost effectiveness, performance continuously improves. Leaders will then be in a much better position to justify current and especially future investment in the face of competing needs.

Essentially, the supporting argument is composed of three simple parts:

- The *cost-effectiveness* statement – You make the case that what you produce and how you produce it is efficient, effective, and continuously being enhanced. Operations and personnel management are measurably improving because you have tracked trends moving in the right direction. One sentence is all you need to make the point, which you can then elaborate upon in one paragraph and a chart of improving trends.

- The *profit* statement – This states that budgeting for your program has a healthy return on investment beyond costs, which allows more opportunities. Simply put, for every dollar invested, the organization makes that dollar back *and more.*

- The *tradeoff* statement – Most important, this simply states in a sentence or two what can be done with the profit accrued from investing in the New Wave Leadership program. For example, we can say, if we invest in this program, we can depend on W dollars to do more of the same or to spend on X, Y, and Z priorities. Remember, most people can tolerate only one page of explanation, in terms they understand, which they can then use to make decisions. Use bullets.

Experience has proven that budgeting in this way is amazingly effective in justifying what you need and projecting your ideas for continued progress. Plus it's self-fulfilling if you do it well. One successful round of budget justification leads to the next and so on. Why? Because everyone from the line on up understands all are doing well, becoming better and better.

Cost Effectiveness – An Example

The public sector provides a good example of cost effectiveness concerning a problem every municipality in the country has: reentry. Why reentry for New Wave Leadership? It's based on true collaboration between individuals and between agencies. It's the epitome of what we're trying to do as New Wave individuals, agencies, and communities.

Reentry concerns "rescuing" people from expensive public services such as detention and jails and keeping them in the community as productive members. Decriminalizing the mentally ill (DMI) is the primary overall program for a municipal strategy of reentry. Other angles concern keeping children in school and supporting juvenile and adult reentry from justice agencies. DMI is the model for other programming and governance. It's extremely cost effective, which can be measured and *monetized*. This proven program involves collaboration between law enforcement, mental health, social work, and medical professionals to prevent individuals living with mental health concerns from becoming involved in the criminal justice system. Instead, they're referred to local, many times private, mental health services or to their families, for example.[260] Many are able to return to or find productive jobs. Reentry here involves a New Wave matrix of services targeted to one purpose.

Why is this population so important? The mental health population is the most expensive to serve when involved in the criminal justice system, while less expensive community-based alternatives abound. A mental health subject can become involved in the criminal justice system some 13 expensive times from the moment of arrest up to but not including incarceration, at which point costs accelerate dramatically. Every time an arrest and involvement in public systems are avoided, that savings—at the very least in man hours—can be documented and summed, contributing to the cost effectiveness of intervention. At the same time, the results determine the efficacy of the New Wave solution of working in a matrix—a permanent solution to a permanent problem. It can be measured.

From experience with the budgetary process, no matter how noble a cause, any spending requires rational, proven dollars-and-cents arguments. While a well-considered cost-effectiveness statement won't guarantee approval for a particular budget item—especially if it's a new idea—it will be compelling.

Conclusion

Thus we rest our case for adopting then assessing your New Wave Leadership program—perhaps only in one section of your organization as a start. Remember the S^3 formula and keep it Simple, Suitable, and Sustainable. Share the data and any good news with the team members on the line as it shows they're getting the job done! Even cursory data supporting cost-effectiveness in one area or with one program will provide justification, experience, and the means to proliferate New Wave Leadership. Everyone wins.

References

Ambrose, S. E. *Nothing Like It in the World: The Men Who Built the Transcontinental Railroad.* New York: Simon and Schuster, 2000.

Apter, M. J. "Developing Reversal Theory: Some Suggestions for Future Research," *Journal of Motivation, Emotion, and Personality*, 2013, v1, No. 1.

Apter, M. J. & Carter S. "Mentoring and Motivational Versatility: An Exploration of Reversal Theory," Career Development International, 2002, 7/5. Last viewed June 7, 2021: *https://apterdevelopment.com/wp-content/uploads/2019/01/AI019-Mentoring-and-Motivational-Versatility.pdf*

Apter, M. J. *Personality Dynamics: Key Concepts in Reversal Theory.* Loughborough, UK: Apter International Ltd., 2005.

Apter Solutions. "8 Ways of Being. How to adjust your view on a situation to manage your motivation," 2019. Last viewed June 3, 2021: *https://content.web-repository.com/ s/2223599942595654/uploads/Images/livret_v11_ENG-0686555.pdf*

Apter, M. J. *Zigzag: Reversal and Paradox in Human Personality.* Leichestershire, UK: Matador, 2018.

Aristotle. *Aristotle's Politics: Writings from the Complete Works: Politics, Economics, Constitution of Athens.* (Jonathan Barnes, ed. and trans., Melissa Lane, intro.) Princeton, NJ: Princeton University Press, 2017.

Aristotle. *The Ethics of Aristotle: The Nicomachean Ethics*, rev. ed. (J. K. Thomson, trans.) New York: Viking, 1955.

Bar-On, R. "The Bar-On Model of Emotional-Social Intelligence" (ESI, 2006). Psicothema, 18, supl.

Benioff, M. R. & M. Langley, *Trailblazer: The Power of Business as the Greatest Platform for Change.* New York: Random House, 2019.

Benson, H. *The Relaxation Response.* New York: HarperCollins, 1975.

Benson, H., M. Greenwood, & H. Klemchuk. "The Relaxation Response: Psychophysiologic Aspects and Clinical Applications," *The International Journal of Psychiatry in Medicine*, 1975.

Blanc, S. The Focus Course (blog), "*The Simplicity of Benjamin Franklin's Daily Schedule.*" Last viewed June 8, 2021: *https://thefocuscourse.com/franklin-schedule/*

Boaler, J. *Limitless Mind: Learn, Lead, and Live Without Barriers*. New York: Harper Collins Publishers, 2019.

Bryson, B. *At Home: A Short History of Private Life*. Toronto: Doubleday Canada, 2010.

Cattell, R. B. *Personality: A Systematic Theoretical and Factual Study*. New York: McGraw Hill, 1950.

Chaleff, I. *The Courageous Follower: Standing Up to & for Our Leaders,* 3rd ed. San Francisco: Barrett-Koehler Publishers, Inc., 2009.

Chechik, G., I. Meilijson, & E. Ruppin. "Neuronal Regulation Implements Efficient Synaptic Pruning," 1998. Last viewed June 3, 2021: *https://papers.nips.cc/paper/1554-neuronal-regulation-implements-efficient-synaptic-pruning.pdf*

Cherry, K. "Fluid Intelligence vs. Crystallized Intelligence," 2019. Last viewed June 3, 2021: *www.verywellmind.com/fluid-intelligence-vs-crystallized-intelligence-2795004*

Churchland, P. *Conscience: The Origins of Moral Intuition*. New York: W. W. Norton, Inc., 2019.

Cicero, M. *On Living and Dying Well*. (Thomas Habinek, trans.) London, England: Penguin Books, 2012.

Cicero, M. *Selected Works*. (Michael Grant, trans.) Middlesex, England: Penguin Books, 1971.

Crum, A. J., M. Akinola, A. Martin, & S. Fath. "The role of stress mindset in shaping cognitive, emotional, and physiological responses to challenging and threatening stress." Routledge Taylor and Francis Group, 2017. Last viewed June 3, 2021: *https://mbl.stanford.edu/sites/g/files/sbiybj9941/f/crumetal_roleofstressmindset_0.pdf*

Csikszentmihalyi, M. "Flow: The Psychology of Optimal Experience," *Journal of Leisure Research*, 1990, 24(1).

Dalio, R. *Principles: Life and Work*. New York: Simon & Schuster, 2017.

Davidson, R. "Well-being is a Skill: Perspectives from Contemplative Neuroscience," Wisdom 2.0, 2015. Last viewed June 3, 2021: *https://www.youtube.com/watch?v=EPGJU7W0N0I*

De Tocqueville, A. *Democracy in America*. (G. Bevan, trans.) New York: Penguin Putnam Inc., 2003.

Elinson, Z., D. Frosch. *Wall Street Journal*, July 15, 2015. Last viewed June 3, 2021: *https://www.wsj.com/articles/cost-of-police-misconduct-cases-soars-in-big-u-s-cities-1437013834*

Epictetus. *The Art of Living: The Classical Manual on Virtue, Happiness, and Effectiveness.* (Interpreted by Sharon Lebell) New York: HarperCollins Publishers, 1995.

Forum, Police Executive Research 2016, "Guiding Principles on Use of Force." Last viewed June 3, 2021: *http://www.policeforum.org/assets/30%20guiding%20principles.pdf*

Franklin, B. *The Autobiography of Benjamin Franklin.* New York: Modern Library Edition, Random House, Inc., 2001.

Fredrickson, B. "The Role of Positive Emotions in Positive Psychology: The Broaden-and-Build Theory of Positive Emotions," 2001, *American Psychologist*, 56(3), 218–226.

Gates, B. & M. Gates. "The Better World You Will Build," *The Wall Street Journal*, May 2-3, 2020.

Goleman, D. & R. Davidson. *Altered Traits: Science Reveals How Meditation Changes Your Mind, Brain and Body.* New York: Penguin Random House, 2018.

Goodwin, D. K. *Leadership in Turbulent Times.* New York: Simon and Schuster, 2018.

Hall, E. *Aristotle's Way: How Ancient Wisdom Can Change Your Life.* UK: Penguin Random House LLC, 2018.

Hawkins, D. R., J. T. Monroe, M. G. Sandifer, & C. R. Vernon. "Psychological and physiological responses to continuous epinephrine infusion: An approach to the study of the affect, anxiety," Psychiat Res Rep Amer Psychiat Ass. 1960, 12:40–52.

Hedrick, L. (ed) *Xenophon's Cyrus the Great: The Arts of Leadership and War.* New York: Saint Martin's Press, 2006.

Heifetz, R. & M. Linsky. "Leadership on the Line," Boston: *Harvard Business Review*, 2017.

Heitman, D. "'Clean Curtains' and New Year's Resolutions," *The Wall Street Journal*, Dec. 31, 2018.

Housel, M. *The Psychology of Money.* Hampshire, GB: Harriman House, 2020.

Isaacson, W. *Benjamin Franklin: An American Life.* New York: Simon and Schuster, 2003.

Johnson, P. *Socrates.* New York: Penguin Group, 2011.

Josephson, M. *Making Ethical Decisions.* (Wes Hanson, ed.) Los Angeles: Josephson Institute of Ethics, 2002.

Keegan, J. *The Mask of Command: A Study of Generalship.* New York: Viking Penguin Inc., 1987.

Keis, K. & Javidi, M. *Deliberate Leadership*. Abbenford BC, CA: Consulting and Resource Company, 2014.

Kesebir, P. & E. Diener. "In Pursuit of Happiness: Empirical Answers to Philosophical Questions," *Perspectives on Psychological Science*, 2008; 3:117–125.

Klopovic, J., M. Javidi, N. Klopovic, & J. Franklin. *Decriminalizing Mental Illness: A Practical Guide for Building Sustainable Crisis Intervention Teams.* Holly Springs, NC: New Wave Publishers, 2019.

Klopovic, J., M. Javidi, A. Normore, & M. Garcia. *Your Moral Compass: A Practical Guide for New Wave Leaders.* Holly Springs, NC: New Wave Publishers, 2020.

Kraut, R. "Aristotle's Ethics," *The Stanford Encyclopedia of Philosophy.* (Edward N. Zalta, ed.) Summer 2018 ed. Last viewed June 3, 2021: *https://plato.stanford.edu/archives/sum2018/entries/aristotle-ethics*

Kringelbach, M. & K. Berridge. "Towards a Functional Neuroanatomy of Pleasure and Happiness," 2009. Last viewed June 3, 2021: *https://www.ncbi.nlm.nih.gov/pmc/articles/PMC2767390/*

Kyeong, S. et al. "Effects of Gratitude Meditation on Neural Network Functional Connectivity and Brain-Heart Coupling," *Scientific Reports* 7, no. 1 (July 2017): 5058.

Lyubormirsky, S. *The How of Happiness: A New Approach to Getting the Life You Want.* New York: Penguin Group, 2007.

McChrystal, S., J. Eggers, & J. Mangone. *Leaders: Myth and Reality.* UK: Penguin Random House, 2018.

McConnell, C. "Malcolm Gladwell on Legitimacy," *The New Yorker*, 2011. Last viewed June 3, 2021: *https://www.newyorker.com/culture/new-yorker-festival/malcolm-gladwell-on-legitimacy*

McKay, B. & K. McKay. *Young Benjamin Franklin's Plan of Conduct*, 2014; updated 2021. Last viewed June 3, 2021: *https://www.artofmanliness.com/articles/manvotional-young-benjamin-franklins-plan-of-conduct/*

Mencken, H. L. "Days of Innocence: Recollections of Notable Cops," *The New Yorker*, Sept. 20, 1941, p. 27.

Mencken, H. L. (Alistair Cooke, compiler) *The Vintage Mencken.* New York: Vintage Books, 1990.

Minerd, M. *Leisure: The Basis of Everything*, 2017. Last viewed June 3, 2021: *https://www.hprweb.com/2017/01/leisure-the-basis-of-everything/*

Moore, C. "What is Flow in Psychology? Definition and 10+ Activities to Induce Flow," PositivePsychology.com. Last viewed June 3, 2021: *https://positivepsychology.com/what-is-flow/*

Moore, M. "The Evolving Strategy of Policing," Semantic Scholar.org, 2008. Viewed June 3, 2021: *https://pdfs.semanticscholar.org/ a614/21a27a6c4fa0e2 5962ef30e95a22371c1b9c.pdf*

Morris, T. V. *If Aristotle Ran General Motors: The New Soul of Business.* New York: Henry Holt and Company, Inc., 1997.

Moskos, P. *Cop in the Hood: My Year Policing Baltimore's Eastern District.* Princeton, NJ: Princeton University Press, 2008.

Moskos, P. *History of Police.* John Jay College of Criminal Justice, 2015. Last viewed June 4, 2021: *http://petermoskos.com/files/ppt/history.pdf*

Musashi, M. *A Book of Five Rings.* (Victor Harris, trans.) Woodstock, NY: The Overlook Press, 1974.

Nutt, A. E. "There's a Scientific Reason to Speak, Not Write to Those Who Disagree With You," *The Washington Post*, 2017. Last viewed June 3, 2021: *https://www.sciencealert.com/there-s-a-scientific-reason-to-speak-not-write-to-those-who-disagree-with-you*

Oishi, S. & E. Diener. "The Optimum Level of Well-being: Can People Be Too Happy?" *Perspectives on Psychological Science*, 2(4), Dec. 2007.

Orr, D. W. "Reflections on Resilience in a 'Black Swan' World," *Resilience: A Journal of the Environmental Humanities*, V 1, No. 1, Jan. 2, 2014, University of Nebraska Press.

Page, A. *9 Successful Characteristics Embodied by Ben Franklin.* (n.d.) Last viewed June 3, 2021: *https://www.lifehack.org/articles/communication/9-successful-characteristics-embodied-ben-franklin.html*

Peterson, C. & M. Seligman. *Character Strengths and Virtues: A Handbook and Classification.* Oxford: Oxford University Press, 2004. ISBN 0-19-516701-5

Pieper, J. *Leisure: The Basis of Culture.* (Alexander Dru, trans.) New York: Mentor-Omega, 1963.

Pinker, S. *Enlightenment Now: The Case for Reason, Science, Humanism, and Progress.* New York: Viking, 2018.

Pollard, W. Lead from Your Current Position (blog). "VUCA: The chaotic 'new normal,'" 2018. Last viewed June 3, 2021: *http://leadfromyourcurrentposition.com/wordpress/2018/05/23/vuca/#.XinsdGhKjOg*

Ryan, M. & E. Deci. "On Happiness and Human Potentials: A Review of Research on Hedonic and Eudaimonic Well-Being," *Annu. Rev. Psychol.* 2001. 52:141–66. Last viewed June 3, 2021: *http://wisebrain.org/papers/HappinessLR.pdf*

Santos, L. "The Science of Well-being" course. Yale University with Coursera. Take the course at *https://www.coursera.org/learn/the-science-of-well-being*. Last viewed June 3, 2021.

Schwab, K. "The Fourth Industrial Revolution: What It Means, How to Respond," 2016. Last viewed June 3, 2021: *https://www.weforum.org/agenda/2016/01/the-fourth-industrial-revolution-what-it-means-and-how-to-respond/*

Schwartz, B. & K. Sharpe. "Practical Wisdom: Aristotle Meets Positive Psychology," *Journal of Happiness Studies,* 2006, vol. 7.

Seligman, M. "The Pursuit of Happiness," lumen learning, 2000. Last viewed June 4, 2021: *https://courses.lumenlearning.com/atd-bhcc-intropsych/chapter/the-pursuit-of-happiness/#:~:text=Elements%20of%20Happiness,%2C%20%26%20Peterson%2C%202005)*

Taleb, N. N. *Antifragile: Things That Gain from Disorder.* New York: Random House, 2012.

Tilgher, A. *Work, What It Has Meant to Men Through the Ages.* (Dorothy Canfield Fisher, trans.) New York: Arno Press, 1977.

USAF, *United States Air Force Core Values,* 1 January 1997. Last viewed June 4, 2021: *https://www.gocivilairpatrol.com/media/cms/Little_Blue_Book_60E272ED66993.pdf*

USAFA, *United States Air Force Academy Outcomes,* 2009. Last viewed June 4, 2021: *https://www.usafa.af.mil/Portals/21/documents/Leadership/PlansAndPrograms/USAFA%20Outcomes.pdf?ver=2015-11-24-175408-140*

Wall Street Journal, "The Science of Late-Blooming Brains," Saturday/Sunday, May 5-6, 2019.

Waterman A. S. et al. "The Questionnaire for Eudemonic Well-Being: Psychometric Properties, Demographic Comparisons, and Evidence of Validity," *Journal of Positive Psychology* 5, no. 1 (Jan. 2010).

Waxman, O. "How the U.S. Got Its Police Force," *TIME,* May 18, 2017. Last viewed June 4, 2021: *http://time.com/4779112/police-history-origins/*

Wilkinson, D. "Changing Mindsets: Evaluation Report and Executive Summary," Education Endowment Foundation, 2015. Last viewed June 4, 2021: *https://www.niesr.ac.uk/sites/default/files/publications/Changing_Mindsets.pdf*

World Bank. "Decline of Global Extreme Poverty Continues but Has Slowed: World Bank," 2018. Last viewed June 4, 2021: *https://www.worldbank.org/en/news/press-release/2018/09/19/decline-of-global-extreme-poverty-continues-but-has-slowed-world-bank#:~:text=%E2%80%9COver%20the%20last%2025%20years,ever%20been%20in%20recorded%20history*

Zacks, R. *Island of Vice: Theodore Roosevelt's Quest to Clean up Sin-Loving New York.* New York: Anchor Books, 2012.

Major Resources

Reading and soaking up new insights and information can benefit your life immensely. Make it a habit to read, learn, and expand your experience as well as your personal and professional growth. What you read, study, and listen to matters. Following are resources that support New Wave Leadership and becoming the best you can be. Choose one to begin and then continuously enhance your journey.

Course

The Science of Well-Being

(Free course offered by Yale University through Coursera)

Millions have taken this course. It's based in extensive science and effective practices. According to the course description: "In this course you will engage in a series of challenges designed to increase your own happiness and build more productive habits. As preparation for these tasks, Professor Laurie Santos reveals misconceptions about happiness, annoying features of the mind that lead us to think the way we do, and the research that can help us change. You will ultimately be prepared to successfully incorporate a specific wellness activity into your life."

https://www.coursera.org/learn/the-science-of-well-being

Publications

Trailblazer: The Power of Business as The Greatest Platform for Change

by Marc Benioff

(New South Wales: Currency Press, October 15, 2019)

According to author Marc Benioff, the premise of *Trailblazer* is that values create value, and a well-led business is the ". . . greatest platform for change." This book supports the case for New Wave Leadership in affirming that doing well means doing good and a company is only as strong as its principles.

https://www.salesforce.com/trailblazerbook/

Selected Works

by Marcus Tullius Cicero. Michael Grant, trans.

(Middlesex, England: Penguin Books, 1971)

New Wave Leadership is rooted in and gets its strength from the Ancients, and one

of the most profound of these teachers is Cicero. This volume includes some of his most important writings on oration, religion, and philosophy. It reveals how to live a purposeful life based on virtue and character—the Good Life.
https://www.barnesandnoble.com/w/selected-works-marcus-tullius-cicero/1101542425

Limitless Mind: Learn, Lead, and Live without Barriers
by Jo Boaler
(New York: Harper Collins Publishers, 2019)
In this revolutionary book, Jo Boaler, professor of education at Stanford University and acclaimed math educator, reveals the six keys to unlocking learning potential based on the latest scientific findings and practices. She discusses why and how to embrace mistakes, how our beliefs physically change and improve our brains, how ideas optimize neural pathways, and that collaboration enhances brain functioning. This engaging book is a must read as the advice is proven and practical.
https://www.youcubed.org/limitless-mind/

Conscience: The Origins of Moral Intuition
by Patricia Churchland
(New York: W. W. Norton, Inc., 2019)
Conscience is an examination of the roots behind our moral beliefs. With wisdom and unflinching scientific and philosophical insight, Patricia Churchland has written an eye-opening, thought-provoking book that may seriously challenge everything we thought we knew about our best behavior. This enjoyable and easily understood read is a must for your New Wave Leadership library.
https://patriciachurchland.com/

Principles
by Ray Dalio
(New York: Simon & Schuster, 2017)
Principles are ways of successfully dealing with reality to get what you want out of life. This book is a master class in rational thinking about life and work. The main theme is that finding truth is the best way to make decisions, and that ego, emotion, and blind spots prevent you from discovering that truth. The author shares his major strategies to circumvent these weaknesses, including radical open-minded-

ness, thoughtful disagreement, radical transparency, and believability-weighted decision making. This book is a must for New Wave Leaders and thinkers. Dalio is realistic, practical, optimistic, and inspiring.

https://www.principles.com/#get-the-books

Leadership in Turbulent Times
by Doris Kearns Goodwin
(New York: Simon and Schuster, 2018)
This book by acclaimed historian Doris Kearns Goodwin discusses four of the presidents she has studied most closely: Abraham Lincoln, Theodore Roosevelt, Franklin D. Roosevelt, and Lyndon B. Johnson (in civil rights). She shows how they first recognized leadership qualities within themselves and then were recognized by others as leaders. The book offers rare insight into the means, manner, and motivations of these significant presidents, how adversity contributed to their growth, and especially how they successfully led.

https://doriskearnsgoodwin.com/

Team of Rivals: The Political Genius of Abraham Lincoln
by Doris Kearns Goodwin
(New York: Simon and Schuster, 2012)
In *Team of Rivals*, Goodwin illuminates Lincoln's political genius "as the one-term congressman and prairie lawyer rises from obscurity to prevail over three gifted rivals of national reputation to become president." When you read this book, consider how Lincoln may be our greatest president, not only for his genius but by being the man of the moment. You will learn much from how Lincoln lived, led, and changed the world for the better. A compelling read, the book provides insights on how to navigate life.

https://www.simonandschuster.com/books/Team-of-Rivals/Doris-Kearns-Goodwin/9781451688092

Aristotle's Way: How Ancient Wisdom Can Change Your Life
by Edith Hall
(UK: Penguin Random House LLC, 2018)
Aristotle understood that all but a few of us can have happiness if we understand what it is and how to create it. Hall captures the essence of this lasting state of

contentment, which we achieve by having purpose, realizing our potential, and continuously striving to be the best version of ourselves. Living the Good Life is a matter of having meaning, exercising creativity, and exhibiting positivity. The focused study and continuous practice of the wisdom in this book will enrich your life.
https://www.barnesandnoble.com/w/aristotles-way-edith-hall/1128615831?ean=9780735220829

The How of Happiness: A New Approach to Getting the Life You Want
by Sonja Lyubomirsky
(New York: Penguin Group, 2007)
A research psychologist and professor of psychology, Lyubomirsky offers more than a dozen strategies to increase happiness based on science and practice. We can determine our own path to thriving as a New Wave Leader.
http://thehowofhappiness.com/

If Aristotle Ran General Motors: The New Soul of Business
by Tom Morris
(New York: Henry Holt and Company, Inc., 1997)
In this book, Tom Morris, a philosophy professor at Notre Dame, shares the knowledge of history's wisest thinkers and shows how to apply their ideas in today's business environment. He describes the organization of the future, in which truth (excellence), beauty (creativity), goodness (ethics), and unity (collaboration) matter. He shows how these qualities work synergistically to build strong, successful organizations that persevere and make a profit as a measure of their contribution to the greater good.
https://www.barnesandnoble.com/w/if-aristotle-ran-general-motors-tom-morris/1103850630?ean=9780805052534

Enlightenment Now: The Case for Reason, Science, Humanism, and Progress
by Steven Pinker
(New York: Viking, 2018)
The future may be quite bright after all! The author argues for optimism with facts, figures, research, and graphics, proving that much in the world is going right and getting better. He makes the case for reason, science, and humanism, the ideals we need to confront our problems and continue our progress.

https://stevenpinker.com/publications/enlightenment-now-case-reason-science-humanism-and-progress

Websites

Principles YOU: *https://www.principles.com/*

Here you will find a helpful self-assessment, books, and an app for putting Ray Dalio's principles to work.

Bar-On Multifactor Model of Performance: *https://www.mmp2perform.com/*

This website provides current information about Reuven Bar-On's Multifactor Model of Performance. This tool represents the next big paradigm shift in understanding, assessing, and improving performance and in psychology in general. It goes beyond the paradigm shift ushered in by emotional intelligence. It has greater implications for parenting the next generation, education and academic performance, occupational performance and leadership, and healthcare. Dr. Bar-On's assessment is easy to take and can be used as a pre-hire tool to assess the fit of job applicants and their potential for performance. The benefit of this assessment for New Wave Leadership is that the test can be administered periodically to monitor and improve performance, advance career development, and prepare for more responsibility on the job.

The McChrystal Group: *https://www.mcchrystalgroup.com/*

The McChrystal Group led by General Stanley McChrystal (ret.) is about the future of leadership. It helps organizations tap into human potential in service of stronger business outcomes. The Group tackles this work by applying their Team of Teams framework to shared knowledge, common purpose, trust, and empowerment to develop leaders, implement strategy, and measure organizational performance. McChrystal believes that when people are empowered, engaged, and aligned around one mission, business can achieve its full potential.

(All Resource websites last viewed June 17, 2021.)

List of Figures

Acknowledgments

This work is a culmination of much learning and many associations over a long and continuing life of education, experiences, travel, and the toing and froing of life.

I would like to acknowledge all the brilliant leaders, writers, scientists, and philosophers—past and present—whose work contributed to this book's foundation of New Wave Leadership. They have enriched my life and that of countless others and will continue to do so.

Just as important are the many acquaintances and friends who have come in and out of my life. These connections, each in their own way, have left me a little changed, a little better, a little more hopeful. How do I acknowledge all of them and everything they've contributed to my life? I cannot. Every one of them flow through these pages.

Therefore, to represent them, I return to the person to whom this book is dedicated, my friend of a lifetime, Don Martin, to illuminate the value acquaintances, friends, and such a singular true friend have provided me. How it is that we are blessed beyond measure by that kind of friendship has been well elucidated by Cicero, the Ancient Great who observed and knew it over 2,000 years ago:

Among the many great benefits of friendship, one stands out above all the others: friendship shines the light of hope into the future and keeps the spirit from becoming weak or stumbling. Looking at a true friend is like seeing an image of yourself. Even when absent, friends are near; although poor, they bring riches, although weak they are strong, and what is especially hard to express, although dead they live – for respect, memory and the longing to pursue them. In this way the dead are blessed and the living are worthy of praise.
– Marcus Tullius Cicero

About the Authors

JAMES KLOPOVIC, Major, USAF, retired, holds a Doctor of Public Policy (DPP) from Charles Sturt University, Sydney, Australia, with concentration on service program capacity building at the organizational and community levels.

James continues to work in the private and public sectors. He's helping cultivate the next generation of New Wave Leaders via continuous values- and character-based education and development. He combines this passion with developing better ways to deliver municipal public services with collaborative capacity building.

After retiring from the United States Air Force, James completed 45 years of experience in the public sector, providing leadership at federal, state, and local levels. He served as a senior staffer for 25 years on the North Carolina Governor's Crime Commission, where his responsibilities encompassed strategic planning, municipal governance, financial development, federal granting, and community and organizational development, implementation, and evaluation.

One of the numerous programs he created detailed the processes and procedures for School Resource Officers, which resulted in continuously improving learning environments statewide while making schools safer.

As the principal investigator/program director on a series of research programs, he analyzed and proposed model local programs leading to grant proposals for dozens of municipal and state initiatives.

James has broad experience in logistics, training, and education. His expertise in program design, implementation, and management includes ensuring program and organizational permanency. His technical support to numerous local government entities created and enhanced service ideas such as delinquency prevention, reentry, and decriminalizing people living with mental illness.

He has authored or collaborated on numerous publications regarding community policing, community development, and effective/efficient delivery of public services as well as books for fun. In addition to *Becoming a New Wave Leader: Principles and Practices to Live and Lead Well*, his books in descending order of date include the following:

Your Moral Compass: A Practical Guide for New Wave Leaders. J. Klopovic, M. Javidi, A. Normore, & M. Garcia. (New Wave Publishers, 2020) Available through Amazon and *http://www.affinitaspublishing.org*.

Capacity Building: Volume II. *Decriminalizing Mental Illness: A Practical Guide for Building Sustainable Crisis Intervention Teams*. J. Klopovic, M. Javidi, N. Klopovic, & J. Franklin. (Holly Springs, NC: New Wave Publishers, 2019) Available through Amazon and *http://www.affinitaspublishing.org*.

Little Stories: A Legacy of Living, Laughing and Loving. B. D. Martin and J. Klopovic. (Morrisville, NC: Affinitas Publishing, 2019) Available through Amazon and *http://www.affinitaspublishing.org*.

The Honest Backpacker: A Practical Guide for the Rookie Adventurer over 50. J. Klopovic and N. Klopovic. (Morrisville, NC: Affinitas Publishing, 2017) *http://honestbackpacker.com/* Available through Amazon and *http://www.affinitaspublishing.org*.

Effective Program Practices for At-Risk Youth: A Continuum of Community Based Programs. J. Klopovic, M. L. Vasu, & D. L. Yearwood. (Kingston, NJ: Civic Research Institute, Inc., 2003). Available through Amazon and *http://www.civicresearchinstitute.com/epy.html*.

Three more books in the Capacity Building series are in the writing and publication pipeline:

Volume I: *Capacity Building from the Bottom Up: The Key to Sustaining Local Services*. Affinitas Publishing.

Volume III: *Accelerating Juvenile Reentry: A Practical Capacity Building Model for Sustaining Aftercare*. Affinitas Publishing.

Volume IV: *Accelerating Adult Reentry: A Practical Capacity Building Model for Sustaining Post-Release Transitional Services*. Affinitas Publishing.

Contact: *jklopovic@gmail.com*

NICOLE KLOPOVIC, daughter of James Klopovic, is a certified Physician Associate (PA). She was class president of her PA program at the University of California Davis and graduated with honors in 2016. Currently residing in northern California, Nicole practices in the areas of Emergency Medicine, Urgent Care, Aesthetics, Weight Management, and Primary Care. Her application to join the USAF Reserves is pending approval with the Office of the Secretary of Defense.

Nicole stays active through dance instructing, weightlifting, hiking, and cycling and enjoys cooking and traveling. She strives to embrace the motto *carpe diem* while maintaining her passion to mentor, help, and teach others.

Support for a Thriving New Wave Leadership

If you would like guidance or have questions as you explore the New Wave Leadership program, Dr. James Klopovic is available to help as an advisor, consultant, or mentor. He would be honored to support you as you implement part or all of the program for yourself, your agency, company, or organization. Your initial consultation is free. You're invited to contact him at *jklopovic@gmail.com*.

Whatever you can do, or dream you can, begin it. Boldness has genius,
power and magic in it.
– Goethe

Endnotes

1   S. Pinker, *Enlightenment Now: The Case for Reason, Science, Humanism and Progress* (New York: Viking, 2018), pp. 3-4.

2   N. N. Taleb, *Antifragile: Things That Gain from Disorder* (New York: Random House, 2012). The term antifragility means the ability to transcend resilience and improve by enduring shocks and difficulties.

3   Watch for *Building Capacity from the Bottom Up: The Key to Sustaining Local Services*, in the pipeline for publication from Affinitas Publishing. See Vol. II in the Capacity Building Series: *Decriminalizing Mental Illness: A Practical Model for Building Sustainable Crisis Intervention Teams*, 2019.

4   W. Isaacson, *The Code Breaker: Jennifer Doudna, Gene Editing, and the Future of the Human Race* (New York: Simon and Schuster, 2021), p. 73. CRISPR stands for Clustered Regularly Interspaced Short Palindromic Repeats.

5   Ibid., p. 336.

6   J. Klopovic, M. Javidi, A. H. Normore, & M. A. Garcia, *Your Moral Compass: A Practical Guide for New Wave Leaders* (Holly Springs, North Carolina: New Wave Publishers, 2020).

7   G. Chechik, I. Meilijson, & E. Ruppin, "Neuronal Regulation Implements Efficient Synaptic Pruning," 1998.

8   G. L. Keiling and M. H. Moore, "The Evolving Strategy of Policing," *Perspectives on Policing*, NIJ, 1988, Nov, no. 4. A fascinating account of how American policing evolved and from which we derived the "waves" of policing evolution as we see it. Article by M. H. Moore, "The Evolving Strategy of Policing," SemanticScholar.org, 2008. Last viewed June 7, 2021: *https://pdfs.semanticscholar.org/a614/21a27a6c4fa0e25962ef30e95a22371c1b9c.pdf*

9   A. de Tocqueville, G. Bevan, trans., *Democracy in America* (New York: Penguin Putnam Inc., 2003).

10   Op. Cit., Keiling & Moore.

11   H. L. Mencken, "Days of Innocence: Recollections of Notable Cops," *The New Yorker*, September 20, 1941, p. 27.

12   Op. Cit., Keiling & Moore, p. 4.

13   Ibid., p. 6.

14   "Peelian Principles." Last viewed June 7, 2021: *https://en.wikipedia.org/wiki/Peelian_principles*

15   Op. Cit., Keiling and Moore.

16   Ibid., p. 13.

17   National Night Out, begun in 1984, exemplifies a community-oriented program. It builds a better community by allowing public safety representatives to connect with people in their neighborhoods. Thus it breaks down a culture of separation by building personal relationships and mutual understanding, which enhances mutual trust. Last viewed May 1, 2021: *https://natw.org/about/*

18   Op. Cit., Isaacson, *The Code Breaker*.

19   Ibid., p. 436. Based on the study of DNA, Jennifer Doudna, Ph.D., first recognized the potential of RNA in the development of vaccines and cures, such as the vaccine for the coronavirus.

20   S. E. Ambrose, *Nothing Like It in the World: The Men Who Built the Transcontinental Railroad* (New York: Simon and Schuster, 2000).

21   Ibid.

22 World Bank, "Decline of Global Extreme Poverty Continues but Has Slowed: World Bank," 2018. Last viewed June 4, 2021: *https://www.worldbank.org/en/news/press-release/2018/09/19/decline-of-global-extreme-poverty-continues-but-has-slowed-world-bank#:~:text=%E2%80%9COver%20the%20last%2025%20years,ever%20been%20in%20recorded%20history*

23 S. Pinker, *Enlightenment Now: The Case for Reason, Science, Humanism and Progress* (New York: Viking, 2018).

24 Op. Cit., J. Klopovic et al, *Your Moral Compass.*

25 Op. Cit., S. Pinker, 2018, and M. R. Benioff & M. Langley, *Trailblazer: The Power of Business as the Greatest Platform for Change* (New York: Random House, 2019).

26 K. Schwab, "The Fourth Industrial Revolution: What It Means, How to Respond," 2016. Last viewed June 3, 2021: *https://www.weforum.org/agenda/2016/01/the-fourth-industrial-revolution-what-it-means-and-how-to-respond/*

27 B. Gates & M. Gates, "The Better World You Will Build," *Wall Street Journal,* May 2-3, 2020.

28 B. Schwartz & K. Sharpe, "Practical Wisdom: Aristotle Meets Positive Psychology," *Journal of Happiness Studies,* 2006, vol. 7, pp. 377-395.

29 E. Hall, *Aristotle's Way: How Ancient Wisdom Can Change Your Life* (UK: Penguin Random House LLC, 2018), p. 103.

30 S. McChrystal, J. Eggers, & J. Mangone, *Leaders: Myth and Reality* (UK: Penguin Random House, 2018).

31 Ibid.

32 Ibid., pp. 371-81.

33 The first monumental revolutionary discovery was harvesting the energy of the atom, which led to nuclear power and, of course, the bomb. The second was the revolution of the bit (short for binary digit), the smallest unit of data in a computer, with a single binary value of either 0 or 1, which can be electronically transmitted. This discovery enabled the internet, which gave much of humanity access to unlimited information.

34 Op. Cit., Isaacson, *The Code Breaker,* 2021.

35 R. Dalio, *Principles: Life and Work* (New York: Simon & Schuster, 2017), p. 48.

36 Ibid.

37 Ibid.

38 Ibid.

39 Ibid., p. x.

40 Ibid., pp. 187-88.

41 T. V. Morris, *If Aristotle Ran General Motors: The New Soul of Business* (New York: Henry Holt and Company, Inc., 1997).

42 Ibid., p. 61.

43 D. K. Goodwin, *Leadership in Turbulent Times* (New York: Simon and Schuster, 2018).

44 Please add Doris Goodwin's *Leadership in Turbulent Times* to your bookshelf. Also add her opus *Team of Rivals: The Political Genius of Abraham Lincoln.* Appreciate the mind and soul of one of history's greatest men—and be inspired.

45 Op. Cit., Goodwin, p. 10.

46 Wikipedia, Theodore Roosevelt. Last viewed June 4, 2021: *https://en.wikipedia.org/wiki/Theodore_Roosevelt*

47 Op. Cit., Goodwin, p. 39.

48 Ibid., p. 40.

49 Ibid., p. 51.

50 Ibid., p. 71.

51 Ibid., p. 32.

52   Op. Cit., McChrystal et al, *Leaders: Myth and Reality*, p. 397.

53   Ibid., p. 396.

54   Ibid., p. 397.

55   Ibid., pp. 398-99.

56   Ibid., p. 397.

57   Op. Cit., Hall, *Artistotle's Way*.

58   Ibid.

59   Ibid., p. 135.

60   Ibid., pp. 102.

61   Ibid., p. 103.

62   Ibid., p. 38.

63   If you wish to get to know this remarkable gentleman and gentle man, Don Martin, read his memoir, available on Amazon: *Little Stories: A Legacy of Learning, Laughing and Loving* (Morrisville, NC: Affinitas Publishing, 2019). Your eyes will betray you with tears, you will touch a good, even great, man, and you will laugh—a lot. Enjoy!

64   P. Churchland, *Conscience: The Origins of Moral Intuition* (New York: W. W. Norton, Inc., 2019).

65   B. Bryson, *At Home: A Short History of Private Life* (Toronto: Doubleday Canada, 2010).

66   Op. Cit., Apter, 2018.

67   Op. Cit., Taleb, *Antifragile*.

68   Op. Cit., McChrystal et al, *Leaders: Myth and Reality*.

69   Op. Cit., Churchland, *Conscience*.

70   M. J. Apter, *Zigzag: Reversal and Paradox in Human Personality* (Leichestershire, UK: Matador, 2018).

72   S. Lyubormirsky, *The How of Happiness: A New Approach to Getting the Life You Want* (New York: Penguin Group, 2007).

72   Amish challenge. Last viewed June 7, 2021: *https://www.pinterest.com/pin/welcome-to-simply-jeans—478437160395814417/*

73   Wikipedia, Benjamin Franklin. Last Viewed June 6, 2021: *https://en.wikipedia.org/wiki/Benjamin_Franklin*

74   B. Franklin, *The Autobiography of Benjamin Franklin* (New York: Modern Library Edition, Random House, Inc., 2001), pp. 91-93.

75   O. Waxman, "How the U.S. Got Its Police Force," *TIME*, May 18, 2017. Last viewed June 4, 2021: *http://time.com/4779112/police-history-origins/*

76   M. Cicero, *Cicero: Selected Works*, Michael Grant, trans. (Middlesex, England: Penguin Books, 1971). Begin with Chapter 5, Cato The Elder on Old Age. His classic treatise on old age provides some of the greatest insights and wisdom about living well so one can die well. Highly recommended.

77   A. E. Nutt, "There's a Scientific Reason to Speak, Not Write to Those Who Disagree With You," *The Washington Post*, 2017. Last viewed June 3, 2021: *https://www.sciencealert.com/there-s-a-scientific-reason-to-speak-not-write-to-those-who-disagree-with-you*

78   W. Isaacson, *Benjamin Franklin: An American Life* (New York: Simon and Schuster, 2003), pp. 90-101.

79   B. Franklin, *The Autobiography of Benjamin Franklin*. Modern Library Edition (New York: Random House Inc., 2001), pp. 90-95.

80   Op. Cit., Isaacson, *Benjamin Franklin*.

81   Ibid., p. 90.

82   Aristotle, *The Ethics of Aristotle: The Nicomachean Ethics*, J. K. Thomson, trans., rev. ed. (New York: Viking, 1955), p. 104.

83 Op. Cit., Hall, *Artistotle's Way*, p. 99.

84 Ibid., pp. 123-25.

85 Adapted from daily meditation, *Wisdom*, Aug. 5, 2020. Last viewed June 4, 2021: *https://app.www.calm.com/homepage*

86 Op. Cit., Franklin, 2001, p. 98.

87 Op. Cit., Hall, p. 123.

88 In the fall of 1727, Benjamin Franklin and a group of friends founded the Junto Club, also known as the Leather Apron Club, leather being the symbol of a tradesman. The 12 members were tradesmen and artisans who met Friday evenings to discuss issues of morals, politics, or natural philosophy. The club lasted 38 years. Franklin proposed that the group be formed of "ingenious men—a physician, a mathematician, a geographer, a natural philosopher, a botanist, a chemist, and a mechanician (engineer)." It was guided by a list of probing questions devised by Franklin. The Junto, it could be said, was the roots of forming the new American republic. Last viewed June 4, 2021: *http://www.benjamin-franklin-history.org/junto-club/*

89 Op. Cit., Hall, *Artistotle's Way*, p. 183.

90 Ibid., p. 200.

91 S. Blanc, The Focus Course (blog), *"The Simplicity of Benjamin Franklin's Daily Schedule."* Last viewed June 4, 2021: *https://thefocuscourse.com/franklin-schedule/*

92 Benjamin Franklin was a genius and a true polymath. However, he was the product of continuous, intense study and thought. Although he had only a second-grade education, he was inducted into the Royal Society in 1756, with the likes of founding giants such as Sir Francis Bacon, Sir Isaac Newton, and more recently, Charles Darwin, Albert Einstein, and Stephen Hawking. Franklin left a library of over 4,000 books. No doubt he was familiar with them all and studied most of them.

93 Op. Cit., Nutt, "There's a Scientific Reason . . . ," 2017.

94 Op. Cit., Franklin, *The Autobiography*, pp. 104-05.

95 B. McKay & K. McKay, "Young Benjamin Franklin's Plan of Conduct," 2014; updated 2021. Last viewed June 3, 2021: *https://www.artofmanliness.com/articles/manvotional-young-benjamin-franklins-plan-of-conduct/*

96 M. J. Apter, *Zigzag: Reversal and Paradox in Human Personality* (Leichestershire, UK: Matador, 2018).

97 P. Churchland, *Conscience: The Origins of Moral Intuition* (New York: W. W. Norton, Inc., 2019).

98 Ibid.

99 Ibid., p. 5.

100 Ibid., pp. 23-24.

101 Ibid., pp. 96, 103.

102 Op. Cit., Klopovic, et al., *Your Moral Compass,* 2020.

103 Brainfacts.org. Last viewed June 4, 2021: *https://www.brainfacts.org/in-the-lab/meet-the-researcher/ 2018/how-many-neurons-are-in-the-brain-120418*

104 Op. Cit., Churchland, p. 83.

105 Ibid., p. 82.

106 From a lecture presented by Nicole Klopovic, PA

107 Medicine.net. Last viewed June 4, 2021: *https://www.medicinenet.com/neurotransmitter/definition.htm*

108 P. Zak, "The Top 10 Ways to Boost Good Feelings," *Psychology Today*, November 7, 2013. Last viewed June 4, 2021: *https://www.psychologytoday.com/us/blog/the-moral-molecule/201311/the-top-10-ways-boost-good-feelings*

109   Our endocrine system is an evolutionary marvel that fits into the whole of our autonomic nervous, respiratory, and digestive systems. Physiologically, our endocrine system controls major functions of reproduction, growth, and metabolism. Now we know it has a major function in controlling our emotions and moral growth.

110   M. Kringelbach & K. Berridge, "Towards a Functional Neuroanatomy of Pleasure and Happiness," 2009. Last viewed June 3, 2021: *https://www.ncbi.nlm.nih.gov/pmc/articles/PMC2767390/*

111   The Yale University course "The Science of Well-Being" is the school's most popular course ever. Students engage in a series of challenges designed to increase happiness and build more productive habits. "Professor Laurie Santos reveals misconceptions about happiness, annoying features of the mind that lead us to think the way we do, and the research that can help us change." The course references hundreds of studies that suggest the essence of achieving well-being. Course skills are the science and practice of gratitude, happiness, meditation, and savoring. Last viewed June 4, 2021: *https://www.coursera.org/learn/the-science-of-well-being*

112   Op. Cit., Kringelbach & Berridge, p. 174.

113   Ibid., p. 176.

114   Ibid., p. 177.

115   D. Goleman & R. Davidson, *Altered Traits: Science Reveals How Meditation Changes Your Mind, Brain and Body* (New York: Penguin Random House, 2018), p. 57.

116   R. Davidson, "Well-being is a Skill: Perspectives from Contemplative Neuroscience," Wisdom 2.0, 2015. Last viewed June 3, 2021: *https://www.youtube.com/watch?v=EPGJU7W0N0I*

117   Ibid.

118   Op. Cit., Churchland, *Conscience*, p. 151.

119   Ibid., pp. 89-91. Kenneth Kishida's study with Parkinson's patients was highly creative, ethical, and groundbreaking. The team studied patients who were being treated for Parkinson's disease by having a probe deeply and safely inserted into the cortex to help cure their disease. This gave the research team, with patient permissions and proper human studies, review and approval to design electrodes to measure dopamine releases. The patients then "played" the stock market and had their dopamine levels read with corresponding losses and wins big and small. This led to conclusive, safe, scientific evidence about the connection of hormones to behavior. And it opened a new way to study the interaction of how our endocrine system works to shape behavior.

120   Ibid., p. 181.

121   Ibid., p. 189.

122   Wilkinson, D. "Changing Mindsets: Evaluation Report and Executive Summary" (Education Endowment Foundation, 2015). Last viewed June 4, 2021: *https://www.niesr.ac.uk/sites/default/files/publications/Changing_Mindsets.pdf*

123   M. J. Apter, *Personality Dynamics: Key Concepts in Reversal Theory* (Loughborough, UK: Apter International Ltd., 2005), p. 83.

124   Ibid., p. 82.

125   Op. Cit., Apter, *Zigzag*, p. 113.

126   Ibid., p. 243.

127   Ibid., p. x, pp. 242-280.

128   Apter Solutions, "8 Ways of Being. How to adjust your view on a situation to manage your motivation," 2019. Last viewed June 3, 2021: *https://content.web-repository.com/s/2223599942595654/uploads/Images/livret_v11_ENG-0686555.pdf*

129   Ibid., p. 6.

130   Op. Cit., Apter, *Zigzag*, pp. 280-281.

131   Ibid., p. 281.

132   Ibid., p. 242.

133   Apter, M. J. & S. Carter, "Mentoring and Motivational Versatility: An Exploration of Reversal Theory," *Career Development International*, 2002, 7/5. Last viewed June 7, 2021: *https://apterdevelopment.com/wp-content/uploads/2019/01/AI019-Mentoring-and-Motivational-Versatility.pdf*

134   L. Santos, "The Science of Well-being" course. Yale University with Coursera. Take the course at *https://www.coursera.org/learn/the-science-of-well-being*. Last viewed June 3, 2021.

135   M. Ryan & E. Deci, "On Happiness and Human Potentials: A Review of Research on Hedonic and Eudaimonic Well-Being," *Annu. Rev. Psychol.* 2001. 52:141–66. Last viewed June 3, 2021: *http://wisebrain.org/papers/HappinessLR.pdf*

136   Op. Cit., Churchland, *Conscience*, p. 169.

137   Ibid., p. 144.

138   Ibid., p. 147.

139   La Farm Bakery. Last viewed June 4, 2021: *https://www.lafarmbakery.com/*

140   D. W. Orr, "Reflections on Resilience in a 'Black Swan' World," *Resilience: A Journal of the Environmental Humanities*, V 1, No. 1 (University of Nebraska Press, Jan. 2, 2014).

141   Op. Cit., Lyubormirsky, *The How of Happiness*.

142   Ibid.

143   McChrystal Group. Last viewed June 4, 2021: *https://www.mcchrystalgroup.com/*

144   The McChrystal Group *Field Manual: Team Resilience*. Last viewed May 21, 2021: *https://mg-website-api-live.s3.amazonaws.com/documents/210315_Team_Resilience_Field_Manual.pdf*

145   A. Jain, "Antifragile: Things that Gain from Disorder." Last viewed May 3, 2021: *https://medium.com/low-pass-filter/antifragile-things-that-gain-from-disorder-8a0e86257edb#:~:text=Fragile%2C%20Robust%2C%20Antifragile,Let%20us%20call %20it-%20antifragile*

146   B. Fredrickson, "The Role of Positive Emotions in Positive Psychology: The Broaden-and-Build Theory of Positive Emotions," *American Psychologist*, 56(3) (2001), pp. 218–226.

147   Ibid., p. 1367.

148   Ibid.

149   Ibid., p. 1369.

150   Ibid., p. 1370-73.

151   J. Boaler, *Limitless Mind: Learn, Lead, and Live Without Barriers* (New York: Harper Collins Publishers, 2019).

152   Ibid., p. 13.

153   Ibid., p. 47.

154   Ibid., p. 77.

155   Ibid., p. 101.

156   Ibid., p. 133.

157   Ibid., p. 165.

158   Op. Cit., Boaler, *Limitless Mind*.

159   Op. Cit., Lyubomirsky, *The How of Happiness*, p. 8.

160   Ibid., pp. 24-26.

161   Ibid., p. 23.

162   Ibid., p. 26.

163   Ibid., pp. 101-11.

164   M. Csikszentmihalyi, "Flow: The Psychology of Optimal Experience," *Journal of Leisure Research*, 24(1) (1990), pp. 93–94. Last viewed June 4, 2021: *https://positivepsychology.com/what-is-flow/*

165   Op. Cit., Lyubomirsky, pp. 101-111.

166   K. Schwab, "The Fourth Industrial Revolution: What It Means, How to Respond" (2016). Last viewed June 3, 2021: *https://www.weforum.org/agenda/2016/01/the-fourth-industrial-revolution-what-it-means-and-how-to-respond/*

167   Op. Cit., Lyubomirsky, p. 106.

168   Ibid., p. 109.

169   Ibid., p. 169.

170   Ibid., pp. 176-180.

171   Ibid., pp. 193-198.

172   Ibid., p. 198.

173   M. P. Seligman, T. A. Steen, N. Park & C. Peterson, "Positive Psychology Progress: Empirical Validation of Interventions" (2005). Last viewed June 4, 2021: *https://pubmed.ncbi.nlm.nih.gov/16045394/*

174   S. Kyeong, K. Joohan, D. Kim, et al, "Effects of Gratitude Meditation on Neural Network Functional Connectivity and Brain-Heart Coupling." *Sci Rep* 7, 5058 (2017). Last viewed June 4, 2021: *https://doi.org/10.1038/s41598-017-05520-9*

175   A. Wood, J. Maltby, R. Gillet, A. Linley, S. Joseph, 2008, "The Role of Gratitude in The Development of Social Support, Stress, and Depression: Two Longitudinal Studies." *Journal of Research in Personality*, vol 42, iss 4 (Aug 2008), pp. 854-871. Last viewed May 31, 2021: *https://www.sciencedirect.com/science/article/abs/pii/S0092656607001286*

176   D. Danner, D. Snowdon & W. Friesen, "Positive Emotions in Early Life and Longevity: Findings from The Nun Study." Pers Soc Psychol (May 2001), pp. 804-13. Last viewed May 31, 2021: *https://pubmed.ncbi.nlm.nih.gov/11374751/*

177   P. C. Watkins, L. Cruz, H. Holben & R. L. Kolts, "Taking Care of Business? Grateful Processing of Unpleasant Memories." *Journal of Positive Psychology*, 3 (2008), pp. 87-99.

178   DailyHealthPost Editorial, "Neuroscience Reveals: Gratitude Literally Rewires Your Brain to be Happier." Oct. 10, 2020. Last viewed June 4, 2021: *https://dailyhealthpost.com/gratitude-rewires-brain-happier/*

179   Op. Cit., Lyubormirsky, *The How of Happiness*, pp. 257-81.

180   Ibid., pp. 258-66.

181   Ibid., pp. 258-59.

182   Ibid., pp. 266-70.

183   Ibid., pp. 270-73.

184   Ibid., pp. 273-77.

185   Ibid., p. 80.

186   Op. Cit., Churchland, *Conscience*, p. 98.

187   Ibid., p. 171.

188   Ibid., p. 173.

189   Ibid., p. 146.

190   Ibid., p. 167.

191   C. Peterson & M. Seligman, *Character Strengths and Virtues: A Handbook and Classification* (Oxford: Oxford University Press, 2004).

192   "The 24 Character Strengths," VIA Institute on Character. Last viewed June 7, 2021: *https://www.viacharacter.org/character-strengths*

193   Ibid.

194   Op. Cit., Hall, *Aristotle's Way.*

195   Op. Cit., *Calm.com.* Last viewed June 7, 2021: *https://app.www.calm.com/homepage*

196   Ibid.

197   *Healthline.com.* Last viewed June 4, 2021: *https://www.healthline.com/nutrition/top-10-evidence-based-health-benefits-of-coconut-oil*

198   *Rush.edu/news.* Last viewed June 7, 2021: *https://www.rush.edu/news/daily-leafy-greens-may-slow-cognitive-decline#:~:text=While%20cognitive%20abilities%20naturally%20decline, University% 20Medical%20Center%20in%20Chicago.*

199   M. Cicero, *On Living and Dying Well,* Thomas Habinek, trans. (London: Penguin Books, 2012), pp. 33, 227.

200   Epictetus, *The Art of Living: The Classical Manual on Virtue, Happiness, and Effectiveness,* Sharon Lebell, int. (New York: HarperCollins Publishers, 1995), p. xiv.

201   Op. Cit., Hall, *Aristotle's Way.*

202   Another best use of our time, which isn't within the scope or purpose of this book, is wealth building toward retirement. This relates to becoming MAGNUS–OVÉA, as retiring from a job as early as possible and still being vital and vigorous leaves a lot of time to enjoy life and continue to make a good and positive impact. We recommend *The Simple Path to Wealth* by J. L. Collins. Basically, he recommends: Avoid debt, invest early and regularly by paying yourself first, set it and forget it. You'll learn it doesn't take much to live well.

203   Adapted from *https://www.calm.com/,* April 3, 2019. Last viewed June 7, 2021: *https://app.www.calm.com/homepage*

204   K. Nowak, M. Rossman, M. Chonchol, & D. Seals, 2018, *Strategies for Achieving Healthy Vascular Aging,* US National Library of Medicine NIH. Last viewed June 7, 2021: *https://www.ahajournals.org/doi/pdf/10.1161/HYPERTENSIONAHA.117.10439*

205   R. B. Cattell, *Personality: A Systematic Theoretical and Factual Study* (New York: McGraw Hill, 1950).

206   K. Cherry, "Fluid Intelligence vs. Crystallized Intelligence," 2019. Viewed June 3 2021: *www.verywellmind.com/fluid-intelligence-vs-crystallized-intelligence-2795004*

207   Ibid.

208   *Wall Street Journal,* "The Science of Late-Blooming Brains," Saturday/Sunday, May 5-6, 2019, p. C2.

209   M. Musashi, *A Book of Five Rings,* Victor Harris, trans. (Woodstock, NY: The Overlook Press, 1974), p. 49.

210   Ibid.

211   Ibid.

212   Op. Cit., Epictetus, *The Art of Living,* 1994, p. 89.

213   J. Klopovic & N. Klopovic, *The Honest Backpacker: A Practical Guide for the Rookie Adventurer over 50* (Morrisville, NC: Affinitas Publishing, 2019).

214   Op. Cit., McChrystal, *Leaders: Myth and Reality.*

215   Op. Cit., Fredrickson, "The Role of Positive Emotions," p. 1396.

216   L. Hedrick (ed), *Xenophon's Cyrus the Great: The Arts of Leadership and War* (New York: Saint Martin's Press, 2006).

217   Op. Cit., McChrystal, *Leaders: Myth and Reality,* pp. 243-44.

218   Ibid., p. 405.

219   Op. Cit., McChrystal, *Leaders: Myth and Reality.*

220   Biography Online, Lord Nelson. Last viewed June 7, 2021:*https://www.biographyonline.net/military/lord-nelson.html*

221   Op. Cit., McChrystal, *Leaders: Myth and Reality,* p. 375.

222 Op. Cit., McChrystal, *Leaders: Myth and Reality.*

223 Steve Jobs revolutionized personal computers, animated movies, music, phones, tablet computing, and digital publishing, all before his premature last birthday of 57. It's safe to say nearly all the world's people don't complete a day without somehow benefitting from his genius and perseverance, and his influence continues to expand geometrically.

224 Op. Cit., McChrystal, *Leaders: Myth and Reality,* p. 372.

225 Ibid., p. 400.

226 Op. Cit., Frederickson, "The Role of Positive Emotions," p. 1375.

227 J. Keegan, *The Mask of Command: A Study of Generalship* (New York: Viking Penguin Inc., 1987).

228 Op. Cit., McChrystal, *Leaders: Myth and Reality.*

229 Op. Cit., Goodwin, *Leadership in Turbulent Times.*

230 *Wall Street Journal,* May 23-24, 2020, p. C4

231 I. Chaleff, *The Courageous Follower: Standing Up to & for Our Leaders,* 3rd ed., (San Francisco: Barrett-Koehler Publishers, Inc., 2009).

232 Op. Cit., K. Schwab, "The Fourth Industrial Revolution."

233 Ibid.

234 J. Klopovic et al, *Decriminalizing Mental Illness: A Practical Model for Building Sustainable Crisis Intervention Teams* (New Wave Publishing, 2019).

235 Ibid. *Decriminalizing Mental Illness* describes an example of how to build service project capacity to ensure permanence.

236 H. Joly, "How Hubert Joly Changed Best Buy Without Everyone Hating Him," *Wall Street Journal* (Apr. 23, 2021). Adapted from *The Heart of Business: Leadership Principles for the Next Era of Capitalism* by Hubert Joly (Harvard Business Review Press, May 4, 2021).

237 Op. Cit., Keegan, *The Mask of Command,* 1987.

238 R. Davidson and S. Begley, *The Emotional Life of Your Brain: How Its Unique Patterns Affect the Way You Think, Feel, and Live—and How You Can Change Them* (New York, Random House, 2012).

239 Ibid.

240 Op. Cit., Dalio, *Principles,* p. 272.

241 W. Pollard, Lead from Your Current Position (blog), "VUCA: The chaotic 'new normal,'" 2018. Last viewed June 3, 2021: *http://leadfromyourcurrentposition.com/wordpress/2018/05/23/vuca/#.XinsdGhKjOg/*

242 Ibid.

243 Ibid.

244 Ibid.

245 Ibid.

246 R. Heifetz & M. Linsky, "Leadership on the Line," (Boston: *Harvard Business Review,* 2017).

247 Op. Cit., Klopovic, et. al, *Decriminalizing Mental Illness.*

248 Ibid.

249 Op. Cit., Klopovic et. al, *Your Moral Compass.*

250 Z. Elinson & D. Frosch, *Wall Street Journal* (July 15, 2015). Last viewed June 3, 2021: *https://www.wsj.com/articles/cost-of-police-misconduct-cases-soars-in-big-u-s-cities-1437013834*

251 Ibid.

252 R. Bar-On, "The Bar-On Model of Emotional-Social Intelligence" (ESI, 2006). *Psicothema,* 18, supl., 13-25.

253 Op. Cit., Klopovic et. al, *Your Moral Compass.*

[254] S. Pinker, *Enlightenment Now: The Case for Reason, Science, Humanism, and Progress* (New York: Viking, 2018).

[255] S. Pinker, "The Enlightenment Is Working," *Wall Street Journal* (Sat/Sun, Feb. 10, 2018).

[256] Ibid.

[257] Op. Cit., Dalio, *Principles.*

[258] D. Heitman, "'Clean Curtains' and New Year's Resolutions," *Wall Street Journal* (Dec. 31, 2018), p. A15.

[259] Reuven Bar-On EQ-i assessment. Last viewed July 15, 2021: *https://www.mmp2perform.com/*

[260] Refer to *Decriminalizing Mental Illness: A Practical Model for Building Sustainable Crisis Intervention Teams.* This book defines in detail and in checklist form practical ideas to implement this community reentry strategy. (Available through *www.affinitaspublishing.org.*)

Index